Helping Your Child *with* Autism Spectrum Disorder

A STEP-BY-STEP WORKBOOK *for* FAMILIES

STEPHANIE B. LOCKSHIN, PH.D., BCBA
JENNIFER M. GILLIS, MA, BCBA
RAYMOND G. ROMANCZYK, PH.D., BCBA

New Harbinger Publications, Inc.

Distributed in Canada by Raincoast Books

Copyright © 2005 by Stephanie B. Lockshin, Jennifer M. Gillis, and Raymond G. Romanczyk
New Harbinger Publications, Inc.
5674 Shattuck Avenue
Oakland, CA 94609

Cover design by Amy Shoup
Acquired by Catharine Sutker
Edited by Karen O'Donnell Stein
Text design by Tracy Marie Carlson

ISBN 1-57224-384-8 Paperback
Library of Congress Cataloging in Publication Data on file

Printed in the United States of America

New Harbinger Publications' Web site address: www.newharbinger.com

07   06   05

10   9   8   7   6   5   4   3   2   1

First printing

Contents

Introduction   1

1   Autism Spectrum Disorder Is a Family Affair   9

2   Coping   17

3   Enhancing Family Communication   31

4   Identifying Family Needs   46

5   How to Teach Your Child New Skills   74

6   Getting the Help You Need   105

7   Teaching Family-Friendly Skills   117

8   Strategies for Increasing Your Child's Communication Skills   132

9   Strategies for Increasing Your Child's Self-Control   154

10   Strategies for Increasing Your Child's Independence   165

11   Increasing Your Child's Participation   180

12   Balancing Child and Family Needs   193

13   How Do We Know When We're in Trouble?   204

14   Evaluating Outcomes   215

      Resources   224

      References   228

Introduction

Autism spectrum disorders (ASD) is the name given to a group of neurobiological disorders that are identified in early childhood. Five separate disorders fall on the spectrum: *autistic disorder* (commonly referred to as *autism*); *pervasive developmental disorder not otherwise specified (PDDNOS)*; *Asperger's disorder*; *Rett's disorder*; and *childhood disintegrative disorder*. Although there are important differences between these disorders, a core set of symptoms is common to all five: significant impairment in social interaction and a consistent pattern of restricted, repetitive, and stereotyped behavior. It is this set of core symptoms that places each of these disorders in the diagnostic category of autism spectrum disorders.

Of the five disorders that make up the autism spectrum disorders, autistic disorder, PDDNOS, and Asperger's disorder are the most common. Rett's disorder and childhood disintegrative disorder are relatively rare. For this reason, the strategies outlined in this book are most applicable with children diagnosed with autistic disorder, PDDNOS, and Asperger's disorder.

WHAT IS ASD, AND WHEN IS IT DIAGNOSED?

The age at which the autism spectrum disorders are first detected and diagnosed can be different for each of the three disorders that we are considering. The symptoms of autism are usually not noticed at birth but instead become obvious when some aspect of development goes awry, usually during the first three years. Early clues that may raise parental concern include delays in communication (both verbal and nonverbal) and in social development. Other early signs include the child's limited range of interests, insistence on sameness, and repetitive, nonfunctional routines and behaviors. In some cases, children appear to be developing normally, but at some point before the age of three they either regress (losing skills they had already acquired) or simply stop progressing. The symptoms of Asperger's disorder and pervasive developmental disorder not otherwise specified may become apparent after the age of three.

In the most widely used diagnostic system in psychology and psychiatry, the *Diagnostic and Statistical Manual of Mental Disorders*, (DSM-IV-TR; American Psychiatric Association 2000), the autism spectrum disorders are considered to be pervasive developmental disorders. *Pervasive* in this context means that the disorder affects multiple areas of functioning. It's not surprising, then, that a diagnosis of autistic disorder, one of the ASDs, requires that a child exhibit symptoms that satisfy multiple criteria. The three areas that are critical for a diagnosis of autistic disorder include deficits in the areas of socialization (a qualitative impairment in social interaction), communication (a qualitative impairment in communication), and behavior (patterns of restricted, repetitive, stereotyped behavior, interests, and activities). A diagnosis of autistic disorder requires that these symptoms are present before the age of three.

As you can see from the above description, a diagnosis of one of the ASDs reflects more than just a delay in development; it also indicates the presence of "atypical" behavior (meaning that the behaviors are not often seen in children at the same level of development). The chart below further illustrates this concept.

Criteria	Typical behavior for a child with a developmental age of two years old	Atypical behavior for a child with a developmental age of two years old
Social functioning	Plays near other children with similar toys, but does not play cooperatively with others; initiates interactions with (brings toys to show, share) and responds to social initiations of others	Does not use toys or doesn't use them in the way they are intended to be used (for example, they may continue to mouth toys or bang, spin, or manipulate isolated parts of toys repetitively); avoids interactions with others; does not initiate or respond to the social initiations of others
Communication	Uses single words to communicate basic wants and needs, to share experiences, to ask for information, and uses gesture to supplement communication when language is insufficient	Delayed speech development or the absence of speech; odd or unusual use of language (such as use of *jargon*—strings of sounds, words, or syllables that have no meaning— repetitive words, phrases, or previously heard dialogue that have no communicative value, and idiosyncratic language or words that are meaningful only to the child); absence of gestures or eye gaze (alternating gaze between objects of interest or desire and people) to communicate basic wants, needs, share experiences, or ask for information

The table shows that while typical two-year-olds do not yet play cooperatively with others (playing with shared toys in a give-and-take manner), they do use toys appropriately (in the way they are intended to be used) and engage in social behavior, initiating interactions with others and responding to others' attempts at social engagement. When development is atypical, many of the behaviors normally seen at specific developmental levels are absent. For example, a child with ASD who has an overall developmental age of two years (as measured by standardized tests of language, achievement, and social functioning) may avoid social interactions (perhaps turning away and becoming fussy if others persist at trying to engage them) and may not use toys in the way that they were designed to be used (for example, spinning the wheels of a toy car rather than pushing or rolling it).

In addition, children with ASD may exhibit a variety of other behaviors, above and beyond those required for a diagnosis, that complicate their clinical picture and increase the challenge involved in raising a child with ASD. These include problems with attention, learning, and behavior, some of which are listed below:

- Problems with attention

  - Difficulty focusing attention (auditory and visual)

  - Difficulty sustaining attention

  - Difficulty shifting attention

  - Focusing on details that are not important for a specific task

- Cognitive delays

  - Specific learning problems

  - Mental retardation

- Additional problems with communication

  - Delayed language comprehension and expression

  - Limited use of gesture (body language) or other forms of nonverbal communication (such as sign language) to make up for poor expressive vocabulary

  - Odd or unusual language (for example, words or phrases used to label objects or events that are not universally recognized)

  - Repetition of words or phrases heard in other contexts that have little communicative value in the present context

  - Limited use of social language (for example, for purposes of sharing interests or providing or asking for information)

  - Inability to sustain a conversation when adequate vocabulary is present

  - Poor understanding of the rules of social communication (such as maintaining appropriate distance from the speaker, turn taking during informational exchanges, etiquette related to beginning and ending conversations, and restricted range of conversational topics)

  - Impaired use of inflection in speech (for example, asking a question in a monotone voice or using a questioning tone when making a statement)

- Atypical learning styles

  - Slow acquisition of new skills

  - Poor maintenance of skills learned

  - Rote learning (is able to memorize specific facts using specific language but cannot supply the same information when the question is asked in a different way)

  - Difficulty applying knowledge learned in one context (taught by a specific person, in a specific setting, with specific materials) in a different context (poor generalization)

- Insistence on sameness

  - Emotional outbursts or tantrums triggered by changes in schedules and routines (such as having breakfast before getting dressed or taking a different route to school), changes in the physical environmental (such as rearranging furniture or changing curtains), and changes in interpersonal interactions

- Self-injurious behaviors

  - Head banging

  - Tissue rubbing (excessive rubbing of skin, eyes, or other body parts to the point where the skin may become irritated or develop abrasions)

  - Self-biting, scratching, hitting, or pinching

- Self-stimulatory behaviors

  - Odd, repetitive vocalizations

  - Unusual hand, finger, or whole-body movements (such as finger flicking, body twirling, body rocking)

- Repetitive actions that seem to have no purpose or function (for example, ritualistic and compulsive behaviors)

- Poor behavior regulation

  - Difficulty regulating behavior in response to situational demands (either too active or too passive)

  - Unusual emotional reactions to situations or events (either an excessive reaction or the absence of reaction)

  - Tantrums

  - Sudden changes in mood

  - Poor response to typical forms of discipline

- Aggressive behaviors

  - Striking or pushing others

  - Biting and scratching others

  - Throwing objects at others

It is important to note that these disorders are syndromes. That is, the disorders are defined by a variety of symptoms, but an individual does not have to have all of the symptoms to be diagnosed with the syndrome. To help you distinguish autistic disorder from Asperger's disorder, which sometimes appear similar to each other, we've included the table below, which outlines the major criteria for these two disorders. A discussion of the other disorders follows the table. Check marks in the two columns on the right indicate that the criteria must be met for a diagnosis of that syndrome.

Major diagnostic criteria	Autistic disorder	Asperger's disorder
1. Significant impairment in social interaction (Two or more symptoms out of four possible symptoms are needed for a diagnosis of either disorder.)	✓	✓
2. Significant impairments in communication (including an inability to engage in spontaneous make-believe play or imitative social play consistent with the child's developmental level) (One out of four is needed for a diagnosis of either disorder.)	✓	
3. Pattern of repetitive and stereotyped behavior and restricted range of interests and activities (One out of four symptoms is needed for diagnosis of autistic disorder)	✓	✓
4. Delays in at least one of the following areas: social interaction, language as used in social communication, and symbolic or imaginative play prior to the age of three	✓	

A diagnosis of autistic disorder is made when a total of six symptoms (which meet the major diagnostic criteria given in items 1 through 3, above) are present in the child's clinical presentation, and when the symptoms are present before the age of three.

As the table shows, autistic disorder and Asperger's disorder share two major criteria: a significant impairment in social interaction and a pattern of repetitive, stereotyped behavior and restricted range of interests and activities. Note that these two disorders do not share the criteria for significant impairments in communication. In fact, in Asperger's disorder there is no global language delay; single words are spoken by age two and communicative phrases are spoken by age three. It is also important to note that a diagnosis of Asperger's disorder requires that the child demonstrate typical cognitive development and age-appropriate self-help and self-care skills as well as curiosity about the environment. However, the problems described in the chart above must be associated with clinically significant impairment in important developmental activities (such as socialization, school participation, work, and so on) if a diagnosis of Asperger's is to be made. Early onset of symptoms is not required for a diagnosis of Asperger's disorder.

Pervasive developmental disorder not otherwise specified (PDDNOS) is the appropriate diagnosis when a child presents with a severe and pervasive impairment in any one or more of the three major diagnostic criteria (that is, impairment in social interaction, impairment in verbal and nonverbal communication, and restricted, repetitive patterns of behavior, interests, and activities), but the symptoms do not meet all of the criteria required for any of the other diagnostic categories. PDDNOS may also be diagnosed if onset of the symptoms happens after the age of three.

Childhood disintegrative disorder is characterized by a significant regression in functioning after at least two years of seemingly normal development. The deficits seen in the areas of social development, communication, and behavior repertoires are similar to those seen in autistic disorder. However, childhood disintegrative disorder is usually associated with severe mental retardation.

Rett's disorder occurs almost exclusively in females. In Rett's disorder, there is a normal pattern of physical and motor development that is followed by a loss of skills. Deceleration in head growth is also seen along with syndrome-specific hand movements (hand-wringing). Rett's disorder is associated with severe or profound mental retardation and limited language skills. While social deficits are also present in Rett's disorder, difficulties in social interaction are less persistent in Rett's than they are in autistic disorder.

Clearly, the autism spectrum disorders can present in many different ways. What makes these disorders especially challenging for parents, teachers, and other service providers is that no two children with ASD are alike. Even if two children were to meet the same diagnostic criteria, the symptoms (behaviors) exhibited by these two children could be very different. This means that there is no "one size fits all" solution to ASD. Instead, individualized interventions are needed in order to address each child's unique pattern of symptoms.

Although ASDs are considered to be lifelong disorders—there is currently no cure for them—you don't need to be pessimistic about your child's future. Many ASD symptoms can improve over time if children receive effective treatment and good support. Recent research has shown that the severity and the impact of the symptoms on the children diagnosed with autism (and on their families and communities) may vary as a result of the age at which treatment is started (Fenske, Zalenski, Krantz, and McClannahan 1985; Lovaas 1987; McEachin, Smith, and Lovaas 1993). The characteristics of the treatment (such as the intensity or number of hours of intervention, the actual amount of direct instructional time, and the specificity of the goals for intervention) may also affect outcomes. Although there are many forms of treatment that are described as effective in the treatment of ASD, and autism in particular, very few intervention strategies are supported by solid research evidence. For the teaching strategies used in this book, we have drawn from the field of applied behavior analysis, since the effectiveness of this approach is supported by research. See the box below for more on applied behavior analysis. The symptoms or behavioral characteristics associated with ASD also change with age and maturation, with some symptoms improving with age and others becoming more difficult to manage. However, if you arm yourself with knowledge about ASD and effective intervention strategies, you can minimize its potential negative effects and "stack the deck" to help your child and your family have an easier life.

WHAT IS APPLIED BEHAVIOR ANALYSIS?

Simply put, applied behavior analysis is a set of procedures that are used to teach new skills and reduce problem behaviors by replacing them with more socially acceptable behaviors. What makes applied behavior analysis different from other teaching methods is the attention given to important aspects of learning (such as task complexity, whether or not the child has the building blocks needed to learn the new task, and the child's motivation) as well as a careful analysis of the situations in which the skills or behaviors are expected to occur. Teaching involves breaking skills down into simple steps and providing adequate incentives so that children remain motivated to learn new responses during the early stages of learning. These strategies keep the demand low and motivation high. Ongoing measurement is an important component of applied behavior analysis. Measurement not only helps us identify important triggers for certain behaviors and consequences that maintain behavior but also tells us if the child is making progress. If he is, we know that the teaching plan is effective and we continue teaching with the same methods. If the child is not making progress, we need to investigate why the child is not learning. Once the source of the problem is identified, we can then make the appropriate changes in the teaching programs.

The positive results achieved by using teaching methods based on the principles of applied behavior analysis have had an effect on our thinking about outcomes in ASD. We now know that children with ASD can learn a wide variety of new skills and behaviors that can have a major impact on their lives.

There are currently many books on the market written for parents of children with ASD. This book is similar to others in that it addresses the needs of children with ASD. However, it is different from other books because it focuses on addressing the child's needs within the context of the family.

Why do we focus on the family? As you will see in chapter 1, "Austism Spectrum Disorder Is a Family Affair," all too often ASD becomes a focal point for families and, in some cases, can hold families hostage. Family life becomes shaped by the child's ASD symptoms. In extreme cases, families make extraordinary sacrifices in order to tolerate living with autism, sometimes abandoning personal needs and goals, expending massive amounts of emotional and physical energy in the process. As a result, they deplete their precious internal resources and have little left over to spend on other personal and inter-personal needs. Thus, the functioning of the family as a unit, and the well-being of other family members, may be compromised.

Yes, ASD is a lifelong disorder. However, it does not have to paralyze your child or your family. This book will show you new possibilities for helping your child and normalizing your family life. The information herein will do the following:

- Broaden the way you think about your goals for your child. You'll consider the broader context of the family when selecting teaching goals for your child.

- Provide you with a method for identifying your family's needs and shaping these into instructional goals that are designed to improve the quality of both your child's life and your family life. We will address strategies for improving family communication about each person's needs, prioritization of these needs, and negotiation to manage conflicting needs.

- Prepare you to develop and implement home teaching programs that improve your child's functioning and help you achieve family goals. We will provide a very basic introduction to the techniques and terminology that you will need to know in order to implement the strategies included in the book.

- Outline strategies for coping and problem solving so that family members can work as a team to meet the common goal of improving family life.

- Help you to think creatively about maximizing available resources.

This book focuses on fairly conservative interventions that you can do at home—strategies that don't necessarily promote radical change but instead allow you to gradually endow your child with new skills, which will improve his life and the life of your family, without causing undue stress. When you implement these strategies, you will see that consistent, focused, and systematic teaching can result in behavior change that has a positive impact on family life. More specifically, use of these strategies will increase your child's independence and his ability to participate in social and community events, and they will make your family life calmer, more productive, and more harmonious. However, if your child has consistent, negative reactions to the changes you make, consult an expert in the field before proceeding.

For the sake of simplicity, we have used masculine pronouns throughout the text. This does not mean that we assume that all children with ASD are males. Please take the liberty of substituting *she* for *he*, *her* for *his*, and so on, as you read so that the text reflects the gender of your child.

As you read the chapters in the book, you will find that there are many different ways you can help your child and your family. By applying the recommended strategies, you can design a plan that best fits the needs of your child and your family, so that your efforts to solve problems, teach your child new skills, and nurture yourself and your family will be successful.

Autism Spectrum Disorder Is a Family Affair

Because autism and autism spectrum disorders can manifest themselves in so many different ways, it's easy for families to feel confused and overwhelmed. Since we've already reviewed the major characteristics of the autism spectrum disorders in the introduction, our focus here will be on detailing the many challenges presented by ASD and the ways that these disorders may be affecting your family.

WHY ARE THE AUTISM SPECTRUM DISORDERS SO CHALLENGING?

Take a minute to reflect on the history around your child's diagnosis. Before you sought help, did you have a sense that something was wrong? Did others support your concerns or did they try to reassure you that everything was okay? Did they try to reassure you by telling you that your child was just shy, that he would outgrow his irritable temperament, or, in the case of autistic disorder or PDDNOS, that he would simply be a late talker?

Alternatively, when your child was diagnosed with ASD, did the diagnosis come with dire predictions about your child's future? For example, a mother of a very high-functioning boy with autism was erroneously told, upon diagnosis, that her son would have to be institutionalized. (Despite the health-care provider's negative prediction, this boy is currently living at home and is fully integrated in a regular second-grade classroom in his school district.)

Unfortunately, the truth is that there are many professionals who continue to be naive about the symptoms of ASD and the benefits of early intervention, even though we have made great strides in early identification and treatment. A regrettable outcome of this lack of enlightenment on the part of the professional community is that from the outset, you begin to question or, even worse, doubt your judgment about your child's needs, and you may begin to question your qualifications as a parent. After all, if these professionals are telling you that there is nothing wrong with your child ("He's just acting his age; he'll outgrow those tantrums" or "A lot of children learn to talk late"), there must be something wrong with your parenting ("You probably need to give him more choices"). In some cases, immediate and extended family members support this perception by criticizing your parenting ("You are really too permissive" or "If you disciplined him better, he would not behave that way"). What people don't realize is that typical parenting practices are usually insufficient for managing ASD-associated behaviors.

Thus, you probably encountered challenges from the very moment that you began to recognize the symptoms of ASD. Once you began to seek help, you probably dealt with the challenges of obtaining a competent evaluation, managing your emotional reaction to the diagnosis, seeking out reliable information about ASD and treatment options, and making decisions about educational services—all the while trying to balance the other necessities of life.

You have undoubtedly experienced ongoing challenges related to the impact that the symptoms of ASD have on your family's everyday life. As you already know, living with ASD can be a major stressor and can have a significant impact on the functioning of your family.

How ASD May Affect Your Family

In our clinical work with families of children with ASD, we have learned two very important principles. The first is that the factors that cause stress and the resources available for coping with and managing stress are different for each family. The second is that families are strongly committed to helping their children grow and change and that they will go to extraordinary lengths to make a good life for their child with ASD. As you will see, this latter principle can have both positive and negative outcomes.

Despite the individual differences among families, we have found that specific clusters of ASD-specific behaviors tend to increase stress in families across the board. Check the boxes below if any of these ASD-related behaviors affect your family.

☐ Excessive emotional reactions and an inability to communicate about the source of the upset

☐ Seemingly unpredictable emotional responses

☐ Aloofness and limited emotional responsiveness

☐ Poor response to directions, particularly those that would protect your child in potentially dangerous situations

☐ Limited awareness of danger

☐ Limited ability to communicate about needs and wants

☐ Difficulty delaying gratification; limited tolerance for waiting

☐ Poor understanding of consequences ("If this, then that")

☐ Poor understanding of personal boundaries (e.g., touching people and things that should not be touched)

☐ Aggressive behavior toward others when frustrated that creates concern about danger to others

☐ Self-injury that creates concern about danger to your child

☐ Difficulty tolerating changes in routines

☐   Difficulty tolerating changes in the environment

☐   Heightened responses to sensory stimulation that cause emotional upset and interfere with basic care-giving routines (e.g., bathing, hair brushing, and so on)

☐   Specific food preferences and demands that create concern about child's diet and health

☐   Need for continuous supervision due to an inability to use free time in a constructive and safe manner

☐   Poor peer and sibling relationships

The above child characteristics make it difficult for you to carry out ordinary family activities. At home, do you find it hard to do the following? (Check those that apply to your family.)

☐   Complete routine household activities

☐   Eat dinner as a family

☐   Have company over

☐   Keep the peace among siblings

☐   Have uninterrupted time

☐   Get personal time

☐   Enjoy family leisure and recreational time

As a family do you avoid participating in the following community activities? (Check those that apply to your family.)

☐   Attend religious services as a family

☐   Visit friends or other family members

☐   Participate in community cultural activities

☐   Make spontaneous stops at the grocery store

☐   Go out to dinner

☐   Go to a park

☐   Go to the movies

☐   Attend local sporting events

☐   Attend local fairs, festivals, or parades

You may be responsible for parenting both a child with ASD and other children who may have more typical development. In your family, do your other children complain about the following? (Check those that apply to your family.)

☐   Lack of fairness related to different standards for complying with family rules

☐   Allocation of time and attention

☐   Different expectations

- ☐ Lack of privacy or difficulty protecting personal property

- ☐ Insufficient free time or extracurricular activities because of responsibilities related to caring for the sibling with ASD or the perception of having to help too much with chores

- ☐ Not being able to have friends visit at home because of disruption of activities or feeling embarrassed about the sibling's symptoms of ASD

- ☐ Personal injury that results from the ASD sibling's aggressive behavior

- ☐ Inability to complete homework or practice other skills (e.g., musical instrument) because of limited quiet time

- ☐ Insufficient time for family leisure or recreation activities at home

As the above issues indicate, the impact of ASD on the family can be pervasive. That is, it may have a significant effect on all aspects of family functioning, including the adjustment and emotional well-being of siblings and the nature of parent-child interactions. Research focused on the impact of ASD has identified still other family stressors. Have you experienced any of the following? (Check all of the following that apply to your family.)

- ☐ Increased marital stress

- ☐ Increased conflict with extended family members related to parenting practices, acceptance of ASD as a diagnosis, levels of support, and disagreement over what is "best" for your family

- ☐ Increased strain on your family finances (due to your child's need for full-time care, treatment and respite care expenses, or changing residences because of safety concerns or neighbors' complaints)

- ☐ Withdrawal from social activities

- ☐ Negative impact on your physical and psychological health including reactive depression and heightened anxiety associated with challenging ASD-related behaviors

- ☐ Increased concern about your own physical health, worry related to the possibility of illness, and thoughts about your own mortality (connected to worry over your child's ability to learn the skills needed for self-sufficiency in adulthood)

The final issue that can affect families relates to your expectations for your child. Although as parents we know that we cannot determine the choices that our children make in their adult lives, it is very hard not to have at least some wishes, dreams, or expectations for them as adults. ASD has the potential to upset those hopes and dreams. It's difficult, if not impossible, to predict their future, and any child's path from childhood to adulthood may hold many unpredictable twists and turns. Add ASD to the picture, and the path becomes anything but a smooth, predictable course. Some common expectations are listed below:

- ☐ Good school performance in the elementary school years and completion of high school and perhaps college

- ☐ Participation in age-appropriate social and recreational activities such as sports, scouting, and clubs

☐   Development of stable social relationships

☐   Competence in self-care and self-control, and the ability to make responsible decisions

☐   Selection of a career path and the pursuit of that career

☐   Financial independence

☐   Marriage and children

☐   Acceptance as part of a community

What Can You Do About It?

Recognize That the Stressors Are Real

Despite the multiple sources of stress associated with ASD, many of the families we work with, particularly mothers, have a hard time accepting the fact that living with ASD is difficult and stressful. Many persist in blaming themselves when they feel overwhelmed by ASD-related symptoms; in other words, they believe that they need to be stronger so they can cope with the symptoms more effectively. The truth is that the stressors associated with raising a child with ASD are excessive and they are real. Feeling overwhelmed by ASD is a normal reaction, not an abnormal one. We emphasize this point because acknowledging that ASD is challenging and that it stresses the entire family is the trigger for action.

If you have gone through the checklists above, you have already taken the first positive step toward reducing the impact of ASD on your family. If you have not already done so, please go back and place a check mark next to all of the issues that relate to your family.

The items that you have checked constitute your starting point for problem solving and treatment planning. In subsequent chapters you will have an opportunity to use the checked items to help you formulate goals and strategies to address these important issues.

The stressors resulting from ASD are real. Recognition and acceptance of this fact are essential in order to move toward constructive problem solving. You are not the cause of your child's symptoms of ASD. However, you can change your response to the symptoms in ways that can help your child and your family grow.

Don't Let ASD Hold You Hostage

Loosening the hold that ASD has on your family may not be an easy process. This is because your family, like most others, has learned to respond to ASD in ways that appear to minimize its impact. When your child screams at the top of his lungs at the entrance of the grocery store because he doesn't want to go in or because he's upset that you won't let him have his favorite candy bar at ten o'clock in the morning, you know that talking to him about why you need to do this errand right now and asking him to cooperate won't do any good, since he doesn't understand lengthy verbal explanations. So, you may find it easier to just give in and give him the candy or take him home rather than deal with the consequences of holding your ground—the comments or looks from other customers, feelings of incompetence, and so on. While it may seem to be the best immediate solution, over time your child may learn that his tantrums help him avoid certain situations that he does not enjoy and that they are an effective means for obtaining preferred items or activities.

In an effort to minimize your child's distress, you may go to excessive lengths to prevent change, keep routines constant, anticipate your child's needs, avoid situations that cause distress, and sacrifice your own needs to maintain the status quo. In extreme cases, families may focus entirely on avoiding situations that might tip the delicate balance between the child's contentment and extreme distress. In one family we worked with, their son would control the physical movements of family members: if they did not heed his demand that they stop moving, he would engage in tantrums that included severe head banging. His mother reported feeling helpless and frightened as she stood still for long periods of time in the middle of her living room simply to prevent her child from injuring himself. Other families have placed a moratorium on family vacations until their child with ASD could handle the unpredictable events associated with travel. One mother told us that she had a difficult time doing errands around town because of her son's insistence on going to movie theaters to watch the credits roll at the end of the films.

Unfortunately, many of the families we work with believe that this level of sacrifice is an inevitable consequence of having a child with ASD. Equally problematic is the practice of denying the family's important needs, such as going on family vacations.

Crucial Steps to Freedom

The steps below outline things you can do to minimize the negative effects of ASD on your family. These steps are equally important whether you have just received the diagnosis or have long been living with ASD.

Get good information. Accurate information can be crucial to your understanding of ASD and its treatment options. An enormous amount of information is available on the subject of ASD. Books, articles, and numerous Web sites have been written and created for parents and professionals. The amount of information can be overwhelming and sometimes it is difficult to determine what is worth reading and what is not. To help you sort out the good from the bad, we have included in the Resources section a list of sources of information that we consider to be reputable. These resources have been written by respected people in the field of autism spectrum disorders and the treatment recommendations they give are supported by high quality research. Why is it important to use treatment strategies that are based on well-controlled research? At the risk of being criticized for answering a question with a question, let us ask you this: would you take a medication to treat a specific disease if no research had shown that the medication reduced the symptoms without causing serious side effects?

Be a good consumer. Not everything you read or hear about ASD is true. Be wary of the "cure du jour." Before you invest time, money, or energy in a treatment or intervention strategy, do some research. Your time and financial resources are much too important to squander on wild-goose chases. As mentioned above, be cautious and selective. Any claim of a "cure" is a sure sign that you should be suspicious about the merits of the treatment.

Utilize high-quality services. Early intervention for your child and your family is one of the best preventative measures you can take. Talk to experts in your area and find out the names of professionals who offer the best early intervention services. If your child is beyond the eligible age for early intervention (from birth to three years) but is participating in a treatment or school program, critically evaluate your child's progress in his current program. If there are no or few objective indicators of his progress, reevaluate program options. Interview staff regarding their knowledge of ASD and if their background is limited, look for more effective programs that offer services to families and children.

Debunk myths. Parents often hold incorrect ideas about how to best parent a child with ASD. We have labeled these ideas "myths" because they have little basis in reality. Nevertheless, in many families these myths strongly influence how the parents behave. Debunking the myths is an important first step in the change process. In the table below, the myths are countered with more realistic perspectives, which can help you develop a healthier outlook on parenting. Debunking the myths is an important first step in the change process.

Myth	Reality
Parents must be perfect.	Children build tolerance and develop coping skills when their needs are not immediately met.
Parents are the only ones who can care for a child with ASD.	Children can and need to learn to adapt to other caregivers.
It is essential to always put the needs of a child with ASD first.	Well-adjusted families balance the needs of all individuals in the family unit. Not all needs get met all of the time.
All other family members must sacrifice their own needs in order to provide adequate care for a child with ASD.	All family members, including the child with ASD, must compromise in order to ensure that all family members get their needs met much of the time.
Families in this situation can never approach normal functioning.	Despite the emotional, physical, and at times, financial stressors associated with having a family member with a lifelong disability, families can and should strive for normal family life.
Superman or Superwoman lives at your address.	He or she doesn't.

Evaluate your emotional response. How are *you* doing? Remember that your emotional health is critical to the well-being of your child and your family. If you feel like you are overwhelmed, chronically fatigued, having difficulty sleeping or sleeping too much, frequently crying or feeling sad, no longer enjoying activities or interactions that used to give you pleasure, feeling disinterested in others, or feeling hopeless about your future, you may be depressed. If you are having chronic worry that is difficult to control, difficulty concentrating, muscle tension, trouble sleeping (difficulty falling asleep, staying asleep, or sleeping well), restlessness, feelings of being "keyed up" or on edge, and fatigue, you may be dealing with anxiety. If you are experiencing any of these symptoms of depression or anxiety, consult with your physician to get help.

Be optimistic—there's reason to hope. Despite the absence of a "cure," well-controlled research studies tell us that teaching strategies based on the principles of applied behavior analysis can make a big difference in the functioning of children with ASD. Much research has documented marked changes in receptive and expressive language, the comprehension of nonverbal communication, the quality and frequency of social interactions, and improvement in self-care skills, academic achievement, and self-control.

Adopt a family focus on intervention. During our years of clinical work with families who have a child (or children) with ASD, we have shifted the focus of our interventions from traditional parent training (interventions that largely focus on building skills and reducing challenging behaviors in the child with ASD) to a family-oriented approach. The family-oriented approach has merit because:

- The overall well-being of the family is important for effective treatment, in large part because of the role that families can play in the carryover of skills learned at school (communication, coping strategies, and socialization). Therefore, it is important to place the needs of the child with ASD within the context of the whole family's needs.

- Balancing the needs of the child with ASD and those of other family members can improve the quality of family life.

- Your family environment serves as a training ground where your child will learn how to function in the world. Within the context of your family, your child will learn about relationships (how to get along with others) and responsibilities (working together to accomplish a set of common goals, for example), as well as how to cope with successes and failures.

- Family involvement provides numerous opportunities to teach new skills in a natural environment.

This shift of focus from child to family does not mean that we view the child's needs as unimportant. Rather, by viewing the child within the context of the family, we focus on how to fully include the child as a contributing family member, rather than on how the family can care for the handicapped child. This view parallels the inclusion model in the educational system that you are likely familiar with. You may be thinking, "This is absurd! Of course our child is included in our family!" and you are correct. But our definition of *being included* is "being an independent and contributing member." We have found that using this definition helps families to level the playing field and see their child with ASD in a new way.

Children of all ages and all ability levels can contribute. Every child can perform a skill or chore that benefits the family and, by doing their part, become active partners in the family's everyday life. Of course, the chores and tasks that we expect our children to complete must be within their ability level and must be consistent with expectations for their chronological age and developmental level, whether they are struggling with ASD or not.

By broadening the scope of intervention from the child to the family and by targeting child-centered goals that contribute to family wellness, everyone benefits, and excessive self-denial and self-sacrifice are minimized. Examples of family-focused goals and how these might affect the child and the family are listed below:

Child's contribution	Impact on the child	Impact on the family
Takes care of basic needs (e.g., toileting, grooming) independently	Increased independence	More time for personal and shared activities; less stress associated with getting ready for school, family outings, and so on
Completes routine household chores	Increased independence and preparation for more independent living environment	Decreased conflict among siblings regarding "fairness" and different expectations for each family member; less need for constant child supervision while completing household tasks
Respects the personal belongings of others	Improved social interactions with family members and peers	Decreased conflict and negative emotions related to destruction of personal property
Complies with rules and participates in social and recreational activities	More frequent inclusion and increased competence in social and recreational activities	Increased potential for your child to participate in extracurricular activities, which would provide you with more time to spend with your other children, get things done, or have some personal time
Complies with safety-related rules (such as staying close to you during outings)	Increased social and learning opportunities	Increased interest on the part of family members in going on family outings
Tolerates care providers other than parents	Increased social and learning opportunities	More opportunities for parents to go out together and to maintain a social network

As you can see, intervention that focuses on family issues can impart benefits to the child and to all family members and thereby have a positive impact on family life.

This chapter has provided you with information about the ways in which ASD can affect your family, and it has introduced you to a family-focused approach for decreasing the impact of ASD on your family. The stress of caring for a child with ASD is real, and there are effective strategies that you can use to reduce the negative impact of ASD on your family. However, the process of change (or even anticipating change) from the status quo can be stress producing. Therefore, in the next chapter we provide you with information on how to manage stress.

2

Coping

As we discussed in chapter 1, parenting a child with ASD can be a very stressful endeavor. So, too, are the initial stages in the behavior change process. This is because you will be investing a different kind of energy and your child will need to learn a new set of rules and expectations.

During this challenging process, it is important to be mindful of strategies that you can use to minimize the impact of stress, maintain a positive and optimistic outlook, and manage fluctuations in mood. Keeping your thumb on the "pulse" of your stress levels, mood fluctuations, and attitude, and taking action to prevent or reduce uncomfortable physical and emotional states, can have a number of positive outcomes. First, taking care of yourself is essential for maintaining your physical and emotional health. Second, if you feel physically and emotionally strong, you will likely feel more confident in your ability to make decisions that affect your family. Third, children with ASD (in fact, all children) respond better when their parents are calm and in control.

The sources of stress experienced in families of children with ASD can vary widely. Therefore, our focus in this chapter is not to identify strategies for coping with specific stressors, but rather to provide you with some general guidelines for managing stress. Some of the strategies we recommend involve recognizing heightened stress and using techniques to reduce your stress levels. Others involve using a more proactive approach—that is, having a plan for managing situations that increase your arousal levels.

COPING MEANS MANAGING, NOT ELIMINATING ALL PROBLEMS

It is not always possible to immediately change the things that cause stress in your life. What you can do, however, is change your response to those stressors, and minimize their impact on your physical and emotional health.

Signs of Stress: Observing Your Behavior and Listening to Your Body

Many subtle and obvious signs pop up during your day to inform you that you are reacting to stress in your life. In the table below, we have listed some of the signs of heightened stress. Use the table to monitor your stress levels.

Symptom	Check if present						
	M	T	W	Th	F	Sa	Su
Fatigue							
Restlessness							
Racing heart							
Muscle tension (in your back, neck, or shoulders) and/or headache							
Heightened emotional reactions (shortness of temper, weepiness, irritability)							
Gastric distress							
Difficulty concentrating							
Forgetfulness							
Excessive worry							
Too much or too little sleep, difficulty falling asleep, or nighttime awakenings after which you cannot return to asleep							
Decreased or excessive appetite							

Cumulative, long-term, and chronic stress can have a serious effect on your health and your mood. Since your health is important to you, it is essential that you have tools to minimize your subjective experience of stress. The first step in this process is to identify the ASD-related situations that are contributing to your heightened stress levels.

Identify Things That Make You Feel Stressed

What situations at home heighten your experience of stress? Write your stressors in the spaces below.

Stress-producing situations
1.
2.
3.
4.
5.
6.
7.

Rating Stress Levels

When using strategies to reduce stress, it is helpful to rate the intensity of the stress you're experiencing. This is especially useful when you want to determine if a particular stress-reducing strategy is working. The idea is to rate your stress level before you implement a strategy and then rate it again immediately after using the strategy. If the coping strategy reduces your stress level, it has done its job. If it does not, you'll need to try a different strategy. Using a before-and-after rating scale to identify your stress levels is one way that that you can keep track of your stress level and determine whether the coping strategies you select are working for you.

In the scale below, a rating of one represents the absence of stress, a rating of five represents a comfortable level of stress, and a rating of ten represents the most intense experience of stress you can recall.

Subjective Units of Distress

1	2	3	4	5	6	7	8	9	10

No stress   Comfortable   Most severe

Practice using the rating scale. For each stressor you identified in the table above, rate your subjective stress level in the table below.

Stressor	Subjective stress level
1.	
2.	
3.	
4.	
5.	
6.	
7.	

Tools for Managing Stress

As we mentioned above, there are many different strategies for managing stress. Even if you currently have a repertoire of effective coping strategies, this section may provide you with new tools that can help you manage even better. The strategies outlined below can help you manage your emotional reactions and prevent situations that can make you feel helpless and frustrated. The result is that you will feel more competent and in control. Keep in mind, however, that finding effective coping strategies is a highly individualized process—what works for one person may not work for another. When trying out new strategies, make a commitment to implementing the strategy for a reasonable period of time before rendering judgment. Be patient, plan, implement your plan, and then evaluate the impact of your effort.

Our discussion of coping strategies is organized in several separate sections: maintaining a steady diet of self-nurturing activities, setting realistic goals, generating plans to manage challenging situations, and adopting a can-do attitude.

Maintain a Steady Diet of Self-Nurturing Activities

A big part of managing stress is getting in the habit of taking care of yourself. This means setting aside some time each day just for you (pursuing your interests, pampering yourself, exercising, or socializing), and spending quality time with the ones you love. In addition, you should take care of your health (eating well and getting enough sleep). If you do not currently have a steady diet of self-nurturing activities, the following list of pleasurable, nonstressful activities may give you some ideas so you can get started:

- Listening to music

- Talking or visiting with friends

- Reading for pleasure

- Taking a relaxing bath

- Exercising

- Cultivating a hobby

Most of us know what we are supposed to do, but how many of us actually succeed at taking care of ourselves? If you are among the many who don't, what's stopping you? Below are some frequently encountered impediments to good self-care (nurturing) identified by parents of children who attend our school program.

- *Insufficient time.* The challenge of juggling household and community responsibilities, parenting, devoting the extra time needed to care for an ASD-diagnosed child, and working leaves many parents with very little or no time for taking care of themselves. Stealing time for themselves may be complicated by the fact that many parents have few, if any, options for even a brief reprieve from their parenting responsibilities. While the other children in the family may be able to function independently for short periods of time, children with ASD often need constant supervision. If parents cannot find someone to supervise their ASD child, then they are on call twenty-four hours a day.

- *Limited interests.* A number of parents have told us that that they have lost sight of their personal interests as a result of their parenting, household, and extended-family responsibilities as well as their quest to find new information about treatments or programs that might help their child. Some have said that they wonder what they would do with their free time if they actually had some.

- *Lack of energy.* Exhaustion often prevents parents from pursuing personal interests even when time is available. Many parents tell us that by the end of the day, they have no energy left for pleasurable activities—all they want to do is go to sleep. To make matters worse, for some parents, uninterrupted sleep is not an option, because their child has sleep problems. In addition to the attendant sleep deprivation, these sleep problems increase the length of the parents' day due to the need for round-the-clock parenting

- *Depressed or anxious mood.* Many parents suffer from depression or anxiety. Research suggests that in many cases where mood problems are present, they are the result of stress. If you are experiencing symptoms of depression or anxiety (listed in the chart below) every day for several consecutive days, we advise that you seek professional help.

Review the chart below and place a check mark indicating the symptoms that you experience each day. If problems persist, review your symptoms with your physician so that an appropriate referral can be made.

Week of:							
Symptoms	**Check if present**						
	M	T	W	Th	F	Sa	Su
Depression							
Decreased interest in or pleasure derived from activities or social interactions							
Sadness, excessive crying, or feeling like you want to cry but can't							
Significant weight loss or decrease or increase in appetite							
Inability to sleep or excessive sleep							
Agitation or motor functions slowing							
Fatigue or loss of energy							
Feelings of worthlessness or excessive guilt							
Decreased ability to think or concentrate; difficulty making decisions							
Recurrent thoughts of death and/or suicide							
Anxiety							
Excessive worry							
Difficulty controlling worry							
Feeling restless, keyed up, on edge							
Easily fatigued							
Difficulty concentrating; mind going blank							
Irritability							
Muscle tension							
Sleep disturbance							

	M	T	W	Th	F	Sa	Su
Palpitations, pounding heart, rapid heart rate							
Sweating							
Trembling or shaking							
Panic							
Shortness of breath; difficulty breathing							
Choking sensation							
Nausea and abdominal stress							
Dizziness, light-headedness, feeling faint							
Feeling as if things are not real							
Fear of loss of control or going crazy							
Numbness or tingling sensations							
Chills or hot flushes							

How can you make some time to take care of yourself? Adopt a problem-solving approach. When it comes to doing things for yourself, it's easy to simply say "I have no time for personal time." But once you get the hang of it, you'll find that taking a little time to engage in problem solving is just as easy as *not* making personal time for yourself. Moreover, you'll be glad you did, especially if you can actually squeeze some time for self-nurturing out of your busy day. The problem-solving process typically consists of seven steps:

1. Identify the problem.

2. Brainstorm solutions. In the initial stages of brainstorming, it is important not to dismiss unlikely seeming solutions, since this type of censoring might stifle creative thinking. You might also find it helpful to seek input from others, especially if you have been feeling stuck.

3. For each idea you generated while brainstorming, objectively list the pros and cons.

4. Review the pros and cons and select one or more solutions that seem promising.

5. Try one of the solutions you selected in step 4 and evaluate the result.

6. If the solution you tried in step 5 seems to alleviate the problem, continue using that solution. If not, select another viable option and try it, continuing until you find a solution that works.

7. If no solution provides relief, go back to the brainstorming phase (step 2) and start the process all over again.

Use the worksheet below to get started. Select a problem, brainstorm solutions, and then list the pros and cons for each solution.

Problem:		
Possible solutions	Pros	Cons

For more on using available resources creatively to allow you to solve family-related problems and thus have more time to take care of yourself, see chapter 7. This information may help you generate additional, potentially useful solutions. Another useful resource on managing family schedules and difficulties is *Defying Autism: Keeping Your Sanity and Taking Control* (Lockshin, Gillis, and Romanczyk 2004).

Set Realistic Long- and Short-Range Goals

One very important strategy for feeling good about your efforts is to make sure that you set reasonable goals. If, for example, you have just taken up a new sport, you probably wouldn't enter a qualifying match expecting that you would make it to the championship tournament. Unless you are an exceptional athlete, this course of action would certainly lead to failure, possibly dampening your enthusiasm for the sport and your confidence in your budding abilities. The same logic applies to your efforts to take control of ASD's effects on your family. If you plan to go straight from A to Z (that is, get rid of all of your child's ASD symptoms in one fell swoop), you may be expecting too much.

A more reasonable approach, and one that has a greater probability of success, involves two steps. First, identify the goal that you wish to achieve. Second, identify a sequence of simpler, more easily achieved tasks that contribute to your ability to meet your goal. In the three examples that follow, we present each scenario in the form of an equation in order to stress the idea that the achievement of the goal is the sum of the parts (i.e., the teaching tasks). We also identify the functional level of the child for whom the teaching sequence would be appropriate.

Example 1: Three-year-old preverbal child (that is, words are just emerging) who has the ability to recognize objects by name

Parent goal for child: Expresses needs and wants

Recognizes pictures of objects + gives picture on request + gives picture to receive the object represented + gives picture when asked, "What do you want?" = expresses needs and wants

Example 2: Five-year-old child with good verbal language skills who does not use his language in social contexts

Parent goal for child: Tells parents about his day at school (relates information about activities or events)

Describes self engaged in an activity when asked, "What are you doing?" + describes self engaged in two activities when asked, "What did you do?" + describes two activities when shown a copy of that day's picture schedule from school and asked the same question + describes three or more activities when shown a copy of that day's picture schedule from school and asked the same question = relates information about activities or events

Example 3: Seven-year-old child with a second-grade reading level who is able to do self-care tasks with parent supervision

Parent goal for child: Independently completes self-care routine in the morning (dresses himself, uses the toilet, washes his face, and brushes his teeth without parent supervision)

Child follows single written direction on his morning routine activity schedule ("Brush your teeth") + child follows two written directions on his morning routine activity schedule ("Wash your face" and "Brush your teeth") + child follows three written directions on his morning routine activity schedule ("Use the bathroom," "Wash your face," and "Brush your teeth") + when given an activity schedule and told to "Get ready," the child completes all four written directions independently ("Use the bathroom," "Wash your face," "Brush your teeth," and "Get dressed") = independently completes self-care routine in the morning.

More detailed descriptions about how to teach these skills are given in chapters 8 through 11. These examples were included here to show that you can "stack the deck" for success by teaching new skills in manageable steps that are consistent with your child's ability level. In other words, you can set both short- and long-range goals to gradually get your child where you want him to be.

One way to ensure that you notice successes is to keep track of your child's and your family's progress toward the goals that you have set. The list of resources at the end of this book includes books that explain how to keep track of your child's performance as he acquires tasks, so that you can know when your child is ready to move on to more complex tasks. Here, we will focus on a simplified form of tracking.

Mr. and Mrs. Ross wanted to increase the amount of time that their son, Bobby, played appropriately with toys (that is, used the toys as they were intended to be used). First they taught him how to play with toy cars, build structures with blocks, and use a tape recorder to play his favorite songs and stories. Next, they decided to teach him to occupy his free time productively using these toys. When they started the teaching program, Bobby was able to play without adult supervision for one minute. The teaching program they developed involved reinforcing Bobby for playing with the toys he had learned to use for progressively longer periods of time. When they started the program, Mr. and Mrs. Ross told Bobby that if he played until the timer went off, he would earn a snack. The table below shows how they tracked Bobby's progress on learning this task. They wrote a plus sign (+) in the appropriate box when Bobby responded correctly and a minus sign (-) when he responded incorrectly. When Bobby had played appropriately with toys for one minute on three consecutive occasions, Mr. and Mrs. Ross then moved to the next level of expectation (playing appropriately for two minutes on three consecutive occasions). Each move to a more difficult level of the teaching program was considered a success.

Opportunities										
Task	1	2	3	4	5	6	7	8	9	10
Plays appropriately with toys for 1 minute	-	-	+	+	-	+	+	+		
Plays appropriately with toys for 2 minutes	-	-	-	+	+	-	+	+	+	
Plays appropriately with toys for 3 minutes	-	-	+	-	+	+	+			
Plays appropriately with toys for 5 minutes	-	-	-	-	+	+	-	+	+	+
Plays appropriately with toys for 10 minutes	-	-	-	+	+	-	+	+	+	
Plays appropriately with toys for 15 minutes	-	+	-	-	+	-	-	+	+	+

Mr. and Mrs. Carrero wanted to teach their daughter, Theresa, to help sort laundry. They used the following worksheet to record her progress.

Opportunities										
Task	1	2	3	4	5	6	7	8	9	10
Sorts 5 pieces of laundry into baskets of colored and white clothing	-	-	+	-	+	+	-	+	+	+
Sorts 10 pieces of laundry into baskets of colored and white clothing	-	-	-	+	-	-	+	+	+	
Sorts 15 pieces of laundry into baskets of colored and white clothing	-	-	+	-	+	+	+			
Places laundry in washing machine	-	-	+	+	+					
Places laundry in washing machine and puts in a capful of laundry detergent	-	-	-	+	-	+	+	+		
Places laundry in washing machine, puts in a capful of laundry detergent, and turns dial to designated setting	-	-	-	+	+	-	+	+	+	
Places laundry in washing machine, puts in a capful of laundry detergent, turns dial to designated setting, and pulls dial out to start washing machine	-	-	+	+	-	+	-	+	+	+

Mr. and Mrs. Carrero applauded Theresa's success when she was able to successfully sort five pieces of clothing on three consecutive occasions, and whenever she moved to the next level of teaching, since she had never assisted with household chores before.

Generating Plans to Manage Challenging Situations

Having a plan for how you will manage your child's routine upsets or disruptions is important for a number of reasons. First, most of us do better when we have a strategy for addressing problems, since it eliminates the guesswork, makes us feel less helpless and frustrated, and can help prevent heightened stress levels. And you probably know from experience that matching your child's out-of-control behavior does not usually help resolve the problem.

Second, if you consistently use a specific strategy in difficult situations, you can begin to evaluate which parts of the plan are helpful and which are not. This point is particularly important because research in the area of ASD has demonstrated that many of the challenging behaviors observed are not random, but fit into a system and serve a communicative function (Carr and Durrand 1985). That is, many behaviors (such as tantrums and aggression) seem to be triggered by specific events (when access to preferred tasks or activities is denied, for example), and yet others may be a way for the child to escape or avoid unpleasant interactions (such as having a tantrum when it's time for a bath). If you consistently react to your child's behavior in a particular way, it may be possible to identify what function the behavior serves and to generate a plan for reacting to the behavior in a different way that has a more desirable effect. These issues will be addressed in much greater detail in chapter 5 and chapters 8 through 11.

The third benefit of having a response plan for dealing with challenges is that you can provide a real-life example for your children (those with ASD and those without) about how to manage emotionally charged situations. As your children continue to develop their communication skills, you can use these situations as teaching opportunities—you can talk about your feelings and explain how you are managing your behavior or resolving the situation.

In the following paragraphs, we describe two examples of different plans families have developed to cope with their child's emotional behavior and manage their own responses.

Rhonda, a five-year-old with a moderate number of autistic symptoms including minimal verbal communication, would sometimes have bouts of intermittent, high-pitched screaming and crying, sometimes lasting as long as half an hour, that did not appear to be related to any physical pain or medical problems. Thorough medical examinations and workups had turned up no possible causes of her behavior. When these episodes occurred, both of Rhonda's parents felt helpless, frustrated, and worried about whether they should be doing something more to help their daughter.

We suggested the following plan:

- Each time an episode occurs, write down the time it started, how long it lasted, any identifiable event that occurred just before it began, and your responses. (The idea was for Rhonda's parents to provide us with information that we could use to identify events or behaviors that might be triggering or maintaining the episodes.)

- Every ten minutes during each episode, follow the procedures below:

  - Check Rhonda for bruises or injury to make sure she has not hurt herself.

  - Check Rhonda's diaper to see if she is wet or dry.

■ Open her communication book (a book containing pictures that Rhonda used as an alternative method for communicating her wants and needs), and ask her if she wants anything.

■ Make notes about Rhonda's reactions, whether she was injured or soiled, and what, if anything, she requested.

■ Be sure to pay attention to Rhonda when she is playing quietly by telling her that you like the way she is playing or by joining her in her play activities to provide her with positive attention for appropriate behavior.

Rhonda's parents told us that their anxiety and distress decreased once they had a plan for what to do. They also took comfort in knowing that they were collecting information that might provide an explanation for Rhonda's screaming episodes.

Mr. and Mrs. Hernandez had deduced that their seven-year-old son Joey's post-breakfast tantrums on weekdays were triggered by their requests to brush his teeth and get dressed for school. It seemed that Joey had his mind set on eating breakfast and then watching his favorite television shows as he always did on the weekends. Because neither parent could tolerate Joey's tantrums, they would dress him, brush his teeth, and make sure he had time to watch television before he had to go off to school, even though he was perfectly capable of dressing himself and brushing his own teeth. Joey was happy with this routine because he got to watch television, and Mr. and Mrs. Hernandez tolerated the situation because they avoided having to cope with Joey's tantrums. The problem was that Joey was not dressing himself or brushing his own teeth despite the fact that he had the skills to do so.

We advised Joey's parents to use the following plan:

■ Have Joey get dressed and brush his teeth before breakfast. (Joey always woke up with a good appetite, so breakfast would be a natural reward for finishing his morning routine.)

■ Lay out his clothing beforehand and give him a checklist showing his responsibilities: get dressed, brush teeth, eat breakfast, and watch TV. Show Joey how to check off each item once it's completed.

■ If Joey comes down to breakfast before he's finished getting dressed and brushing his teeth, send him back upstairs in a calm but firm voice informing him that he needed to dress and brush before breakfast.

■ To screen out Joey's protests, listen to your favorite CDs using headphones.

■ Give verbal praise and hugs when Joey arrives ready for breakfast with clothes on and teeth brushed.

The result? Within three days, Joey was independently completing his morning routine. Mr. and Mrs. Hernandez felt that the plan they used to resist Joey's complaints and tantrums had really helped them achieve their goal. Everyone was pleased.

Mr. and Mrs. Hernandez's story highlights the importance of having a plan for managing your own emotions and behavior when your child is having a tantrum. Below are some ideas that have worked for some parents we know. Write in any of your own coping strategies on the blank lines at the end of this list.

- Listen to music using headphones during a tantrum or screaming episode to screen out noise and minimize your emotional response. This strategy is most appropriate when tantrums and screaming are thought to function as a means of getting attention or escaping a task demand, and if you periodically check to make sure that your child is not in any danger or obvious physical distress you can be reasonably confident that your child is not in any danger. Allowing the tantrum or screaming to increase your arousal level would be counterproductive; listening to music may help keep you calm, prevent you from reinforcing tantrums or screaming, and allow you to follow through on your response plan. Of course, if tantrums or screaming are unusual events for your child, a different response might be more appropriate.

- Do mindless but engaging tasks that keep you productively occupied (such as cleaning, folding laundry, or clipping coupons).

- Use relaxation strategies.

- Call a friend or family member for support.

- _____

- _____

Adopt a Can-Do Attitude

Although some people might be reluctant to admit that they talk to themselves, self-talk can play a big role in how we interpret situations that we encounter and how we feel about ourselves. Patterns of self-talk that are negative and self-defeating can contribute to sad or depressed mood. In contrast, patterns of self-talk that are self-affirming can contribute to a positive mood and the ability to face challenges with an air of confidence and competence. Adopting a can-do attitude involves the following actions:

- Remind yourself that change is a process that takes time and that you are actively working toward change.

- Generate positive self-statements to help you stick to your plan.

- Look for the positive in everyday events.

- Recognize even small successes.

- Interpret false starts as learning experiences.

- Don't compare your child or your progress to that of other children—strive for your family's personal best.

Generate positive self-statements to help you stick to your plan. Your self-talk is powerful. Thinking negatively can affect how you feel and can contribute to your feeling defeated. Statements like "I can't do this," "This will never work," and "I'm not good at this" can be self-fulfilling prophecies. In other words, if you tell yourself that you can't, you likely won't.

Finding a way to restate your feelings in a more positive, self-supportive way can have the opposite effect. Instead of saying "I can't," try saying "I'll give it a shot." A more positive substitute for "I'm no good at this" might be "I'm getting better at this." Restating "I can't" as "I can't right now, but I'll figure out how to do this" is also adaptive. Using these strategies, you turn a defeatist attitude into constructive resolve.

Look for the positive in everyday events. Is your glass half full or half empty? Focusing on your child's positive developments, no matter how small, will make you feel more in control and optimistic. A trip to the grocery store that only takes five minutes should be viewed as a success when you're dealing with a child who has trouble managing behavior in public places. Similarly, a five-minute play session in a group of three or four other children should be seen as a success for a child who has trouble using toys appropriately. And a meal in which the child actually stays at the kitchen table long enough to eat a quarter of his dinner is a success if he has trouble staying still.

Recognize successes, even small ones. Taking time to recognize and acknowledge the successes that you and your child share is extremely important for a number of reasons. First, success breeds more success, which keeps you and your child motivated and rewards your collective efforts. Your child's success also gives you information about the effectiveness of your teaching strategies. If your child responds well to a particular teaching method, you will likely want to use that strategy to teach other skills.

Enhancing Family Communication

Autism spectrum disorder is a family affair, and so is the struggle to achieve and maintain a healthy family environment. As you begin to focus on how to normalize family life, you initiate the process of protecting your family from the potential negative effects of ASD. However, you cannot do all the work alone.

WORKING TOGETHER AS A TEAM

Using the concept of teamwork is useful for families who are confronting challenging situations. For our purposes, we define *team* as a number of people who are organized to work together as a group, and *teamwork* as a cooperative effort by members of that group. The group, of course, is your family. Defining your family as a team does not mean that all family members should be expected to assume the same workload or that everyone will need to expend the same amount of emotional and physical energy helping your child with ASD. It *does* mean that no family member will have to sacrifice his or her needs because of ASD. Working together as a team has the following advantages:

- *Everyone helps.* This means that no one person is responsible for everything and that family members will work to help and support each other to meet both personal and shared or family goals.

- *Division of labor.* Tasks and responsibilities can be assigned on the basis of age, ability, level of dependability, preference, and family needs.

- *Increased flexibility.* Tasks and assignments do not have to be permanent; they can change as individual or family needs change, either temporarily or permanently.

- *Increased sense of camaraderie.* Teamwork provides multiple opportunities for family members to work cooperatively toward a mutual goal.

Mobilizing your family to work as a team will take some time and practice. Below, we've outlined several steps you can take to get the process started and to maintain the team concept.

Step One: The Rationale

Explain to your family why you want to adopt a team approach. Offer information about ASD and how you think ASD has affected your family's functioning. The amount and complexity of the information given to each family member will depend on their age and their ability to understand these rather complex concepts. When explaining ASD to young siblings, it is important to point out that the child with ASD, though still an important part of the family, is different from other children in that he has difficulties learning (language, play skills, self-help skills, rules, and/or coping with his feelings) and that he may have a restricted range of interests and a desire for routine and sameness. Other important areas to cover when talking with all family members include the following:

■ Although the child with ASD is capable of learning, he may not learn as quickly as other children in the family and he will likely not learn new skills the same way they do.

■ If the child with ASD is nonverbal and tends to be aggressive, you can explain that the child uses aggression in part because he has difficulty telling people what he needs and therefore gets very frustrated when people do not understand his efforts to communicate. If the child has language skills, you can explain that controlling his behavior related to his emotions is difficult for him. It may be helpful to explain that in most cases the child does not intend to hurt others, but that sometimes others can get hurt if they block goal-directed activity (that is, they prevent the child from getting what he wants) or if they annoy the child. A similar explanation could be used for self-injurious behavior.

■ Seeing a sibling engage in repetitive and stereotyped behaviors such as rocking or hand or arm flapping can be confusing to young children without ASD. You can explain this behavior by saying that children with ASD may enjoy the physical sensation of these movements, or that these activities may help them reduce stress or frustration, and so they repeat them. A young sibling can also be helped to understand that since age-appropriate play activities are not very enjoyable for children with ASD, they tend to do other things that make them feel good.

■ In order to provide a balanced view of the child with ASD, it is important to point out the child's (and his sibling's) strengths *and* limitations. Ask the child's siblings to think about things that they themselves do very well and those things that are more difficult for them. This can open up a discussion regarding the fact that we all have strengths and weaknesses; in ASD, the weaknesses are just more obvious.

■ Be sure to tell the siblings that children with ASD can and do learn and one of the team's goals will be to help the child with ASD learn new skills so that he can become more independent, better able to communicate with others, more socially oriented, more successful in school, and better able to enjoy a wider range of activities.

See the Resources section for sources of information on ASD.

Step Two: The Team Members

Inform your family that while you would like all members, including your child with ASD, to be part of the team, you understand that everyone may not want to join in. Assure family members that you will respect their decision and that they will not be penalized for nonparticipation. However, make it clear that you will expect everyone, even those who do not actively participate, to support the team's efforts and not interfere with the team's game plan.

Step Three: Team Responsibilities

Explain that each member of the team has certain roles and responsibilities, just as members of a sports team do. If each team member does his part, the team is more likely to be successful than if only some members contribute. The contributions of each team member can vary depending on the age and special abilities of each team member. When each member performs his expected role to the best of his ability, no one person has to bear the entire workload, which makes everyone's work easier.

Step Four: The Team Leaders

Explain the administrative structure of your team. One person should be assigned the role of manager, another should be given the role of head coach, and the rest of the family will be the team members. The team leaders (responsible adults) will make the tough decisions and take responsibility for overseeing the game plan. The manager takes the lead role in putting together the team's strategy (the team members' suggestions, the ASD child's needs, and the personal needs identified by family members) into a viable plan, assigning roles, and establishing and prioritizing a list of team goals. The head coach consults with the manager and helps him or her implement the plan by making sure that all the team members do their part. Ideally, both leaders help team members meet their responsibilities, assist members with motivational issues if they arise, and monitor the plan to make sure that it is working. Even though the team leaders have authority, it is important to make it clear to the other family members that their input is crucial; let them know that their ideas, needs, and wishes will be included in the game plan, and that their observations of the team's functioning will be valued by the team manager and the head coach.

Step Five: Creating an Environment That Is Conducive to Teamwork

We have found that there are three prerequisites for building an effective team: mutual respect, mutual support, and good communication skills.

Mutual respect is an understanding among family members that each person values the others—their interests, abilities, concerns, and goals. Mutual respect enables family members to accept the aspirations of others even if they differ from their own.

Mutual support is the result of both providing and accepting emotional encouragement and assistance; team members acknowledge the efforts of others, and individual and group successes are celebrated. Providing support helps each team member to function at his peak. This means that team members rally to help each other achieve individual goals, handle disappointments, and work on alternative solutions when the strategies being used are unsatisfactory. At times, it can also mean providing financial support to fund specific pursuits. Accepting support shows other team members that you recognize their efforts to help and that you value their contributions. All too often, parents reject offers of assistance from their spouse or older children who live at home. But there are multiple consequences of habitually refusing support: family members may start to feel that you do not value their support and may come away with hurt feelings, and as a result you may ultimately become more isolated.

Good communication means that team members need to not only express their ideas clearly but also be skilled at listening, a complex art. Good listening involves the following behaviors:

- Looking attentive, making eye contact with the speaker, and nodding or making comments to let the speaker know that his or her message is being heard.

- Asking questions to clarify information given, or rephrasing what the speaker has said to show the speaker that the message was understood.

- Refraining from interrupting.

- Acting on the information given is another way to show the speaker that you have really understood what was said. For example, if a sibling expresses sadness, other siblings would offer emotional support or other types of assistance, or if a parent asks the siblings to ignore an ASD-related behavior when it occurs, they would abide by their parents' wish.

Step Six: Assess the Climate in Your Home

How is your family doing? Complete the worksheet below to assess your family's readiness for teamwork.

Behaviors conducive to teamwork	Never	Sometimes	Often	Very often
Mutual respect				
Do family members value other family members?				
Do family members regard the others' interests, abilities, concerns, and goals in a favorable light?				
Mutual support				
Do you make time to check in with each family member to see how he or she is doing?				
Do members of your family provide each other with emotional support?				
Do members of your family provide each other with assistance?				
Do members of your family accept support?				
Do members of your family accept assistance?				

Do members of your family acknowledge others' efforts?				
Communication				
Do family members practice good listening skills?				
Do family members take turns speaking during family discussions?				
Does the family set aside specific times to talk about family-related issues?				
Do members feel safe expressing all feelings in your home?				
Do members feel safe disagreeing with others?				
Are family members open to hearing opinions from all family members?				
Do family members show interest when you express concerns or share information?				
Does your family talk openly about the impact of ASD?				
Can family members ask questions about ASD without offending anyone?				

If you have put the majority of your answers in the "often" or "very often" range, you are in great shape and ready to begin your teamwork. If many of your responses fall in the "never" or "sometimes" range, you will need to do some preliminary work to set the stage for teamwork. Your first goal should be to isolate the areas where your family scores low and make improvements in these areas. Step seven, below, will provide you with ideas and strategies to help you work on problem areas and develop a climate that is conducive to teamwork.

Step Seven: Improving Your Family's Communication, Mutual Respect, and Support

Four strategies can be used to improve your family's communication, which will also result in improvements in mutual respect and support:

- Scheduling family meetings

- Setting an agenda for family meetings

- Developing rules for family discussions

- Preparing for subsequent meetings

Scheduling Family Meetings

In busy families, it is sometimes difficult to find a time when everyone is available and not in a hurry to get to another activity. Creating a regular meeting time can be the first challenge that you encounter. Perhaps a weekend morning, just before a family breakfast, might work. While finding an ideal time might be difficult, you might find the guidelines listed below to be useful:

1. Start by scheduling short meetings. These will probably be adequate when you're getting started, giving you enough time to explain the purpose and benefits of the meetings and to review meeting protocol. As you go along, family business will require more time, and the meeting time can then be extended. However, it is important to let family members know how long each meeting will be, and to try to stick to the time limit as best you can.

2. Avoid scheduling meetings when family members are tired, since fatigue may reduce tolerance, listening skills, and patience during discussions.

3. Avoid scheduling meetings at "prime times" that are likely to coincide with other activities such as sports, church, and so on.

4. Consider your family's needs when scheduling meetings. Some families prefer short, frequent meetings and do best when the meetings are held at the same time each week so that everyone can plan ahead. For other families, members may view these meetings as a burden. If your family agrees with the latter perspective, you might try scheduling longer family meetings less frequently (biweekly or monthly) so you can update the family on progress, make changes to responsibilities, and check in to find out how everyone is doing.

Setting an Agenda for Each Meeting

Establish an agenda for each session. The agenda for each meeting will be different, since as you become immersed in the process of change, your priorities will evolve and you'll have more business to discuss.

The first meeting. Below is a sample of the agenda for an initial meeting.

FAMILY MEETING AGENDA: THE FIRST MEETING

Date: _____

1. Why we are meeting

2. How meetings will be run

3. Rules for communication

4. Questions and comments

5. Family commitment: the team pact

6. Preparation for next meeting

    a. Be clear about what you expect each team member to do between this and the next meeting. Posting a list of expectations for each team member is often useful.

    b. Keep track of the concerns or issues raised by family members so you can make sure they do not get forgotten and so you can expand upon the lists and show family members how their concerns are being addressed.

We've already given most of the information you'll need in order to conduct your first meeting. The two issues that we have not yet addressed are establishing rules for communication during team meetings and making a commitment to the team. Let's discuss rules for team meetings first.

Developing Rules for Family Discussions

Every family has their own style of discussing important issues. In some families, everyone speaks up and it is hard to get a word in edgewise. Unfortunately, sometimes in these kinds of discussions information gets lost. Too many people speak at once and not enough people listen. In other families, some team members may be less than eager to participate or may not be sure of how to participate; they may worry that they will say the wrong thing or that other family members may be critical of their opinions. In these same families, other members may tend to do most of the talking. In order to even the playing field, you can create your own rules for meetings so that everyone has a chance to speak and be heard. Below is one example of family meeting guidelines. You may choose to use these rules as they stand, add other rules that are suited for your family, or rewrite the rules completely. The important thing is that you have a set of rules that encourage fairness in communication and that you review them at the start of each meeting.

RULES FOR FAMILY DISCUSSIONS

- The team manager chairs the meeting (the team manager is responsible for creating the agenda and helping other family members abide by the rules for family discussions).

- Only one person speaks at a time.

- Listen to the speaker.

- Don't interrupt. Everyone will get a turn to speak.

- Stay on topic.

- Be respectful.

- Avoid destructive criticism.

- Focus on your own feelings and use feeling statements to describe how you feel. In other words, if you disagree with something someone has said, you wouldn't say, "Oh, that's ridiculous! How could you feel that way?" Instead, you could say, "I understand that _____ makes you feel _____ . I'm sorry you feel that way."

Preparing for Subsequent Meetings

Once the team members understand the rationale for the team effort and the contract is signed, the agenda for subsequent family meetings should be somewhat different, so that it provides a structure for addressing the next steps in the change process. As indicated in the example, Family Meeting Agenda, each session should begin with a review of family rules. The next step involves making a wish list that consists of desirable changes. Asking the question "What would make our family better?" may be a useful starting point for generating wishes. Common responses to this question might include "less noise," "protecting personal property," "more family activities," "being able to have friends and relatives visit at the house without major incidents," or "fewer tantrums and disruptive behaviors."

The number of planning meetings is not fixed. Rather, it will depend on the amount of time that it takes your family to identify needs and translate them into goals that the family can address. Keep in mind that the family's wishes, or priorities, may change as behaviors and needs evolve. Remember, change is a dynamic process, not a fixed target.

The team commitment. Formalizing the family's commitment to work together toward common goals is important. Below is an example of a contract that your family can sign to show their willingness to be part of the team.

THE TEAM COMMITMENT

1. I understand that the goal of our team is to improve our family life through team effort and cooperation.

2. I understand that as a member of the team, I will have to make specific changes in my behavior. I may have to help out more or help in different ways. I understand that the other members of the team will also be making changes so that we can reach our goal.

3. I understand that the team leaders will write down the team's goals and responsibilities so we all know what is expected of us.

4. I understand that I must honor my team commitments. I know that when I take on a responsibility, the other team members will be counting on me.

5. I understand that if I run into trouble taking care of my responsibilities I must let the team know so we can work on a solution.

6. I understand that there may be times when, in order to help the team, I will have to be more flexible than I have been in the past.

7. I agree to participate in team discussions about making changes in the family.

8. I agree to talk openly about my feelings about the team's activities and goals. I will state how I feel and what is making me feel that way, but I will not blame other team members or intentionally hurt their feelings.

9. During team discussions, I agree to do the following:

   a. to not criticize team members

   b. to listen to what other team members say

   c. to give everyone a chance to talk

10. I agree to try to use coping strategies when I am frustrated or upset, and not to hold grudges against team members over differences of opinion, having to postpone satisfying my needs, or being asked to share responsibilities.

11. If I can't help the team directly, I agree to support the efforts of the team to the best of my ability.

_____   _____

Signature   Date

_____   _____

Signature   Date

_____   _____

Signature   Date

The insert below shows what an agenda for planning meetings might look like.

FAMILY MEETING AGENDA: A PLANNING MEETING

Date: _____

1. Review rules for family discussions.

2. Make a wish list ("What would make family life better?").

3. Translate the wish list into goals (both teaching tasks and family goals).

4. Establish priorities for teaching tasks (see chapter 4).

5. Establish priorities for family goals (see chapter 4).

6. Determine how family members can help.

   a. Assign family responsibilities

   b. Schedule family responsibilities/activities

Now that you have team goals and teaching tasks, and team responsibilities have been assigned, you will need a new agenda format for your family meetings. The focus at this point is to evaluate how your plan is working for your family, to monitor your child's progress on learning new tasks and your family's progress toward achieving team goals, to modify the plan, and to monitor family wellness overall. A sample agenda that covers important topics at this stage of the process is presented below.

FAMILY MEETING AGENDA: ALL OTHER MEETINGS

Date: _____

1. Review rules for family discussions.

2. Review progress of family and child with ASD.

3. Recognize family members for meeting responsibilities and being supportive and adapting to changes.

4. Examine progress made on previously identified issues.

5. Identify new issues.

6. Make changes to teaching program.

7. Make changes to assigned responsibilities.

8. Organize the family schedule for the week.

9. Update goals.

TOOLS FOR IMPLEMENTING THE GAME PLAN

In this section, we will provide you with examples of how you can use tools such as schedules, goal and progress charts, and lists to help you implement and monitor your family's game plan. Below is a schedule that the Smith family used in order to organize their Saturday mornings. The family was made up of Mom, Dad, Joey (age ten), Susan (age three), and Bobby (age seven; diagnosed with autistic disorder).

Time	Saturday
7:00 A.M.	Bobby, Mom, and Dad wake up. Mom exercises and Dad watches TV with Bobby.
7:30 A.M.	Mom showers and dresses. Dad helps Bobby get dressed and groomed, using teaching strategies to help Bobby become more independent in his ability to dress himself. In other words, Dad uses naturally occurring activities (the morning routine) as a teaching opportunity.
8:00 A.M.	Joey and Susan wake up. Mom makes breakfast and Joey, Susan, and Mom eat while Dad exercises.
8:30 A.M.	Joey and Susan get dressed. Bobby helps Mom clean up breakfast dishes. This is a teaching session for Bobby in which Mom teaches Bobby to help by clearing the dirty dishes from the table.
9:00 A.M.	Mom takes Joey to soccer practice. Susan and Bobby go along for the ride. Dad cools off after his run, showers and dresses, eats breakfast, and pays bills. Mom takes Susan and Bobby to the playground near the soccer field.
9:30 A.M.	Same.
10:00 A.M.	Same.
10:30 A.M.	Mom takes Bobby and Susan to the store to get drinks for her children. Pick up Joey from soccer practice.
11:00 A.M.	Mom stops at grocery store with Bobby, Joey, and Susan. While Mom shops, Joey helps Bobby find items on his grocery list, which contains pictures of some of Joey's favorite foods. Mom has found that if Bobby is actively engaged in this kind of structured task, he does not run off or have tantrums, and the task strengthens Bobby's emerging skill of following a sequence of directions.
11:30 A.M.	Mom and kids travel home. Mom and Susan unpack groceries and make lunch. Joey plays with Bobby. Dad has free time.
12:00 A.M.	Family has lunch.

Take another look at the schedule above, and then complete the following questionnaire to evaluate how well the schedule addresses the individual family's needs.

1. What needs were met for Mom? _____

_____

_____

2. What needs were met for Dad? _____

_____

_____

3. What needs were met for Joey? _____

_____

_____

4. What needs were met for Susan? _____

_____

_____

5. What needs were met for Bobby? _____

_____

_____

6. What teaching tasks were addressed? _____

_____

_____

7. How did Mom use her resources (the people in her family) to help her accomplish important tasks? _____

_____

_____

Did you notice the following?

- Family responsibilities were well specified.

- At least one need was met for each family member. Although it may seem as though Susan's needs were ignored, it so happened that Susan loved to help unpack groceries and "help" with the cooking. She also got some special time with Mom when they made lunch together.

- Mom utilized her resources well. She did not shop for groceries until Joey was available to help keep Bobby productive and busy.

- Bobby worked on learning several tasks, which would ultimately benefit both Bobby and his family: independent dressing, cleaning up dirty dishes, and managing his behavior.

It's always beneficial to keep track of the child's progress as you implement your game plan. The chart below is an example of how the management team can share the progress made by the child with ASD with the rest of the team. This type of chart is useful because it clearly identifies the goal, the child's ability at the start of the teaching program, and his weekly progress. If you decide to use this type of progress chart, it is important to keep in mind the following issues:

- Be sure to break the new skills being taught into small enough units so that it is possible to document progress. In the example below, if the management team chose to report on Bobby's progress toward independence in activities of daily living without dividing the task into smaller task components (such as dressing independently), at the end of the second week there might be little progress to report. In addition to the fact that breaking complex skills down into simpler components is a good teaching practice, documenting these small gains can also reinforce team effort.

- If progress is not made, the management team should specify how the teaching plan will be changed in the upcoming week to improve progress.

Bobby's progress chart			
	Ability prior to teaching	**Progress week 1**	**Progress week 2**
Goal 1			
Increase independence in activities of daily living			
Teaching tasks			
Dresses self independently	Raised arms when parent held up shirt	Put on shirt independently	Put pants and shirt on independently
Puts dishes in sink after meals	Ran away from table when finished eating	Carried plate to sink when told, "Put your dishes away"	Carried plate and cup to sink when told, "Put your dishes away"
Goal 2			
Manages behavior on community outings	Unable to be in grocery store for 5 minutes without running away or having a tantrum	Able to be in grocery store for 5 minutes without running away or having a tantrum while "helping to shop"	Able to stay in grocery store for 10 minutes without running away or having a tantrum while "helping to shop"

The next example demonstrates how to use a chart to share progress made toward family goals. The chart is organized in the same way as Bobby's individual progress chart above.

Family's progress chart				
	Status prior to family intervention	**Progress week 1**	**Progress week 2**	**Progress week 3**
Parent goals				
Daily exercise for both parents	Dad exercised on a regular basis, but Mom did not	Dad continued to exercise daily; Mom exercised on 4/7 days	Dad continued to exercise daily; Mom exercised on 6/7 days	Dad continued to exercise daily; Mom exercised on 7/7 days
Uninterrupted time to take care of household financial management (paying bills and balancing checkbook)	Dad was taking bills to work and staying at the office late in order to get them paid in a timely manner	Dad was able to complete one-quarter of the financial management tasks at home	Dad was able to complete half of the financial management tasks at home	Dad was able to complete three-quarters of the financial management tasks at home
Sibling goals: Sibling #1				
Individual time with parents; participation in age-appropriate leisure activities	Bimonthly shopping trips with Mom, including eating lunch out; weekly soccer skills practice with Dad during season	Half hour of Mom's time doing activity of choice (craft project, cooking/baking, playing preferred game) once a week	Half hour of Mom's time doing activity of choice (craft project, cooking/baking, playing preferred game) once a week *and* soccer skills practice with Dad for half hour twice a week. Projects that could not be completed in one sitting were preserved so that they could be worked on during other scheduled times	Half hour of Mom's time on activity of choice (craft project, cooking/baking, playing preferred game) twice a week *and* soccer skills practice with Dad for half hour twice a week

Sibling goals: Sibling #2				
Individual time with parents; participation in age-appropriate leisure activities	"Catch as catch can" time with Mom playing favorite board games; homework assistance from Dad on an as-needed basis; and time with Dad in the car on the way to basketball practice	Weekly time with Dad shooting hoops for half hour	Weekly time with Dad shooting hoops for half hour; ongoing assistance with homework; and playing chess with Mom once a week. Mom and child agreed that chess or other games would not necessarily be completed in one sitting; they would preserve the game so they could continue play over time	Biweekly time with Dad shooting hoops; ongoing assistance with homework; and playing chess or other board game with Mom twice weekly

Again, breaking goals down into smaller components is a useful strategy for maintaining an upbeat and positive attitude, since these mini goals are easier to achieve in the short term.

In this chapter you learned about the importance of teamwork and encouraging your family's commitment to support changes that will benefit the entire group. You also learned about the importance of communicating about both individual and family issues (including information about ASD and how it affects your family) and how to establish rules to make these discussions more productive. Finally, you learned about how to use schedules and charts to provide visual representations of current goals, ensure that tasks get completed, and help you progress toward individual and family goals. Chapter 4 will provide a more detailed discussion of family needs and how to meet them.

Identifying Family Needs

We begin our discussion of family needs with four basic truths underlying the content of this chapter:

1. Every family has needs and so does every family member.

2. At times, individual needs conflict with the needs of the family unit.

3. Even under the best of circumstances, it is impossible to meet all needs at the same time.

4. Every family struggles to meet the conflicting needs of its members.

While conflicts about competing needs are a part of every family's life, the challenges associated with living with a child with autism spectrum disorder may make your task even more complex. As you begin to apply the principles of our family-centered approach, you will become more aware of the range of your family's needs and you will learn strategies that will help you develop viable plans for satisfying these needs. We will help you use specific problem-solving techniques to generate solutions and help you learn how to identify teaching tasks. During this process, you will begin to see that the challenges, while real, are not insurmountable.

HOW DO THE SYMPTOMS OF ASD AFFECT YOUR ABILITY TO MEET FAMILY AND CHILD NEEDS?

It is generally accepted that there are basic needs that, when fulfilled, establish a foundation for stable family functioning. Lockshin, Gillis, and Romanczyk (2004) created a list of the top ten family needs, presented below, which represents a compilation of family needs that have been identified by experts in family therapy and ASD.

Top ten family needs
1. Adequate income
2. Shelter
3. Sense of belonging
4. Acceptance
5. Autonomy
6. Intimacy
7. Support
8. Leisure and recreation (both personal and family)
9. Flexibility
10. Growth

The same authors also generated a list of the top ten child needs. This list can serve as a good starting point when you are examining how your children's needs are being addressed.

Top ten child needs
1. Unconditional love
2. Protection
3. Consistent parenting
4. Relationships with family members, peers, and others
5. Developing independence
6. Play
7. Education
8. Ability to communicate needs and wants
9. Nurturance
10. Positive role models

How ASD Can Interfere with Meeting Family Needs

The challenges associated with ASD can often make it difficult to meet everyone's needs. Some examples of complications encountered by parents of children with ASD are presented in the checklist below. As you read them over, check all of the obstacles that apply to your family, since you will be using these in later exercises.

ASD-Related Obstacles to Satisfaction of Family and Parent Needs

Financial. Having a child with ASD can stress a family's ability to manage their finances in many ways, including the following:

☐ One parent may have to stay home in order to care for the child and meet his needs, placing an enormous strain on financial resources.

☐ Caregivers experienced in working with children with ASD are extremely difficult to find and their services are expensive.

☐ Medical expenses and the cost of supplemental therapies can deplete financial resources.

☐ Expenses incurred in multiple consultations in an effort to find the best treatment and therapy programs can also deplete family finances.

Shelter. Some families report that the challenging behaviors associated with ASD limit their housing options. Keeping children safe is an ongoing concern for parents and is especially challenging for parents of children with ASD. Examples of housing-related worries include the following:

☐ The child may be at risk of injury due to excessive traffic.

☐ He may have poor safety awareness and tend to do things that are dangerous.

☐ He may have a tendency to leave home unaccompanied by a parent or caregiver, roaming about unsupervised.

☐ He may go into other people's homes or swimming pools without permission and get lost or hurt.

☐ The child may make a lot of noise, causing apartment-dwelling parents to change residences due to their neighbors' complaints.

☐ City noises may be disturbing to the child.

Sense of belonging and acceptance. Research focused on family issues related to autism tells us that it is not unusual for family members to experience isolation. Below are several reasons why families may be at risk for isolation:

☐ Members of the extended family and the community at large may have limited knowledge about ASD, and limited tolerance for individual differences, making participation in family and community events difficult.

☐ Parents are often preoccupied with the tasks of caregiving and household management and have little time to pursue social or recreational interests.

☐ When parents finally get some free time, they are too exhausted to do anything for fun.

☐ Children with ASD may have difficulty tolerating family or community events, making it difficult for the whole group to stay connected with friends and relatives.

Autonomy. For better or for worse, extended family members and other concerned individuals are free to give their opinions and advice regarding how to parent a child with ASD and they frequently do so without understanding the issues involved. This barrage of input can make parents feel uncertain and inadequate.

☐ Some parents find themselves continually questioning their decisions because of feedback received from others that conflicts with their judgment and parenting decisions.

☐ In a related problem, parents often feel unable to act independently when confronted with various parenting issues. Instead, they feel a need to consult with others (psychologists, teachers, or family members) before making even simple choices.

☐ Parents may feel that ASD limits their range of choices in important areas, such as their career, personal interests, and lifestyle, which translates to a loss of independence.

Intimacy. Many factors can influence a family's ability to sustain intimate relationships with friends and relatives, and a couple's ability to maintain emotional connectedness to each other, including the following:

☐ The parents feel exhausted and overwhelmed and have little time or emotional energy to invest in sustaining relationships.

☐ Parents can be so preoccupied with the child's needs that their sensitivity to others' needs is diminished.

☐ Parents' feelings of inadequacy, stemming from well-meaning advice from others that comes across as criticism, can cause them to feel defeated, and as if no one truly understands their situation.

Support. Parents who have few, if any, intimate relationships with people outside their immediate family can also suffer from a lack of emotional and practical support. ASD can affect family support in other ways as well. Below are some of the reasons why families don't get enough support:

☐ The complexity of ASD often confuses and intimidates others, so that they feel incapable of helping despite their good intentions.

☐ Some parents subscribe to the myth that they should be able to manage everything on their own (see chapter 1). One outcome of accepting this myth is that they refuse assistance and emotional support when it is offered.

☐ In some families the stress of ASD can limit the amount of time that family members are able to spend keeping up with each other and enjoying time spent together. As a result, camaraderie and companionship within the family are stifled.

☐ Another source of support is family members' recognition of each other's efforts and achievements (for example, parents telling their children that they appreciate their efforts to help, spouses expressing gratitude when the other helps out, or making time to celebrate accomplishments such as good grades, receipt of awards, or promotions at work). In families who have a child with ASD, the focus is often on "what's wrong" rather than "what's right."

Leisure and recreation. Research also tells us that autism in a family can result in limited opportunities for family recreation and leisure activities. When a child with ASD has restricted interests, difficulty dealing with delayed gratification, and disruptive behaviors, and does not follow directions to stop annoying, dangerous, destructive, or embarrassing behaviors, parents may come to the conclusion that family outings are not possible. Does your child exhibit specific ASD-related behaviors that prevent your family from enjoying recreational or leisure activities? Use the checklist below to identify the behaviors that interfere with your families activities:

☐ The child has limited ability to follow directions regarding regulating impulsive behaviors (such as touching, grabbing, running, and pushing others out of the way) that keep everyone on edge, making it necessary for a responsible adult to closely supervise the child.

☐ The child's loud, attention-drawing vocalizations can be embarrassing to family members (especially siblings).

☐ The child's limited understanding of personal boundaries and related behaviors (such as touching strangers, taking things from others, or standing too close to strangers) can make supervision an issue.

☐ The child may talk to strangers and fail to recognize when others are not interested in participating in conversational exchanges, making family members and strangers uncomfortable.

☐ Tantrums occur when the family needs to wait in order to participate in an activity (for example, in line at an amusement park or at a table in a restaurant), raising stress levels and causing embarrassment.

☐ The child's rigidity or inflexibility can spoil everyone's good time in situations like hiking (the family wants to follow one trail and your child with ASD wants to follow a different trail) and choosing a restaurant (your child with ASD may have a tantrum because the family members agree on a specific type of food that he does not like).

☐ The child's tendency to wander off to look at items of interest or to engage in preferred activities requires caregivers to be vigilant in monitoring the whereabouts of the child and interferes with the family's ability to focus their attention on having fun.

Flexibility. One characteristic of families that function well is flexibility (that is, the ability to recoup from disruptions, disappointments, or role changes, and go with the flow). The rigidity and desire for sameness in many children with ASD can make it difficult for a family to be flexible. These traits may be expressed in the following ways:

☐ The child's fear of new people or situations may limit the spontaneity that some families enjoy or may restrict the range of activities that the family can explore.

☐ Inability to perform previously learned skills in new settings or with new people may limit family activities. Parents may expect that their child will be able to handle specific situations because he has done well with similar situations at school or at home (for example, standing in line, carrying a lunch tray in a cafeteria-style restaurant, or using the bathroom), only to find that he cannot use these skills in new situations.

☐ The child's excessive emotional reactions to changes in routines or schedules may prevent the family from changing plans on the spur of the moment.

Growth. In this context, *growth* is the freedom to pursue interests, try new things, and broaden one's range of experience. ASD can limit growth within the family, since it often inhibits change. Thus, ASD can affect family members' growth in the following areas:

☐ Parents are often reluctant to change jobs, especially when this would result in a change in work hours, distance from home (and therefore availability when child needs require parental involvement), and the amount of work they would need to bring home.

☐ Parents may put off plans to pursue an advanced education, since this usually requires being able to carve out study time and have a quiet place to complete coursework.

☐ Some families reject job offers that would involve relocating, even when the move would be beneficial for career and financial reasons, because the move would be too distressing for the child with ASD. Moreover, parents may conclude that arranging for services (finding adequate school and therapy services, medical care, and so on) in a new geographic area would be too overwhelming.

☐ Parents may be reluctant to make new friends because their child with ASD has difficulty adapting to new people and new situations.

☐ Parents may avoid pursuing new interests or routinely engaging in personal leisure and recreational activities because this would take time away from the child with ASD. Also, as discussed previously, if pursuing these interests involves leaving home, finding competent child care may become an impediment.

Privacy. Although not included in the top ten needs listed above, privacy is a universal need of all family members. Everyone needs to have a reasonable level of confidence that personal belongings will be left alone by others. Additionally, in order to take care of personal business, socialize with friends at home, or have personal and intimate discussions, everyone needs to know that they will have at least some uninterrupted time. Children with ASD often do not pay attention to personal boundaries, a trait that can reduce the privacy of other family members. Specific aspects of privacy that may be affected by ASD are listed below:

☐ Because children with ASD don't understand the concept of personal boundaries, individual family members may have trouble protecting their personal belongings and teaching the child about appropriate boundaries related to personal space and property.

☐ The social and language deficits in ASD can make it so that your child cannot recognize and understand others' messages communicating a desire to be left alone, a situation that can be quite frustrating to family members.

ASD-Related Obstacles to Satisfaction of Child Needs

The symptoms of ASD can also affect the ability to satisfy the needs of the children in the household, including both the child diagnosed with ASD and his siblings.

Unconditional love. All children need to feel loved and truly valued. As we've discussed, dealing with the symptoms of ASD can be both emotionally and physically draining for parents. One possible outcome of this chronic stress is that your reserves of emotional and physical energy become depleted. In addition to the negative impact on your own well-being, your emotional and physical exhaustion can also inadvertently affect your children in the following ways:

☐   Your children may misinterpret your irritability or sullenness as anger or disapproval regarding something that they did or didn't do.

☐   Because you are distracted, you may overlook opportunities to demonstrate or verbally express your love for your children or your pride in their accomplishments.

☐   High levels of stress can also affect parental expectations for children's behavior, such as expecting children to provide more help at home or achieve more at school than is realistic for their age and developmental stage. Under these circumstances, your children might interpret your disappointment over unmet expectations as loss of love.

Protection. It is the responsibility of the parents and caregivers to protect their children from illness and physical and emotional harm. This is no small job for parents of typical children, and the task is significantly more complex for a family of a child with ASD, as you will see below:

☐   One of the ways that parents can protect their children is to set limits and establish consequences for exceeding those limits. These restrictions and consequences discourage children from engaging in dangerous behaviors (climbing on furniture or other unsafe objects, ingesting nonfood items, running into the street, jumping into swimming pools, playing with tools or machinery) and teach them to avoid dangerous situation. Since children with ASD have difficulty understanding limits and have little, if any awareness of risky situations, protecting your child can be an extremely difficult task.

☐   Children with ASD who exhibit aggressive behavior present their parents with another challenge—that of protecting their typically developing children from potential harm. The seemingly unpredictable and random nature of the aggressive behavior may frighten typically developing siblings and make them feel as if they are unsafe in their homes. (Another consequence of ASD-related aggression is that siblings may avoid playing with or near the aggressive child, limiting the ASD child's opportunities for socialization and the family's ability to have fun together.)

☐   The self-injurious behavior that is sometimes observed in ASD poses yet another challenge to parents' ability to protect their child. Reducing or eliminating this behavior may take time and may require professional consultation.

☐   Children with ASD may not distinguish between strangers and familiar people, which makes them vulnerable to others' malicious deeds or acts.

☐   Parents may feel helpless if their efforts to stop their child's dangerous behavior are unsuccessful and they may feel frustrated about their inability to protect their children from harm.

☐   Because children with ASD do not grasp the subtleties of language, they may not always be aware that they are being mocked or ridiculed by peers. Alternatively, they may actually comprehend these remarks and comments and feel sad or hurt by them.

It is important for parents to recognize that treating aggression and self-injury in ASD can be challenging and they may not be able to solve these problems on their own. They should consult with a professional right away if the behaviors do not lessen in response to typical parenting practices.

Consistent parenting. At times, when you're dealing with the symptoms of ASD, the boundaries between effective and ineffective parenting can become blurred. This presents a problem especially in situations where good parenting practices and the need to take care of family business are competing (for example, managing one child's tantrum while trying to get your other child on the school bus). Common parenting issues include the following:

☐ Responding patiently and consistently to rule infractions and misbehavior is challenging with a child with ASD because he may not understand rules and limits. The frequency of rule violations can be high and it may be difficult, if not impossible, to consistently monitor the behavior of your ASD child to make sure that he is minding house rules. In addition, parents may find that it is difficult to consistently respond to particular behaviors in a set or predetermined way. For example, if a parent generated a plan to ignore whining and repetitive requests for between-meal snacks in an effort to improve mealtime behavior, he might find it difficult to follow through on the plan when he is in the grocery store, where the whining and complaining might draw unwanted attention from other shoppers. Or when the parent has had a tough day and is feeling emotionally on edge, instead of ignoring the persistent requests as planned, the parent might raise his voice and reprimand the child, thus changing the consequence for the behavior.

☐ Because you may have different expectations for your child with ASD and your other children (due to differences in their abilities), siblings may feel that you expect too much from them and too little from their sibling.

☐ Siblings may feel angry and resentful about the disproportionate amount of time parents dedicate to their sibling with ASD, and they may feel guilty about feeling angry and resentful. (They may also feel guilty for not offering more help at home, or maybe even for being successful.)

Relationships with family members, peers, and others. ASD symptoms can affect family members' relationships with people outside of the immediate family group in several ways:

☐ Many people are uncomfortable with ASD symptoms and avoid contact with those with ASD. This can have a significant impact on the quality and quantity of close relationships with extended family members, family friends, and peers.

☐ On the other hand, children with ASD may get special attention from members of the family's extended social network. Siblings may resent this "specialness" and feel a need to compete for attention.

☐ Children may feel embarrassed by their sibling's symptoms of ASD and have difficulty explaining the ASD to others, causing them to be reluctant to make friends with others.

☐ Children may have to deal with criticism and ridicule directed at their sibling diagnosed with ASD and feel conflicted about whether to try to fit in or protect their sibling.

☐ As siblings grow older, they may worry about whether they will have a child with ASD when they become parents and they may worry about having to assume caretaking responsibilities for their diagnosed sibling as an adult.

See the Resources section for sources of information on how siblings can be affected by ASD in the family.

Developing independence. During the process of raising a child with ASD, so much caregiving is needed that it is hard to know when to shift gears and foster independent functioning. Roadblocks to promoting independence for children diagnosed with ASD include the following:

☐ You may have difficulty letting go of the caregiving role.

☐ You may be reluctant to place too many demands on your "special needs" child.

☐ Siblings may tend to be more helpful than is needed.

☐ You may worry that your child will not manage well in your absence.

ASD can also affect the development of age-appropriate independence in siblings:

☐ Increased reliance on siblings for child care or completion of household chores may give children more responsibility than is expected for their age group.

☐ Decreased opportunities to socialize with peers or engage in extracurricular activities can adversely affect the developmental process of separating from the family. Peer interaction and participation in extracurricular activities (such as clubs and sports) are a critical part of learning how to socialize and work within group contexts. These experiences are formative experiences that children can later apply in their adult lives.

☐ Siblings may be reluctant to engage in activities outside of the home for fear that they will not be available to you or to the sibling with ASD when they are needed.

Play. Within this context, we are using *play* to mean age-appropriate social interactions. Given that one of the primary symptoms of ASD is significant social impairment, it follows that for children with ASD, opportunities to engage in age-appropriate play may be limited. For siblings, opportunities for play may also be affected by ASD in the following ways:

☐ Siblings may not feel comfortable having friends come to their home to play.

☐ You may be limited in your ability to provide transportation for your children without ASD to go to other children's houses or to participate in activities outside of the home, and the child with ASD may need so much attention that you are not be able to supervise his siblings' play with other children when they visit your home.

Education. The need for education can be subdivided into four categories: the importance of educating siblings about ASD, teaching siblings skills that lead to positive interactions with the child with ASD, finding a good educational placement for your child with ASD, and providing the supports needed for siblings to achieve academic success. Actions you can take in each of these areas are provided in the checklists and discussions below.

☐ Educate typical siblings about ASD in order to allay fears and concerns and to set reasonable expectations regarding how they can help manage their sibling's ASD symptoms.

When they are old enough to understand the vocabulary and concepts involved in describing ASD, siblings should be provided with accurate information, including identification of core symptoms and related problems, and explanations about possible causes of ASD. These areas are particularly important because lack of knowledge can result in faulty beliefs. For example, a sibling might misinterpret a child's "aloofness" as rejection ("My brother never pays attention to me. He must hate me"). Inadequate information about ASD can also lead to unnecessary worry on the part of siblings, such as the belief held by some siblings that ASD is contagious, or that if they tried hard enough their brother would behave better.

☐ Teach typical siblings ways of interacting with their ASD-affected sibling in order to increase opportunities for mutually enjoyable shared time. Skills training for siblings that teaches them how to play successfully with the child with ASD is very important for maintaining good sibling relationships. This kind of training focuses on how to choose games that use the strengths of their diagnosed sibling, how to use prompts and cues to provide help when needed, and how to handle problem behaviors if and when they occur. Armed with this information and a feeling of competence gained from successful supervised play sessions, siblings should be able to have fun playing together.

☐ Become knowledgeable about the components of good educational programs for children with ASD to ensure that your child gets the best services available. Finding an educational program that meets the needs of both your diagnosed child and your family can be a challenge. As you well know, the educational needs of ASD are diverse and, until recently, specialized teacher training in ASD was limited. Decisions about class size, the range of disabilities included within a given classroom, the teaching methods used, segregated or integrated classroom placement, whether to have a one-to-one aide, and the degree of mainstreaming can seem overwhelming.

When making decisions about school programs or classroom placement, remember that each child with ASD is different. A classroom placement that is a success for one student could be a disaster for another. Below is a list of questions you should consider as you make choices about your child's educational placement.

- What is the teacher's experience and training in ASD?

- How many children are in the class?

- Will my child receive instruction alongside typically developing children? How much time will he spend with typically developing children?

When considering support services (such as speech, occupational, and physical therapy), it is important to ask the following questions:

- How often will my child receive these services?

- What is the experience of the provider in working with children with ASD?

- How much instructional time will actually be spent on skill development and how much time will be spent managing behavior?

- Will the services be provided in a "pull out" format (that is, taking the child to a designated area outside of the classroom for therapy) or a "push in" format (one that provides instruction within the classroom setting)?

- How much time will be devoted to what educational tasks?

- What settings offer the most flexibility and time for teaching tasks that challenge the child?

- How is progress monitored and reported to parents?

In your search for school or classroom placements, you may find yourself at odds with school officials over your desire to find the "best" educational program for your child and their desire to find an "appropriate" educational program, as defined in educational law. However, determining the best educational program for a given child is not always a simple, straightforward process. It is also important to understand that the committees on special education, the body of people who make decisions about educational services, are required to make sure that schools meet state and federal mandates (which include educating special-needs students in "least restrictive" educational settings where they can intermingle with nonhandicapped students to the "extent possible") and generate a plan that is acceptable to parents.

However, if you are dissatisfied with the services offered by the school, you have the legal right to challenge them and initiate due process procedures. However, it is always wise to weigh your desires against the cost of developing an adversarial relationship with the very agency that will be responsible for providing your child with services throughout his school career.

ASD can also be an impediment to meeting the educational needs of your other children. For siblings, the symptoms of ASD (noise, disruptions) may interfere with their educational pursuits in the following ways:

- ☐ Disruptions during study time may decrease their ability to learn effectively.

- ☐ Helping your child with ASD may occupy much of your time, making it so that you are not readily available to help your other children with homework.

- ☐ Siblings may not have sufficient time to study due to other household responsibilities.

Ability to communicate needs and wants. It is important that your typically developing children feel that it is safe for them to express their feelings about ASD and feel comfortable making their wants and needs known without upsetting you. Therefore it is important that you provide opportunities to do the following:

- ☐ Acknowledge and validate your child's feelings and talk about how these needs might be addressed, since this process is an important part of your family's ability to cope with ASD.

- ☐ However, you need to remind your children, and yourselves, that not everyone's needs and wants can be met at once.

It is also important to provide opportunities to solicit information about the needs of your child with ASD. While this may be complicated by your child's inability to communicate, several strategies can be employed to gain this important information:

- ☐ If your child is nonverbal and has limited communication skills, observing how family members interact with your child with ASD (that is, how they initiate social contact and respond to social approaches and communicative efforts) and how they react to ASD-related behaviors can help you identify ways in which the family can be more sensitive to the child's needs.

☐ When your child becomes somewhat skilled at communicating, it is possible to offer him choices (using words, pictures, or gestures) about how he would like others to respond to him in specific situations.

☐ If your child is more verbal, it may be possible for you to get information about his needs or preferences by asking him to finish incomplete sentences such as "I like it when _____ " and "It makes me mad when _____ ."

☐ If your child has strong verbal abilities, you may be able to get his input in the same way that you would get information from your typically developing children.

Nurturance. All children need tender care, protection, and encouragement in order to grow, develop, and be successful. ASD can affect your ability to provide adequate nurturance to both your child with ASD and your typically developing children in the following ways:

☐ Many children with ASD resist soothing, comforting, caregiving, routine self-care tasks, and medical care, making it hard for you to meet these needs.

☐ With children who hurt themselves and others, stopping or preventing this behavior can be extremely challenging and dangerous for everyone involved. In many cases, professional consultation (both medical and psychological) is needed to address these confusing and sometimes life-threatening behaviors.

☐ It may be difficult, if not impossible, to assure your typically developing children that you can eliminate their sibling's aggressive behavior immediately. What you can do is validate their concern, let them know that you are looking for solutions, teach them ways to avoid triggering aggression (if you know what the triggers are), and teach them how to protect themselves without hurting their sibling.

Consistent role models. When you're raising a child with ASD, it is important that you manage your behavior and your feelings in a reasonable manner and seek out professional help when you feel overwhelmed. The reason for this is that, aside from your own emotional well-being, your children will learn strategies for managing stress and emotions by observing your behavior. In addition, parental attitudes and coping strategies can have a profound influence on how children view their diagnosed sibling, and the concept of disability in general. Although we discussed the importance of being consistent in your responses to child behavior (that is, providing consistent limits and consequences for behavior), we view the issue of being a good role model as related, but separate, and therefore worthy of discussion. The checklist that follows highlights ways that you can model appropriate responses and coping strategies for all of your children.

☐ When you begin to lose patience, take a break and come back to the task after you have composed yourself.

☐ Label your feelings. It's okay to let your children know that you are feeling frustrated, angry, disappointed, and so on. It is also good practice to verbalize your coping strategies or a plan for addressing the issue at a later time. For example, "I'm so frustrated right now, I think it's a good idea to stop working on this now and try again later when I feel better about this" or "I'm feeling so angry now. I need a little time to calm down so I don't do or say something I'll regret."

☐ When you're frustrated or upset with child behavior (typically developing or ASD-related), be sure to label the behavior that is causing the reaction instead of labeling the child. For example, say "That whining is so annoying" instead of "You're being such a baby."

☐ Provide examples of how to apply problem-solving strategies when confronted with challenging situations.

Thus far, we have talked about many of the problems that can arise when raising a child with ASD. This is largely because this workbook is designed to offer a family-focused, problem-solving approach to minimizing the impact of ASD on the family. However, research focused on family issues has shown that not all families of a child diagnosed with ASD experience high levels of distress. In fact, a number of experts have indicated that living with a child with ASD can provide unique growth and bonding opportunities for family members. Moreover, some evidence suggests that having a sibling with autism can be related to a positive self-image, good interpersonal skills, and good nurturing skills.

ADDRESSING FAMILY NEEDS

The first step in this process is to identify your family's needs. As you begin to think about your family's needs, you may feel overwhelmed by the number of needs you want to address, and you may begin to feel that you are facing an impossible task. We're not saying that your task is easy, but it can be done. In our experience, you're most likely to succeed if you are able to do the following:

- Enlist the participation or support of all family members

- Assure family members that their needs will be considered

- Develop an organized plan for how you will address needs

If you have not already done so, review the team commitment in chapter 3, and put it into practice in order to enlist family support. Remind family members that change takes time and that you need to help each other stick with the plan, be patient, participate in discussions and negotiations, and refrain from being critical. Using the family communication skills outlined in chapter 3 should be helpful. To help you do this, complete the worksheet below. The elements included in the table are taken from the preceding discussion regarding how ASD can affect your ability to address family needs.

Family need	Obstacles to need satisfaction	Other needs not listed
Shelter	■ Limited housing options ■ Risk ■ Poor safety awareness ■ Roaming ■ Noise ■ Sensory sensitivities	
Sense of belonging and acceptance	■ Lack of community understanding and acceptance of ASD ■ Parental preoccupation with caregiving and household management ■ Limited energy for leisure activities ■ ASD child's limited tolerance of group activities	
Autonomy	■ Parents' lack of confidence in decision-making abilities ■ Perception that ASD limits options for career choices, personal interests, and so on	
Intimacy	■ Little emotional energy to invest in relationships ■ Preoccupation with ASD results in narrow focus and inattention to needs of friends and extended family members ■ Parental feelings of inadequacy	
Support	■ Feelings of inadequacy on the part of potential "helpers" due to lack of knowledge about ASD ■ Inability of parents to accept the help of others ■ Sacrificing personal relationships due to immersion in ASD-related issues ■ Limited appreciation or acknowledgment of efforts	
Leisure and recreation	■ Excessive ASD behaviors discourage family outings	
Flexibility	ASD child's rigidity limits family activities that involve ■ Novelty (i.e., new activities) ■ Spontaneity	

Growth	■ Parents' reluctance to change jobs ■ Delaying pursuit of advanced education ■ Rejecting offers for job relocation ■ Not expanding social networks ■ Avoidance of engaging in leisure pursuits and recreational activities	
Privacy	■ Keeping personal belongings safe ■ Having space to conduct personal business, intimate discussions, and entertain friends	

You should also complete a similar worksheet for child needs, provided below. When completing this worksheet, refer back to the discussion of child needs, above, and write in those that apply to your children. Listing the needs of your child with ASD and his siblings separately will enable you to keep track of the needs that are unique to each.

Child needs	Obstacles to need satisfaction in child with ASD	Obstacles to siblings' need satisfaction
Unconditional love		
Protection		
Consistent parenting		
Relationships with family members, peers, and others		
Developing independence		
Play		
Education		
Ability to communicate needs and wants		
Nurturance		
Consistent role models		
Other needs		

Prioritizing Needs

As in all other areas of your life, prioritizing means deciding the order in which you will address certain tasks. Often, a number of factors will determine which tasks get done first and which ones can be safely put on hold for a period of time. Some factors that may influence your prioritization in your everyday life include the demand for task completion (that is, who has asked you to complete the task and what, if any, specific deadlines were specified), whether or not a specific task needs to be completed before other tasks can be addressed, how much you will enjoy or benefit from the task, and the degree of difficulty involved (sometimes it is prudent to get the easy tasks done first and save the more challenging tasks for when you have more time and energy).

A similar logic can be applied to prioritizing your family's needs. We generally ask families in our program to identify specific needs and then to rank them according to priority. Below is the list of factors that we ask parents to consider when making decisions about priorities:

- *Safety and protection are always high-priority needs.* This means that any situation or behavior that puts your child or someone else at risk is automatically a priority. *Risk* in this context can mean risk of injury (for example, due to the child's aggressive or self-injurious behavior or inattention to safety issues) or risk to physical health (such as when your child is not eating an adequate diet or is ingesting nonedible or potentially dangerous substances).

- *Behavior that threatens the stability of your current housing situation.* Shelter also ranks high as a priority since having a stable residence benefits everyone in the family. When generating your list of possible solutions, you should also consider child-centered behaviors like teaching alternatives to tantrums, and decreasing destructive or disruptive behaviors.

- *Skills that are viewed as important prerequisites for learning other skills.* Skills that fall in this category include making eye contact, compliance with parental requests, imitation, and delaying gratification (waiting).

- *Solutions that can solve more than one problem.* Teaching a new skill that will address multiple needs (for example, following directions to cease unwanted behaviors, occupying some unstructured time engaged in independent, age-appropriate play activities, and tolerating changes in his schedule) can be part of the solution to many of the ASD-related behaviors that impede need fulfillment.

- *Skills or behaviors that are relatively easy to teach.* The types of skills that we are referring to here include ones for which your child has already mastered the prerequisite skills, and positive behaviors that are already in your child's repertoire but could stand some improvement.

Below, we have provided you with a worksheet to help you with the process of prioritizing your family's needs. To use the worksheet, write in your family's needs (use the list you generated in the previous worksheets). Review the list provided in the "Factors to consider" column to help you make decisions about need prioritization. Then, in the "Rank" column, assign each need a number to indicate the importance of the addressing the need. You may want to review the issues raised in the preceding sections to help you prioritize.

Prioritization worksheet		
Family needs	**Factors to consider when ranking items according to priority**	**Rank**
	☐ Reduces risk to child with ASD and family ☐ Increases sense of stability and organization in the household ☐ Benefits more than one family member ☐ Results in rapid success as the need is relatively easy to satisfy ☐ Has a broad and lasting impact on overall family functioning ☐ Is a prerequisite for addressing other family needs ☐ Improves family relationships ☐ Broadens social contacts and family support ☐ Strengthens family ties ☐ Benefits only one family member, but satisfying this need for this individual is important for this family member's well-being	
	☐ Reduces risk to child with ASD and family ☐ Increases sense of stability and organization in the household ☐ Benefits more than one family member ☐ Results in rapid success as the need is relatively easy to satisfy ☐ Has a broad and lasting impact on overall family functioning ☐ Is a prerequisite for addressing other family needs ☐ Improves family relationships ☐ Broadens social contacts and family support ☐ Strengthens family ties ☐ Benefits only one family member, but satisfying this need for this individual is important for this family member's well-being	
	☐ Reduces risk to child with ASD and family ☐ Increases sense of stability and organization in the household ☐ Benefits more than one family member ☐ Results in rapid success as the need is relatively easy to satisfy ☐ Has a broad and lasting impact on overall family functioning ☐ Is a prerequisite for addressing other family needs ☐ Improves family relationships ☐ Broadens social contacts and family support ☐ Strengthens family ties ☐ Benefits only one family member, but satisfying this need for this individual is important for this family member's well-being	

Developing a Plan to Address Family Needs

Identifying your family's needs was just the first step in the process of improving life in your home. The next step is to develop a plan of action to minimize the effect of ASD on your family.

If you've ever taken a road trip to an unfamiliar destination, you may have used one of the route-planning and mapping programs available on the Internet. Prior to embarking on your trip, you mapped out a route and you may have even identified landmarks that showed that you were on the right path and were getting closer to your destination. Taking family needs and shaping them into a plan of action is similar to mapping out a route. The objective is to identify a series of tasks that will gradually lead you to your goals. Once you have the "map," the next step is to work on the individual tasks either by teaching your child skills that will remedy the ASD behaviors that impede need satisfaction, or by implementing practical solutions to improve life at home.

In this section, we will be using the problem-solving approach explained in chapter 2. However, we will be focusing on two separate sets of possible solutions: viable, practical solutions that address problem areas, and skills that you could teach your child to ease the burden of ASD symptoms.

Remember, the first step in the problem-solving process is to identify the problem. The next step in the process is brainstorming, in which you identify specific problems and generate a list of possible solutions for each problem. (You will probably also recall that in the brainstorming phase it is important not to dismiss unlikely solutions, since censoring might stifle creative thinking.) Once ideas are generated, you consider and evaluate the pros and cons.

The example below demonstrates how Armand's family used the brainstorming technique to decide whether or not to take a ten-day family vacation to Disney World. In the past, they had simply avoided taking vacations, because Armand had difficulty with changes in routine (like sleeping in a different bed, eating at restaurants, enjoying recreational activities, and having to wait for the activities of his choice) and his parents did not want to leave Armand home with a caregiver. However, they now had an opportunity for a special family trip, and they wanted to find out what the best course of action would be. Review the solutions the family came up with, and add any others you can think of at the bottom of the table.

Possible solutions
Don't go on vacation.
Go on vacation, but leave Armand at home with a competent caregiver (grandparents or other relative) or utilize respite services.
Take Armand on the trip, but also take a competent caregiver to help with child care so that the family would have more choices of activities.
Leave Armand at home and keep the vacation brief. This way, the family could assess how Armand and the family coped with the separation from each other.
Take Armand along and keep the vacation brief.
Choose lodging that would best accommodate Armand's needs. Instead of making reservations at a hotel, they could find lodging that had cooking facilities (which minimize problems at mealtime) and more living space so that all family members could be more comfortable.
Plan the vacation far enough in advance so that Armand could learn the skills he'd need for success, such as sleeping in a different bed, eating out at restaurants, waiting appropriately, tolerating changes in routine, and staying close to parents.

The table below lists practical options and teaching tasks that might be useful.

Possible teaching tasks
1. Teach Armand to tolerate sleeping in a different bed.
2. Teach Armand to comply with parental requests when out of the house, such as staying within an arm's reach of a parent.
3. Teach Armand to delay gratification (for example, teach him to engage in quiet play activities when he is required to wait).
4. Teach Armand to follow an activity schedule so that he can anticipate the sequence of events during the vacation.
5. Teach Armand to eat in settings other than at home.
6. Increase Armand's ability to stay with a caregiver in his parents' absence.
7. Teach Armand to tolerate bathing in a bathtub outside of his home.

Brainstorming Examples for Satisfying the Top Ten Family Needs

The tables below illustrate how to apply the brainstorming process to generate possible solutions when any of the top ten needs are not being met. The two examples below address the need for financial stability. In the first example, the brainstorming process generated various practical solutions to the problem of how to pay for medical expenses.

Example 1
Need: Financial
Impediments to having financial stability: Cost of medical examinations and consultations to find out the cause of behavioral problems; cost of treatment
Practical solutions for accessing aid for medical costs
■ Investigate eligibility for Supplemental Security Income (SSI). ■ Set reasonable limits on seeking out professional help to find out the cause of problems. ■ Investigate possible sources of support for accessing services/treatment.

The second example provides some solutions that might be considered by a family having difficulty managing the cost of competent child care, including teaching tasks that the child might learn in order to make the job of child care easier. (See chapter 5 for a detailed discussion of teaching strategies.)

Example 2
Need: Financial
Impediment to having financial stability: The cost of competent child care
Practical solutions for accessing child care
■ Enroll child in a full-day school program. ■ Investigate eligibility for respite services. ■ Have a family member provide child care. ■ Hire a moderately competent person at a moderate cost to watch your child while you are at home. This might allow a parent to take care of business at home (including spending time with your other children). ■ Explore options for participation in after-school programs, including classes at school, sports, scouting, and so on.
Possible teaching tasks to make child care easier
■ Teach child to tolerate separation from parents. ■ Improve compliance with directions from caregivers. ■ Increase ability to occupy unstructured time appropriately by using an activity schedule. ■ Increase independence with self-care activities to make child care more manageable. ■ Teach child to control his behavior. ■ Teach child the skills needed to play specific sports or participate in activities like scouting.

The next example shows some practical solutions and possible teaching tasks that provide options for a family trying to solve problems related to housing.

Example 3
Need: Shelter
Impediments to having adequate shelter: Excessive noise and property destruction by child with ASD and concerns about child's safety
Practical solutions for accessing or maintaining adequate shelter
■ Move to a different residence. ■ Carpet floors to dampen noise from physical activity. ■ Provide more acceptable alternatives for physical activity and appropriate supervision. ■ Secure furnishings. ■ Remove breakables. ■ Replace windows with unbreakable glass. ■ Secure your doors so that they cannot be easily opened by your child with ASD but can be opened by others in case of emergency (for example, install door knob protectors, hook and eye locks placed out of reach, and so on). ■ At the front and back doors, place a bell or touch-sensitive pad that emits a signal to notify you of attempts to leave the house. ■ Use a monitoring device ("electronic nanny") to alert you when your child wanders out of acceptable range. ■ Cover stove burners. ■ Place child-safety locks on cabinets (particularly those containing dangerous substances).
Possible teaching tasks
■ Help your child learn to vocalize in a quieter way. ■ Teach your child to discriminate between indoor and outdoor activity levels and provide plenty of opportunities for outdoor activity. ■ Decrease the frequency of tantrums, jumping, and other noisy behaviors. ■ Increase the amount of time your child spends engaging in enjoyable, quiet activities. ■ Help your child learn to express needs and wants. ■ Increase socially appropriate ways of expressing negative feelings. ■ Increase appropriate use of household objects. ■ Increase compliance with parental limit setting. ■ Increase your child's ability to recognize dangers at home and in the community.

Since leisure and recreational activities have been identified as very important to family well-being, the next example outlines some practical solutions and teaching strategies designed to help a family make this a reality.

Example 4
Need: Leisure and recreation
Impediments to family leisure and recreational activities: The child's rigidity, limited range of interests in activities, difficulty coping with new situations and settings, and difficulty regulating behavior according to situational demands
Practical solutions to enable family to enjoy leisure and recreation activities
■ Find activities that the whole family can enjoy (for example, going to family movies, biking, hiking, bowling, sledding, and skating). ■ Plan to participate in these activities during nonpeak times, in order to avoid lines, crowds, noise, and delays. ■ Avoid outings that will require choices of activities (for example, a county fair, carnival, or amusement park) or those that will require extensive periods of waiting. ■ If traveling to an amusement park, call ahead to inquire about accommodations for children with special needs. ■ Play board games that everyone can enjoy. ■ Consider planning trips that do not include the whole family, perhaps short trips with siblings that focus on their interests. One parent stays home with the children who are not yet ready to participate or are not interested, while the other parent goes with the other children. Alternatively, everyone in the family except the child with ASD could go on a trip, while the child with ASD, not yet ready to tolerate the trip, could be cared for by a relative, close friend, or respite agency. Finally, the entire family could go on the trip and the family could bring along a nanny to care for the child with ASD.
Possible teaching tasks
■ Teach the child to play simple card games, strategy games, or other board games, including how to take turns and display good sportsmanship. ■ Improve on skills already in the child's repertoire. For example, if the child enjoys riding a bicycle, teaching tasks might include gradually increasing the child's endurance so that he can manage family outings, increasing his ability to follow directions during bicycle rides, and increasing his understanding of safety issues (such as the need to wear a bicycle helmet when riding). ■ Teach the child to watch films with appropriate etiquette. This can be done with rented videos at home. When the child gets close to being able to go to a theater, do some practice runs: ask the manager if you can attend the last thirty minutes of a movie. Reward the child for his success. ■ Teach the child to bowl by practicing at home with toy pins. When his is ready to try the bowling alley, purchase only one game to start, and alternate turns (that is, you bowl five frames apiece). Depending upon the child's skill level, arrange to have the child bumpers placed on the alley. When the child is able to handle this modified game format, gradually increase the number of frames played until the child can successfully play an entire game by himself. ■ Teach the child to use an activity schedule to help him anticipate events during family outings. With this strategy he will understand the sequence of events, so that he will know when his preferred activities will take place.

One last example, addressing the issue of privacy, is presented below.

Example 5
Need: Privacy
Impediments to having privacy: The child's poor understanding of limits and personal boundaries, disruption of conversations or social interactions amongst family members or friends, no distinction between what's "mine" and what's "yours," refusal to sleep in his own bed, and limited ability to occupy unstructured time independently and productively
Practical solutions to ensure privacy for family members
▪ Keep valuable personal possessions in a secure place. Lock bedroom doors. ▪ Arrange for in-home or out-of-home respite when planning social events at home.*
Possible teaching tasks
▪ Increase the child's ability to occupy his free time appropriately. ▪ Teach the concept of "mine" and "not mine." ▪ Teach physical limits and boundaries. ▪ Teach him to follow directions, so that you are able to redirect your child's activities and move him to a more appropriate area. ▪ Teach the child to sleep in his own bed.

Creating a Family Action Plan

Now, let's look at how a family can use the results of the brainstorming process to create a family action plan. When Mr. and Mrs. Lang, whose eight-year-old son, Jimmy, has ASD, reviewed their family needs, they noticed that all members had identified the desire for increased privacy as a priority. They used the worksheet template below to brainstorm possible solutions and they identified two strategies, adapting their home environment and teaching Jimmy new skills in order to provide each family member with additional privacy.

---

*   Respite care is often provided by county government or local human services organizations. Respite provides trained staff to provide short-term child care. This can be done within a family's home or at an agency equipped to supervise activities during the day (a few hours or an entire day) or overnight. This service could be used to create opportunities for family members to have uninterrupted time to socialize or engage in other recreational or household activities.

Need: Privacy		
Impediments to having privacy: Jimmy did not understand when his siblings or his parents told him to stay out of their bedrooms and to leave their personal belongings alone and he did not respond to sibling requests to leave them alone when friends visited.		
Practical solutions for increasing privacy		
Solution	**Pros**	**Cons**
Lock up all personal belongings so that they would be inaccessible to Jimmy.	Our "stuff" would be protected. There'd be fewer arguments and emotional reactions related to this issue.	Our stuff would be less accessible (getting things "on the run" would not be possible). Locking things up makes home less "homey." We shouldn't have to lock up our stuff.
Continue to allow Jimmy to have access to all rooms in the house and teach family members to cope better.	Jimmy would be happy.	The privacy issue would remain a problem. Personal property would continue to get destroyed, lost, or misplaced. It's expensive and inconvenient to have to replace items that are tampered with. Family members would frequently be angry with Jimmy.
Lock bedroom doors when no one is occupying them to protect contents.	Personal belongings would be protected. We'd be less mad at Jimmy.	We hate the idea of having to lock our rooms. It would feel like a prison! We couldn't get things easily if we needed them in a hurry. Jimmy might get mad and break the door. Then we'd be faced with an even bigger privacy issue.
Forbid Jimmy to access bedrooms other than his own.	Then Jimmy would have rules he'd have to obey.	Jimmy would probably not remember to stay out of our rooms. Who would enforce the rule?

Solution	Pros	Cons
Teach Jimmy to recognize the "Do Not Enter" sign and teach him not enter bedrooms unescorted. We could also put a list of other choices that Jimmy could choose as alternatives (find the room's owner and ask permission, play with a toy on the "choice list," or go into his own room).	Jimmy already knows how to read and use an activity schedule! If we put the sign on a closed door and we all reinforced him for not opening doors with signs, we could teach him to stay out. It really shouldn't take him long to learn these skills. If we give him a list of other things he could do, he probably would not get mad. He'd likely be content to pick one of the suggested activities.	Extra time would be required to teach Jimmy the new skills. Extra time would be needed to supervise Jimmy.
Teach Jimmy to ask permission to enter bedrooms when the "Do Not Enter" sign is in place.	If Jimmy came and asked permission, I wouldn't mind. At least I could supervise him and make sure he didn't get into anything important. The rules would then be the same for everyone!	
Teach Jimmy to engage in other activities when the "Do Not Enter" sign is in place and access to bedrooms is denied.	We could help Jimmy use skills that are already in his repertoire to solve a family problem. He gets more practice, we get more privacy. If this solution works, maybe we can use a similar strategy to teach Jimmy to give us privacy when we have friends over.	

Their plan included a combination of practical solutions and teaching tasks, as follows:

Practical solutions. The practical solutions that the Lang family generated are listed below:

■ In order to handle Jimmy's lack of understanding that he should leave other family members' personal belongings alone, they purchased lockable cabinets for each of the bedrooms and living areas so that important possessions could be kept out of his reach. They also agreed to keep bedroom doors shut when not occupied and they placed latches on the bedroom doors.

- They arranged for Jimmy to stay with his grandparents overnight one weekend every month so that the other children could have friends sleep over and visit without being disrupted. The children took turns and planned activities in advance so that everyone had equal opportunity.

- Specific times on the weekends were also set aside for Jimmy's friends to come over. The other siblings took turns helping to supervise Jimmy's visits with his friends.

- Jimmy's parents also scheduled special outings with each of the siblings that focused on their interests. They agreed that the activities would not be expensive or require a lot of time but would be mutually enjoyable. Some of the activities that they shared included bicycle rides, fishing trips, afternoons at the local library, hikes in nearby parks and woodlands, and working on model airplanes. The family rule was that, short of an emergency, these activities were not to be interrupted or postponed.

Teaching tasks. The Lang family also generated a list of teaching tasks to change child-specific behaviors that interfered with family need fulfillment. The family agreed that they could teach Jimmy some skills in order to lessen the intensity of the emotions that tended to arise when he violated his siblings' personal space. These skills included the following:

- Reading and comprehending the sign that stated, "Do Not Enter," and was placed on bedroom doors when privacy was desired. Underneath these words were suggestions for alternative activities that Jimmy could engage in. The family implemented a teaching program that taught Jimmy to select one of the "choice activities" when he was prevented from entering a room.

- Following an activity schedule that was designed to be used during times when privacy was very important (for example, during homework time or during times set aside for family meetings). The plan was to decrease interruptions by increasing productive activity.

- Discriminating between his possessions and those of others. The family taught Jimmy to ask permission to use others' possessions and to abide by the response he received.

Below is a template that you can use when you brainstorm to find ways to meet one of your family's needs.

Need:		
Impediments to:		
Practical solutions for		
Solutions	Pros	Cons
Possible teaching tasks		
Solutions	Pros	Cons

In this chapter, we identified the needs of children with ASD and the needs of the family and examined how ASD-related behaviors can impede need satisfaction for all family members. We also provided tools to help you and your family identify the needs that are unique to your family situation and gave you suggestions regarding how to prioritize your family's needs. If you have completed the exercises in this chapter, you are well on your way to devising a plan of action. In chapter 5, we will focus on another very important component of your plan of action: how to teach your child with ASD new skills. This information is very important because, as you saw in the example of the Lang family, above, the best solutions to many family issues may involve teaching your child new skills.

5

How to Teach Your Child New Skills

Teaching new skills to children with autism spectrum disorders can be very complicated and challenging. This is in large part because many children with ASD have multiple problems, such as limited attention span, limited language skills, and challenging behaviors, that make it difficult for them to learn from traditional teaching methods. But despite the challenges, with the right strategies, a good deal of patience, and a positive attitude, you can help your child succeed at learning new skills.

There are many research-based strategies that have been proven to be effective, but it would be impossible to discuss them all here. However, we believe that you can benefit from learning some of the important principles and techniques used in many of these research-based strategies, and we'll explain them in this chapter. You can use these techniques to teach your child a wide variety of useful, adaptive, and functional skills that will make a difference in the way that he and your family function. To help you make sure you're going in the right direction, we've provided a Resources section at the end of the book and a list of warning signs in chapter 13 so that you will be able to recognize when you are getting in over your head or need a professional consultation. In this chapter, you will learn the following information:

- How to select what to teach

- How to play to your child's strengths

- How to keep it simple: starting with skills already in your child's repertoire and moving from the simple to the complex

- Why it is important to have a teaching plan, and how to develop a plan

- How to create the right environment for teaching

- How to structure teaching interactions and keep your child motivated

- How to provide cues that help your child learn

- How to increase wanted skills and decrease unwanted behaviors (such as tantrums, disruptive behavior, and verbal refusals)

- How to teach the appropriate time and place for specific behaviors

In addition, we will be providing you with a crash course in the vocabulary that you will need to effectively use the information contained in the rest of the book.

HOW TO SELECT WHAT TO TEACH

When we are teaching parent-education classes, one of the first tasks that we ask parents to do is to generate a wish list of skills that they would like their child to learn. Not surprisingly, this is not a problem for most parents. Within a few minutes, they produce extensive lists that usually include at least some of the following desires:

- Improved communication and self-help skills

- Increased range of play and leisure skills

- Improved social skills

- Improved toileting skills

- Increased independence in self-care skills

- Increased tolerance for a broader range of foods

- More typical sleep habits

- Increased awareness of environmental dangers

- Increased tolerance of change in the environment

- Less-severe emotional reactions (tantrums, screaming, self-injury)

- Activity levels that more closely match situational demands

While parents have little difficulty making their wish list, the next task, *prioritizing* the skills, presents more of a challenge. That is, ranking the desired skills in the order in which they'd like to teach them is quite difficult. We often use the metaphor of a child in a candy store; having so many highly desired things to choose from can sometimes be overwhelming. Even the basic concept of prioritizing can be frustrating, since many parents want to do everything *right now*. Of course, however, little is accomplished by trying to do everything at once, and "mega teaching" can be stressful for your child. It's far better to address a few skills at a time and to teach logical sequences of skills so that, over time, you can build complex, functional skill repertoires.

Before we get started on prioritizing and sequencing the skills you'd like to teach your child, we need to cover a number of important topics, including playing to your child's strengths, keeping it simple, and having a teaching plan.

HOW TO PLAY TO YOUR CHILD'S STRENGTHS

While you may have a tendency to focus on what your child cannot do, you will find that there are specific things that your child *can* do. Identifying the skills your child already has is very important in the planning process, since it provides a starting point for teaching. These existing skills, no matter how small, become our building blocks. The example of Maria, below, illustrates this point.

Although four-year-old Maria's verbal abilities were extremely poor, she, like many other children with autism, demonstrated the ability to recognize and match pictures. In addition to having this strength, Maria was good at imitating simple motor actions. Capitalizing upon these relative strengths, her parents taught her to use pictures to communicate basic wants and needs. In addition, using her ability to recognize pictures and imitate actions, she quickly learned to perform activity sequences that were displayed in pictures, which resulted in greater independence in self-care skills. Specifically, Maria learned how to dress herself independently and improved her toileting hygiene; she also learned to follow a schedule for her morning routine. The teaching sequences that were used for instruction are offered below.

Task Analyses for Maria's Communication and Self-Help Programs

Using Pictures to Communicate Basic Wants and Needs

Step 1. Matches pictures to objects

Step 2. Imitates giving picture to receive preferred items

Step 3. Uses pictures independently to request preferred items

Step 4. Imitates giving pictures to receive preferred activities

Step 5. Uses pictures independently to receive preferred items and activities

Following Picture Sequences to Complete Self-Care Routines

Step 1. Follows one picture direction

Step 2. Follows two picture directions in sequence

Step 3. Follows three picture directions in sequence

Step 4. Follows four picture directions in sequence

Step 5. Completes self-care sequence when the last picture is removed

Step 6. Completes self-care sequence when the last two pictures are removed

Step 7. Completes self-care sequence when the last three pictures are removed

Step 8. Completes self-care sequence independently (without pictures)

Following a Picture Schedule to Complete Morning Routine

Step 1. One task (using toilet): Responds to timer by walking over to schedule, looking at the picture, completing the task depicted, and placing the activity card in the "Done" pocket

Step 2. Two tasks (using toilet and brushing teeth): Responds to timer by walking over to schedule, looking at the first picture, completing the task depicted, placing the activity card in the "Done" pocket, looking at the second picture, completing the task, and placing the activity card in the "Done" pocket

Step 3. Three tasks (using toilet, brushing teeth, and getting dressed): Responds to timer by walking over to schedule, looking at the first picture, completing the task depicted, placing the activity card in the "Done" pocket, looking at the second picture, completing the task, placing the activity card in the "Done" pocket, looking at the third picture, completing the task, and placing the activity card in the "Done" pocket

Step 4. Four tasks (using toilet, brushing teeth, getting dressed, and eating breakfast): Responds to timer by walking over to schedule, looking at the first picture, completing the task depicted, placing the activity card in the "Done" pocket, looking at the second picture, completing the task, placing the activity card in the "Done" pocket, looking at the third picture, completing the task, placing the activity card in the "Done" pocket, looking at the fourth picture, completing the task, and putting the activity card in the "Done" pocket

Step 5. Completes all four tasks independently within expected time limit

Learning these skills helped Maria communicate her wants and needs better and thus reduced her tendency to have tantrums, making for a calmer household environment. She was able to increase her independence in completing self-care tasks, which allowed her mom and dad more time to spend getting the other children ready for school, gave her more free time before school, and decreased morning stress. As you can see, teaching these skills benefited both Maria and her family.

HOW TO KEEP IT SIMPLE: SMALL STEPS LEAD TO BIG THINGS

Take a minute to think about how you learned arithmetic concepts. You likely learned to recognize a subset of numbers (1 through 10), then to associate a specific quantity with each number, next to memorize their ordinal sequence, and finally to use them for counting objects and for understanding comparative concepts such as "greater than" and "less than." Breaking complex tasks down into logical sequences of simpler skills makes teaching complex skills easier. It also provides you with an idea of which skills need to be mastered before more advanced skills can be taught. For example, a child would need to understand basic quantity concepts (that is, to be able to answer the question "How many?") before being able to master comparative concepts.

Teaching new skills to children with ASD is most successful when the skills are taught in small steps. Breaking tasks into simpler parts has a number of advantages:

- You and your child can feel successful right away.

- Early success in learning keeps you and your child motivated to continue working on skill development. Success breeds more success.

■   By breaking the task down into small steps, you can more easily identify problems and fix them so that learning can continue.

The steps used in Maria's teaching programs progressed from the simple to the complex. More effort and a higher degree of skill were required of her only after she had mastered earlier steps in the teaching program.

Use the checklist below to make a list of your child's relative strengths (we have left room at the bottom to write in skills and abilities that are not included in the checklist). This will get you thinking about how you can use these skills to broaden your child's repertoire.

IDENTIFYING YOUR CHILD'S STRENGTHS

☐   Points to indicate wants and needs

☐   Follows simple verbal directions (when accompanied with gesture, or without gesture)

☐   Imitates simple motor actions

☐   Produces sounds to indicate wants or needs

☐   Recognizes pictures (points to pictures, matches pictures to like pictures, matches pictures to objects, or names pictures)

☐   Recognizes letters of the alphabet (points to letters, matches letters)

☐   Recognizes words (reads words representing common objects, matches words to objects)

☐   Uses some toys appropriately

☐   Enjoys some social interactions with family members

Other strengths:

☐   _____

☐   _____

What Does It Mean to Simplify Tasks?

Now let's apply these concepts to the ability to "follow verbal directions," breaking it down into teachable parts. One example of a teaching sequence that progresses from simple to complex directions is outlined below:

1.   Follows functional directions, such as "Come here," "Stand up," "Sit down," "Raise your arms," and "Give me your foot."

2. Follows functional directions that involve objects, such as "Bring me the toy," "Give me the cup," and "Show me the paper."

3. Follows functional directions involving objects and people, such as "Give the salt to Daddy," "Give the toy to Jamie," and "Bring Mommy your pajamas."

4. Follows directions involving qualifiers, such as "Get your red jacket," "Bring me five napkins," and "Get the big yellow cup."

Sequencing Skills: Using a Curriculum Guide

There are numerous curriculum guides available on the market that can help you identify skills that you can teach your child in important areas such as communication, socialization, and self-care. We highly recommend using such tools to help you break down the skills that you want to teach into logical, sequential steps. We list some of these curricula in the Resources section of this book. (Some of the other books included in the Resources section provide skill sequences even though they are not labeled specifically as "curricula.")

HOW TO DEVELOP A TEACHING PLAN: WHICH TASKS COME FIRST?

Once you've created your wish list, you'll need to organize the skills into meaningful and functional clusters of skills: a teaching plan. (Skills that are used in everyday functioning are termed *functional*.) Why is it important to have a plan for teaching, and how do you develop a plan? Generating a teaching plan is an important step because it prompts you to think about a number of very important aspects of the teaching process before you actually begin instruction. For starters, you'll be prompted to think about how the skills that you want to teach will affect both your child's ability to participate in everyday activities and your family's functioning. Since a teaching plan functions as a guide for the skills you intend to teach, it reflects your priorities, outlines logical teaching sequences (the order in which you will teach specific skills), and ensures that acquired skills are reinforced and maintained by allowing you to select other skills that build upon skills already learned. In the process of generating your teaching plan, you can make sure that you have selected goals that form functional and meaningful skill clusters (skills that can be used on a daily basis to improve your child's interactions with his environment). The following example shows the goals selected for Joel, a ten-year-old boy with ASD who had a sizable verbal vocabulary, but little conversational speech. Joel was able to read fairly well but had poor comprehension, had a difficult time adhering to behavioral limits, and required a lot of parental supervision to complete self-care activities. He also had limited ability with number concepts and had no prior knowledge of the value of money or how to conduct monetary exchanges. In the table below, we have presented a list of the teaching tasks that Joel's parents elected to address. They are listed in order of priority; those that had the most impact on Joel's overall functioning and decreasing stress in the family were addressed first. The table also demonstrates how Joel's parents used skills already in his repertoire to teach new skills and how they maximized teaching opportunities to prepare Joel for instruction in goals that would be addressed later in the teaching sequence.

Parent wish list: Increase Joel's ability to share information with family members

Increase Joel's ability to engage in conversational exchanges

Increase Joel's ability to comply with directions to manage his behavior

Increase Joel's understanding of numbers and quantity

Increase Joel's ability to complete self-care skills more independently (including dressing, showering, tying his shoes, and purchasing items at the store

Strengths: Joel's word recognition skills were at grade level (second grade).

Joel had great matching skills.

Sequence of goals	Teaching methods	Related goals selected
Compliance with directions to manage behavior	Joel was provided with a written rule list that outlined rules and consequences. His parents gradually decreased the number of cues needed to get him to comply. Joel's compliance with his parents' directions was rewarded with points that he was able to exchange for preferred activities (such as video games, choice of favorite TV shows, and selection of dessert for the family on a given night).	In an effort to improve his counting and number recognition skills, Joel's parents and his teachers had him routinely count the points he earned and match the quantities with numerals. This instruction was seen as a prerequisite for teaching him about the value of money.
Independence with self-care skills (dressing and grooming routines)	Joel was taught how to follow a written activity schedule to help him get through routine activities (such as dressing independently, grooming, and showering). When his parents first introduced this goal, they had him use Velcro-fastened shoes since he was unable to tie his shoes.	Tying shoes independently: since Joel was so visually adept, a picture sequence was used to teach Joel to tie his shoes.
Increase Joel's ability to share information with family members	Given Joel's ability to read, his parents and his teachers helped him generate a log of his activities each day. At school and at home, Joel was taught to answer who, what, and where questions. In the early stages of teaching, Joel was able to use his daily logs to answer these questions.	

Increase Joel's ability to engage in conversational exchanges	Once Joel was able to talk about some of his own experiences, he was taught to ask others who, what, and why questions to get information. The teaching program progressed from asking the questions to both asking the questions and listening to the answers.	Joel was then taught to sustain two or three conversational exchanges with others on a variety of topics. At first these were scripted, but later he was able to spontaneously generate questions to sustain short conversations.
Purchasing items at the store	Again, capitalizing on Joel's strengths in the area of visual matching, Joel's parents initially taught him to match coins to a "price card" that showed items he frequently purchased (soda, candy, game cards) and their monetary value, so he was able to make purchases independently. Joel's parents also taught him how to engage in appropriate conversational exchanges with clerks at the store. Initially, these were scripted, and eventually the scripts were eliminated when he became competent at conversing.	At school and at home, Joel worked on discriminating between coins, identifying their value, and using a calculator to compute the cost of multiple purchases. Once Joel had mastered these skills, he no longer required price cards for making purchases.

Prioritizing and Sequencing

The four questions that appear in the following pages highlight core principles that you should consider when prioritizing teaching tasks and planning a teaching sequence.

1. *Does your child have some ability to perform one of the skills that you want to teach?*

Think about skills that are already in your child's repertoire. Observe your child during his everyday activities and look closely at the skills he uses. For example, does he do any of the following, even occasionally?

- ☐   Use toys appropriately

- ☐   Play for short periods of time without close supervision

- ☐   Remain seated without running about or climbing on furniture

- ☐   Play on the swings in the backyard

- ☐   Enjoy coloring

- ☐   Look at you some of the time when you call his name

- ☐   Like to help with chores

☐   Have an affinity for matching or sorting

☐   Have good motor skills

Once you identify the skills in your child's repertoire, begin thinking about how you can expand or refine them in order to improve your child's overall level of functioning.

Let's take a look at how Juan's parents, Mr. and Mrs. Perez, used a skill already in his repertoire to make an important change at home. Juan's parents observed that he enjoyed playing with a train set, but that he was only able to play appropriately for five minutes. Juan's parents thought that it would benefit the family if he could occupy himself appropriately, with minimal supervision, for longer periods of time. Mr. and Mrs. Perez hoped that by increasing independent play with safe toys, they could have some uninterrupted time to take care of important household and personal care tasks. The outcome? They effectively taught Juan to play with his trains in the family room for thirty minutes when his activity schedule indicated that it was time to play with trains, and they felt less stressed because they had extra time to take care of family business.

Dominique loved to sort objects; she did this with her blocks, pop-together beads, and hair bows and ribbons. Her parents wanted to get her involved in helping with household tasks so that they could keep her in sight while they were doing chores around the house. Dominique's parents taught her how to help put safe utensils and unbreakable dishes away. They also taught her to sort laundry and put clothes away after they were folded—when her parents put pictures of clothing items on the dresser drawers, putting away clothes was a breeze for Dominique!

2.   *Does the skill you want to teach relate to other skills and therefore help your child function better in an important area?*

Some skills are important to teach because, when learned, they comprise a solid foundation that enables your child to learn new tasks more easily. These skills have been referred to as *keystone behaviors* or *learning-to-learn skills*. Stated a different way, these skills function as prerequisite skills for new learning. Below are some common learning-to-learn skills:

- Turning toward the speaker

- Following simple directions

- Focusing attention on teaching materials or on objects and activities in the natural environment

- Verbal and nonverbal imitation

- Matching

- Picture recognition

- Pointing or indicating

- Following a picture or activity schedule

If these skills are not in your child's repertoire, it would be wise of you to make them a high priority. Taking the time to teach these early will save you a lot of time and energy later on. Below are two examples of how learning-to-learn skills can make teaching easier.

Janie's parents wanted to teach her to use an activity schedule. They found that Janie's ability to recognize pictures, focus her attention on instructional materials, and match pictures and objects made it easier for her to learn to follow a schedule.

Marsha's parents wanted to teach her to wash her face. Marsha's nonverbal imitation skills made it possible for her to learn to imitate the actions required to complete this task. The teaching program focused on teaching Marsha to wash different areas of her face in sequence via imitation. A similar approach was used to teach her to brush her teeth.

3. *Does your child have the prerequisite skills (for example, adequate attention, comprehension of the concepts required for performance, or imitative skills) needed to be able to learn the skill(s) you want to teach?*

In addition to the learning-to-learn skills, it is important to determine what, if any, *foundation* skills need to be in your child's repertoire before you embark on teaching a new task. In our work with children diagnosed with ASD, we often find that the children have "holes" in their skill repertoires. That is, they may perform some rather advanced skills without having mastered earlier skills that may be necessary for success in that area.

For example, some children with ASD are able to decipher almost any word in print that is put in front of them. However, due to the language difficulties associated with these disorders (such as poor expression and comprehension in autism, and literalness in Asperger's disorder), their comprehension of what they read may be surprisingly inferior to their word knowledge. Comprehension of entry-level reading material, then, is a prerequisite skill for reading at a higher grade levels.

We recently met a child who was not making progress toward a teaching goal that focused on adding two-digit numerals without carrying. When we conducted our assessment, we found that the child could not perform one-digit arithmetic problems without counting on his fingers. Although he had performed well doing single-digit arithmetic problems with sums ranging to ten, he could no longer use finger counting to compensate for his lack of knowledge of basic sums. The solutions were twofold: the child was taught to use a calculator to enable him to succeed at doing functional, everyday calculations, and he received practice doing basic sums to twenty until he learned them in a rote fashion.

4. *Does your plan identify a progression of skills that gradually increase in complexity?*

In order to ensure your child's success, you'll want to teach skills in a logical progression, starting with a relatively easy task and methodically moving on to the next, more complex task. Before elaborating on this concept, we do want to emphasize that this is not the only principle you will apply to selecting tasks for the teaching plan (see the section Organizing Skills into Meaningful Clusters later in this chapter), although it is a useful concept.

Look at the following excerpt taken from the expressive language domain of *Individualized Goal Selection Curriculum* (Romanczyk, Lockshin, and Matey 2000), which offers an example of skill sequences.

Area 5 Expressive Language/Communication

Level 1. Basic communication
    Stage 1. Self-initiated vocalizations
        Task 1. Emits any sound to communicate intent
        Task 2. Emits multi-syllabic vocalizations in social contexts
    Stage 2. Use of gestures
        Task 1. Produces nonspecific gestures/signs to communicate

           Task 2. Uses gestures to indicate desire for object in proximity

           Task 3. Uses gestures to indicate desire for object that is not visible

       Stage 3. Use of Mands [requests or directions]

           Task 1. Uses vocalization to indicate basic wants

           Task 2. Uses single word to indicate want

           Task 3. Uses multiple words to indicate want

   Level 2. Labeling

       Stage 1. Labeling using single word/sign/symbol

           Task 1. Produces consonant-vowel combination in response to an object

           Task 2. Labels familiar objects with a single word/sign/symbol

           Task 3. Labels body parts

           Task 4. Labels pictures of objects

           Task 5. Labels events using a single word/sign/symbol

       Stage 2. Uses two words/signs/symbols to label pictures or events

           Task 1. Uses noun-verb combinations (boy run)

           Task 2. Uses verb-noun combinations (catch ball)

           Task 3. Uses pronoun-verb combinations (I eat)

           Task 4. Uses adjective-noun combinations (red apple)

           Task 5. Uses negatives (no play, no cookie)

           Task 6. Uses verb-adverb combinations (run fast)

The topic headings "Area," "Level," "Stage," and "Task" as used in the *Individualized Goal Selection Curriculum* provide the user with a method of breaking down complex skills into simpler components. As you can see, the "levels" represent a broad skill area and the "stages" represent a further simplification of complex skills. The "tasks" represent the specific tasks that are incorporated into the teaching plans that are developed for each child. For each task that is selected for instruction, an individualized teaching strategy is developed. The teaching strategy outlines the method that will be used to teach the goal and, if necessary, the teaching task will be divided into even smaller steps to make learning easier. The *Individualized Goal Selection Curriculum* subdivisions can also be used to monitor the child's progress. If, for example, a child has mastered the majority of teaching tasks in Stage 1, "Labeling using a single word/sign/symbol" (above), then he should be reasonably competent at labeling objects and events in his environment.

It is important to note that your child does not necessarily need to acquire all of the skills in the exact sequence given in the list above. We've simply offered this sequence as a guideline to help you identify teaching tasks, and to alert you to prerequisite skills that may be needed before you move on to more advanced skills.

Here is an example of a teaching plan for the expressive language domain derived from the *Individualized Goal Selection Curriculum* excerpt above, for teaching a nonverbal, preschool-age child to label familiar objects:

1. Makes multisyllabic sounds in social contexts

2. Uses vocalization to indicate basic wants

3. Produces consonant-vowel combination to label objects (such as "ba" for "ball" or "ca" for "car").

4. Labels familiar objects with a single word, sign, or symbol

5. Uses a single word or sign to indicate a want or desire

The task sequences above begin at or near the child's current level of functioning and progress to more challenging tasks. In the sequence, the earlier tasks represent simpler skills that may be easier to teach in the beginning stages of language instruction. The important point is to begin instruction at your child's current level of language ability and to select more advanced skills that will be addressed once your child has mastered the earlier skills in the sequence.

Try your hand at creating a teaching sequence that will result in a complex, functional skill for your child.

Teaching sequence
Complex, functional skill: _____   In the space below, generate a sequence of teaching tasks that combine to create a complex, functional skill.
1.
2.
3.
4.
5.
6.

Simplifying Tasks Even Further

In the preceding section, we talked about the importance of selecting sequences of skills in order to teach complex, functional skill repertoires. While each of these skills may, at first blush, appear to be simple enough to teach, for many children with ASD it is essential to break these skills into even simpler components so that learning can occur quickly and easily.

We perform so many tasks automatically—without thinking about their individual steps—that we can easily overlook the complexity involved in performing everyday tasks. However, just about any task that you want to teach can be broken down into smaller parts. There are several ways to simplify skills and the learning environment for teaching purposes, including the following approaches:

- Break a specific skill into its sequential component parts (referred to as a *task analysis*). An example of this would be specifying the individual steps needed to learn how to put on a pull-on shirt.

- Teach the child to perform the skill in a familiar environment before expecting him to perform it in an unfamiliar environment.

- Teach the child to perform the skill in an environment where there are few distractions. Once the child performs at mastery levels in this setting, teach him to perform the skill in more complex settings.

Now let's discuss these three strategies in more detail.

The Task Analysis

In the most traditional application of the task analysis, skills are broken down into their component parts. Three examples of this type of tasks analysis (putting on a pull-on shirt, self-feeding with a spoon, and ordering a meal at a fast-food restaurant) are presented below.

Putting on a pull-on shirt

1. Picks up shirt and finds opening at the bottom of the shirt when shirt is placed tag side up on a flat surface

2. Places head inside opening

3. Finds the top opening of the shirt and places head inside

4. Pulls head through the opening

5. Pulls shirt down to shoulders

6. Lifts one arm up and searches for arm opening

7. Places one arm through opening

8. Lifts second arm up and searches for second opening

9. Places second arm through the second opening

10. Pulls shirt down toward waist or hips

Self-feeding with a spoon

1. Picks up spoon when a bowl of semisolid food is placed on table

2. Positions the spoon appropriately for scooping

3. Uses nondominant hand to hold bowl while scooping food from bowl

4. Brings food to mouth and puts spoon into mouth

5. Repeats cycle of holding the bowl in place, scooping, bringing the food to mouth, and eating until the bowl is empty

6. Places spoon on table when the bowl is empty

Ordering a meal at a fast-food restaurant

1. Stands in line while waiting to order and moves to the counter when it's his turn

2. Responds to the greeting of the server

3. Waits until the server asks, "What would you like today?" or "What can I get you?"

4. Tells the server the names of three food items and any preferences for preparation (for example, hamburger without ketchup, but with lettuce, pickles, and mustard; large french fries; and a cola) when he is shown pictures of his favorite foods on a cue card. (Note: As your child demonstrates competence in ordering, you can begin to systematically eliminate the picture cues so that he learns to order without the cue card.)

5. Moves to the pickup area

6. Picks up tray, stops at condiment station, and picks up napkins, utensils, and a straw

7. Carries tray to the table and carefully places tray on the table

Keep in mind that tasks can be broken down into any number of component parts and that no formula tells us how many steps are appropriate. The only way to tell whether your task analysis is adequate is to see if your child is able to master each individual step. If he gets stuck on a step, it may be a signal that you have not subdivided the task into small enough components.

A task analysis could also be developed to teach your child to perform skills in increasingly complex environments. Again, the idea is to identify the environment where you want your child to ultimately perform the skill and then develop a progression of skills, starting with the simplest and gradually increasing the complexity of the environment. For the purposes of the example below, we are assuming that your child already has decent ball-handling skills and can follow basic game rules.

Playing soccer

1. Follows the ball and changes direction at the right times when the soccer game is played on a quarter of the soccer field with a total of four children

2. Follows the ball and changes direction when the soccer game is played on half of the field with a total of six children

3. Follows the ball and changes direction when the soccer game is played on three-quarters of the field with a total of eight children

4. Follows the ball and changes direction when the soccer game is played on the full field with the entire team

Some of the tasks that you may want to teach will require that your child perform or sustain his attention for a specific amount of time. For example, you may choose to teach him to watch a film (typical viewing time is approximately ninety minutes), sit at the dinner table for the duration of the meal (perhaps twenty to thirty minutes), or take a walk with the family. An example of a task analysis that targets increasing duration of activity follows:

1. Remains quiet and in seat while watching a self-selected video with a familiar story line for three minutes

2. Remains quiet and in seat while watching a self-selected video with a familiar story line for five minutes

3. Remains quiet and in seat while watching a self-selected video with a familiar story line for ten minutes

4. Remains quiet and in seat while watching a self-selected video with a familiar story line for fifteen minutes

5. Remains quiet and in seat while watching a self-selected video with a familiar story line for thirty minutes

6. Remains quiet and in seat while watching a self-selected video with a familiar story line for forty-five minutes

7. Remains quiet and in seat while watching a self-selected video with a familiar story line for sixty minutes

8. Remains quiet and in seat while watching a self-selected video with a familiar story line for seventy-five minutes

9. Remains quiet and in seat while watching a self-selected video with a familiar story line for ninety minutes

10. Remains quiet and in seat while watching a video selected by someone else with a familiar story line for ten minutes

11. Remains quiet and in seat while watching video selected by someone else with a familiar story line for twenty minutes

12. Remains quiet and in seat while watching a video selected by someone else with a familiar story line for thirty minutes

13. Remains quiet and in seat while watching a video selected by someone else with an unfamiliar story line for fifteen minutes

14. Remains quiet and in seat while watching a video selected by someone else with an unfamiliar story line for thirty minutes

15. Remains quiet and in seat while watching a video selected by someone else with an unfamiliar story line for forty-five minutes

16. Remains quiet and in seat while watching a video selected by someone else with an unfamiliar story line for sixty minutes

Another application of a task analysis addresses the problem of generalization—that is, an inability to generalize skills learned in one setting to new situations or stimuli. One way to avoid problems with generalization is to create a task analysis that incorporates a broad range of varied learning opportunities. The task analysis below was developed to teach the concept of the color red and to ensure generalization of the concept across various materials and situations.

1. When shown a red flash card and asked, "What color?" the child names the color red or points to a red card from a choice of three color cards on a communication board.

2. When shown pictures of red familiar objects and asked, "What color?" the child names the color red or points to a red card from a choice of three color cards on a communication board.

3. When shown pictures of red objects in books and asked, "What color?" the child names the color red or points to a red card from a choice of three color cards on a communication board.

4. When shown the red clothing of peers or family members and asked, "What color?" the child names the color red or points to a red card from a choice of three color cards on a communication board.

5. When shown familiar red objects outside of the home and asked, "What color?" the child names the color red or points to a red card from a choice of three color cards on a communication board.

6. When shown unfamiliar red objects and asked, "What color?" the child names the color red or points to a red card from a choice of three color cards on a communication board.

Use the examples above to help you create a task analysis for a skill that you want to teach your child.

Task analysis worksheet
Teaching task: _____ _____
Break the task down into smaller, teachable units.
1.
2.
3.
4.
5.
6.
7.
8.

Start in a Familiar Environment before Moving to an Unfamiliar Environment

Sometimes it's easier for children to learn new skills at home than out in public. We applied this strategy when teaching Jasmine how to keep herself occupied appropriately when she had to wait for events. Jasmine had difficulty waiting and, as you can imagine, her behavior often caused her parents and siblings a considerable amount of distress. Several factors led to the decision to start teaching this skill at home, including the difficulty of managing Jasmine's behavior in public, the embarrassment that her siblings experienced because of her behavior, concerns about Jasmine's safety when she had severe tantrums, and the fact that her parents had greater control of the amount of time that Jasmine would have to wait at home. The teaching program was structured to increase Jasmine's ability to do some of her favorite activities while waiting. Supplies for these activities, kept in a "waiting bag," included an Etch A Sketch, a kaleidoscope, crayons and paper, and a CD player with her favorite CDs. The parents systematically increased the amount of time that Jasmine was required to wait while behaving appropriately, from less than a minute to fifteen minutes. Once she reached this point, her parents began using the "waiting bag" during short waits in settings outside of the home, which Jasmine handled reasonably well. Eventually, the teaching program was applied to situations that gave Jasmine the most difficulty.

Teach Learning-to-Learn Skills in a Distraction-Free Environment before Moving to More Naturalistic Settings

Some important skills (such as maintaining eye contact and nonverbal imitation) may need to be taught in a distraction-free environment before they can be transferred to more complex settings. This is in part because these skills are sometimes hard to teach and because multiple teaching trials are often needed to achieve mastery. Since these skills can be useful when teaching many other important skills, it is important that they be strongly established in the child's repertoire. Teaching sequences that can be used to teach and transfer these skills to more complex environments are presented below.

Eye contact

1.   Responds to his name and the direction "Look at me" in a quiet setting with few distractions

2.   Responds to his name only in a quiet setting with few distractions

3.   Responds to his name only in a minimally distracting environment (at home during everyday activities or in a classroom during routine activities)

4.   Responds to his name only when shopping in a grocery store or playing on a playground

5.   Responds to his name only at a community event (such as a town fair)

Nonverbal imitation

1.   Performs functional actions when they are modeled by an adult in a quiet setting with few distractions (such as raising arms for dressing)

2.   Performs functional actions when they are modeled by an adult in moderately distracting environments (such as washing hands in the bathroom at home, or imitating toy use in the family playroom with siblings present)

3.   Performs functional actions when they are modeled by other children (such as toy play modeled by siblings)

4.   Imitates play activities modeled by peers in a classroom or on a playground

Organizing Skills into Meaningful Clusters

At the time of our consultation with her family, Amanda's parents, Mr. and Mrs. Fitch, were feeling frustrated because Amanda's behavior made it difficult for them to run errands with her along—a significant problem because both of Amanda's parents worked and it was extremely inconvenient for them to find after-work child care. And taking care of errands before picking Amanda up from day care meant that they had to take time off from work. Mr. and Mrs. Fitch wanted to teach Amanda to behave in the grocery store and other similar situations, because it would save time, decrease stress, and give them extra family time at home.

Reviewing Amanda's strengths, we identified the following skills that could be refined and expanded into functional "shopping" skills:

Matching pictures

Following an activity schedule

Pushing a toy stroller

Using Amanda's strengths, we helped her parents select a cluster of goals. We refined, expanded, and combined skills already in her repertoire. The result? A new, functional skill, "grocery shopping," which would have a positive impact on family life. In developing her teaching plan, we also included related skills that would increase Amanda's vocabulary, and we added a social component, sharing her successes with her parents. Below are the skills that were involved in Amanda's grocery shopping program:

- Matching pictures of grocery items frequently purchased by the family

- Following an activity schedule (which required Amanda to find items that matched the pictures on her "shopping list," one item per aisle at first, then more as she progressed) in a specific sequence, determined by the layout of the grocery store

- Pushing a shopping cart

- Labeling grocery items on the list

- Getting parent attention to show that item was found ("Look! Frosted Flakes!")

Looking at Amanda's example, above, we could say that she already had the prerequisite skills in her repertoire to learn a simple form of grocery shopping (that is, she was able to match pictures, follow an activity schedule, and push a toy stroller). But what if your child did not have these skills in his repertoire and you wanted to teach the same skill? In order for the teaching program to be effective, you would first have to teach your child the prerequisite skills before teaching the actual shopping part of the task, or you would have to use a different teaching plan that did not require these skills.

Now, using the worksheet below, apply the principles above to create a functional skills cluster.

Functional skill cluster
Functional skill you want to teach: _____
Identify areas of strength that you will incorporate into the skill cluster: 1. _____ 2. _____ 3. _____ 4. _____
What other skills will you need to teach? 1. _____ 2. _____ 3. _____ 4. _____

Learning and Behavior Change

Learning new skills involves behavior change. When you want to teach your child to look at you when you call his name, what you want is for him to respond to you in a way that is different from what he is currently doing. The same is true when you want your child to sit at the dinner table for an entire meal, to respond to greetings initiated by others, to put on pajamas before bedtime, or to play with toys in the company of other children. We can say that your child has learned a new response (or set of responses) when he consistently responds in a new and appropriate way when he encounters the same situation. The table below presents some examples of changed responses as a result of teaching.

	Example 1	Example 2	Example 3	Example 4
Parent's statement or request	"Sally?" (You say your child's name.)	"Stay at the table and eat your dinner."	"Hi! I missed you."	"Go put on your jammies."
A. Child's response *before* teaching	Looks away; doesn't pay attention	Takes a bite of food and wanders away	Looks away; runs off and grabs a toy	Starts to cry and runs into the living room
B. Child's response *after* teaching	Turns and looks in your direction	Remains at the table until meal is finished	"Hi, Mommy!"	Goes into bedroom, takes clothes off, and puts on pajamas

HOW TO CREATE THE RIGHT ENVIRONMENT FOR TEACHING

It is possible to teach new tasks in many different settings. Choosing the right teaching environment depends on the following factors:

- The difficulty of the task

- The amount of practice your child will probably need in order to learn the task

- How many teaching interactions (or teaching trials) you want to conduct at a given time

- How distracted your child becomes in complex environments, and where your child will likely use the skill taught (for example, making the bed is something that is done at home)

As is suggested by the last item in the list above, many tasks are best taught in the environment where you expect your child to perform the skill (this is generally referred to as teaching in the *criterion environment* or *natural environment*. One major reason for this is that children with ASD often have difficulty transferring skills learned in one setting to new settings. By teaching the skill in the setting where you ultimately want your child to perform the skill, you eliminate the need to transfer the skill. Another reason is that children with ASD can be rigid, so once routines are established, they may be hard to change. Therefore, skills like dressing and undressing might be best taught in your child's bedroom or bathroom. When you teach new skills in the criterion environment, you generally have fewer teaching opportunities because it would be unnatural to practice a skill multiple times in this context.

However, children with ASD often learn most effectively in settings that are free of distractions—and afford multiple opportunities. If you have ever tried to learn to shoot free throws or develop a consistent golf swing, then you appreciate the value of repetitive and focused practice for everyone, not only children with ASD. This type of repetitive practice teaching format is highly suited to learning-to-learn skills, early language and communication skills, and skills that need to be performed fluently and automatically, as in the case of basic computation skills and simple spelling patterns. When children perform the learning-to-learn and basic skills automatically or fluently, they can then focus their attention on the important aspects of new tasks that they are learning. This type of repetitive practice is often referred to as massed practice. When teaching your child new skills, you can use both types of teaching formats simultaneously. That is, you could use the massed practice format to teach basic attentional, imitative, and communication skills while at the same time providing additional learning opportunities for your child to use these skills in the natural environment.

BASIC TERMINOLOGY: A CRASH COURSE

Before we jump into the nuts and bolts of how to change the child's behavior from A to B (as shown in the table under "Learning and Behavioral Change" earlier in this chapter), you'll need to become familiar with some of the vocabulary that we will be using, which reflects strategies and techniques that are based on applied behavior analysis. In the pages that follow, as we discuss teaching techniques, we will also define and explain key terminology (set in italics) that will help you teach your child new, functional skills, reduce unwanted behaviors, and replace them with more positive behaviors. Although learning new vocabulary can sometimes be challenging, we will provide many examples to ensure that you understand the concepts and can use them to teach your child using the guidelines we will provide in the rest of the book.

HOW TO STRUCTURE TEACHING INTERACTIONS, AND HOW TO KEEP YOUR CHILD MOTIVATED

When teaching new skills to children with ASD, it is important to structure teaching interactions so that they are focused and maximize learning. In this section, we will introduce the *stimulus, response, and consequence* model, the structure that we use for all teaching interactions regardless of the teaching context. The components of this model are defined below, along with specific examples that illustrate their meaning and use.

Stimulus: A *stimulus*, defined here as a signal that may elicit a response, can be a direction (verbal or nonverbal), a gesture (such as pointing), a facial expression or eye gaze, a question, a verbal statement, the presence of specific materials or objects, or specific environmental events.

We encounter and respond to stimuli continuously in our everyday activities. They provide us with cues and information about which behaviors are required in specific circumstances. One example is the sound of a telephone ringing; it signals that someone is trying to contact us and that we need to answer the call. Another example is the sound of your alarm clock; it tells you that it is time to get out of bed. Many other stimuli in our environment call for specific behaviors in response to them: greeting others when they say, "Good morning," following certain procedures in response to a fire alarm, stopping at a red light, and taking an umbrella to work when we see overcast skies.

Learning new behaviors involves associating new responses with specific stimuli. During early teaching interactions, the stimulus that signals the occasion for a particular response should be clear and unambiguous. A stimulus that is used to set the occasion for a specific response in a teaching interaction is called a *discriminative stimulus*. Before presenting the discriminative stimulus, you want to make sure that you have your child's attention. Once his attention is directed toward you or the task materials, present the task directions using simple forms of communication (verbal, picture, gesture, or sign) that he is most likely to understand. Examples of how to begin structured teaching trials are presented below.

Task	Instructional format	Teaching environment	Stimulus
Labeling objects with a single word	Massed practice	Quiet area at home with minimal distractions	Get your child's attention, saying "Look." Hold up the object to be labeled and ask, "What is this?"
Requesting a desired item	Naturalistic teaching	In the kitchen at snack time	Place snack in a sealed container and place container in front of your child at snack time. Look toward the snack and wait for your child to make a request.

Stimuli that set the occasion for behavior are sometimes called *antecedent events*. Let's talk now about how antecedent events can affect your child's behavior. Imagine that it is dinnertime and you want to call your child, who is watching his favorite television program, to come to the table. You say, "Turn off the TV and come to dinner" (the antecedent event). Your child responds by saying "No!" and starting to cry (the problematic behavior).

Did you know that some intervention techniques focus solely on changing the antecedent events, in order to affect the child's behavior? Now let's return to the example above. Imagine what would happen if, instead of interrupting your child's favorite television show, you wait until it is over. Then you walk over to the TV and turn it off as you inform your child that it is time to eat one of his favorite foods. You have changed the antecedent event and your child may respond in a very different way. Another way that you could change the antecedent is to give a warning before you ask the child to make a transition. For example, you might set a timer and say to your child, "It's almost dinnertime. When the timer rings, it'll be time to eat." A third way that you might change the antecedent event is to create a picture schedule showing that dinnertime comes after the television show ends. During a commercial break, you could direct your child's attention to the picture schedule and show him that when the TV show is over, it will be time for dinner.

Response: A *response* is the behavior your child engages in after the stimulus is presented. During any given teaching opportunity, a response may be placed into one of six possible categories.

Type of response	What does this mean?	Example
Correct response	The intended or expected response	Answering "10," in response to the question "What is "5 plus 5?"
Approximation of a correct response	A response that is close to the desired response but falls short of the desired response in one of several ways (for example, the response may be less precise than the desired response, may be correct but is not sustained for the desired length of time, or may not occur with the speed that is desired)	Labeling a picture of a boat as "bo" (spelling a word almost correctly); playing appropriately, but not for the required length of time; or getting dressed completely, but taking an extraordinary amount of time to complete the task
Incorrect response	A response that is not appropriate for the stimulus	Running in the opposite direction when you say "Come here," or labeling a picture of a dog as "cow"
Prompted response that is correct	The desired response that is given when child is prompted	Touching his nose when you say "Touch your nose," after you bring his hand halfway to his nose
No response	Absence of a response	Doing nothing after being instructed to brush his teeth and being given a toothbrush and tube of toothpaste
Inappropriate response	A definite response to the stimulus, but one that has little connection to the stimulus	Exhibiting tantrums, disruptive behavior, verbal refusals, and so on when asked to perform a specific task; stacking blocks when asked to give the adult a block in a specific color when presented with four blocks (red, green, blue, and yellow)

Being able to differentiate between the types of responses is important because this information is critical for evaluating the effectiveness your teaching strategy and knowing when to make changes to promote learning. In addition, the instructor's behavior (that is, what he or she does next) is determined by the child's response.

Shaping is a technique that focuses on gradually and systematically altering behaviors already in your child's repertoire so that they become functional skills. Shaping is a process that occurs when we reinforce slight changes in the desired response (the child's behavior) so that it gradually comes to resemble the *criterion behavior* (the behavior that we are hoping to teach). The focus is on gradual change in your child's response (the quality or duration of the response) while the stimulus stays basically the same.

Consequences: A *consequence* is an event that follows the child's response. Although there are many types of consequences that result in behavior change, only two types of consequences will be reviewed in this section: *reinforcement* and *extinction* (planned ignoring). See the Resources section of this book for additional reading that will provide you with information about other types of consequences.

Reinforcement is a consequence that strengthens the behavior it follows. Although many people equate the concept of reinforcement with rewards, the two are not the same. Rewards are predetermined objects or events that are assumed, but not proven, to have a positive effect on behavior. In contrast, an activity, event, or experience is accurately labeled a reinforcer only *after* it has been demonstrated to actually result in an increase in the behavior it follows.

REINFORCERS

Many people express the belief that using reinforcers in teaching programs is tantamount to using bribes. First, reinforcers are not the same as bribes; a bribe is something of value given to someone up front to coerce that person into performing an illegal or immoral act. Second, reinforcement, when used appropriately, has been proven to be a critical component of the teaching process. So don't avoid using reinforcers—they can be effective in helping to teach children new skills and behaviors.

Let's look at some examples of how reinforcers work. James is a tenth-grade student who has above-average intelligence. Although he has the capacity to become an honors student and thereby receive recognition (a reward) for good grades, this reward doesn't work as a reinforcer for him because his peer group looks down on academic achievers. As a result, getting only mediocre grades is a reinforcer for James because these grades help him maintain his status in his peer group.

Tony is a nine-year-old boy with autism. His teachers are frustrated because he has not been making progress toward his educational goals, even though they have incorporated rewards into his teaching interactions. The rewards do not seem to be motivating him to perform better on his tasks. When several of the toys and activities that Tony seemed to prefer were put to the test to see if they actually functioned as reinforcers, only two of these actually resulted in behavior change: having the opportunity to play with visually stimulating toys and to jump on a trampoline. When access to these preferred activities was given following Tony's correct responses, his task performance increased markedly. His teachers and parents were thrilled that they had found a way to reinforce his performance and help him succeed.

Reinforcers may be classified into several different groups. Typical groupings and specific examples of each are listed in the table below. Don't worry if you don't understand all of the terminology in the table; unfamiliar terms like "points," "tokens," and "terminating unpleasant or negative events" will be explained further below.

Reinforcers	Examples
Access to favorite foods (primary reinforcers)	Snacks or drinks
Access to favorite toys (tangible reinforcers)	Toys, books, or games
Access to preferred activities (activity reinforcers)	Playground time; getting to help with special tasks; watching a favorite TV program; special time with a parent, friend, or relative engaging in preferred activities; taking walks; biking; and so on
Parent attention (social reinforcement)	Verbal praise, tickles, hugs, snuggling, and good-natured roughhousing
Points, tokens, and external recognition (symbolic or conditioned reinforcers)	One of the following: points, tokens, money, certificates, trophies, or awards
Personal satisfaction (automatic reinforcement)	Sense of accomplishment and sheer pleasure in doing a good job
Terminating nonpreferred or unpleasant events (negative reinforcement)	Ending teaching interactions or social interactions

Symbolic reinforcers: *Symbolic reinforcers* are tangible items (like money, points, or tokens such as stars) that usually do not function as reinforcers by themselves. However, they develop reinforcing value once children learn that these items may be exchanged for highly coveted objects, activities, events, or social recognition and praise. Money is an example of a symbolic reinforcer since the value of the coins and bills is learned through association with what they can purchase. Therefore, in the same way that children learn about the value of money, they can learn to value tokens and points and be highly motivated to earn them.

Teaching children the value of symbolic reinforcers can be done using a common three-step strategy. First, it is important to identify reinforcing objects and events (depending on the child, these may be food reinforcers, tangible reinforcers, or activity reinforcers). Second, you have to teach the child that the symbolic reinforcers can be traded for these reinforcers (often called *backup reinforcers*). This can be done by using the symbolic reinforcer each time a child receives reinforcement. However, immediately after the symbolic reinforcer is given to the child, he has the opportunity to exchange the symbolic reinforcer for one of the backup reinforcers. Once the child demonstrates an understanding of the exchange (one clue would be that his rate of correct responding remains high when symbolic reinforcers replace the original reinforcer), the frequency of the exchange period is increased.

Negative reinforcement: *Negative reinforcement* is another principle that affects behavior. Below we provide three examples of how negative reinforcement affects behavior. The first two examples demonstrate how negative reinforcement increases wanted, or socially desirable, behaviors, while the last two examples demonstrate how it can increase unwanted behaviors and can inadvertently lead to patterns of interaction that can be counterproductive.

The first example involves using negative reinforcement to teach your child to handle social interactions. For many children with ASD, social interactions can be very unpleasant. As counterintuitive as this may seem, your child may be more likely to engage in social exchanges if the unpleasant event (the social interaction) ends after the interaction is completed. Imagine that your child is playing at the playground and another child comes over to him and asks him to play. If your child does not respond, the other child may prolong the interaction by repeating his request, "Do you want to play?" or he may ask other questions, like "What's the matter? Don't you talk?" If your child responds by saying, "No, thank you" or "I don't want to play right now," the other child is likely to go away. As a result, your child has engaged in an appropriate social response that is negatively reinforced by termination of the peer's persistent overtures.

A second example of how negative reinforcement can reinforce an appropriate social response may be seen when your child comes into contact with family friends or relatives. It is not uncommon for parents to persist at "helping" their child with ASD to acknowledge or greet others appropriately. If your child waves, smiles, or says "Hi" when greeted and is then allowed to wander off or play, he can successfully avoid the sequence of prompts and cues that generally follow nonresponding. Therefore, allowing your child to leave the social interaction after making an appropriate response can negatively reinforce appropriate social interactions (in other words, it can help him to learn to interact socially). When using this principle to increase social behavior, during the course of the teaching process you'll need to increase the duration and complexity of the social skills required. As your child becomes more competent, he may even come to enjoy social interactions.

Now, imagine that your child begins to cry loudly when you are in line at the grocery store. In between sobs, your child repeatedly tells you that he wants candy from the display next to the cash register. In an effort to avoid embarrassment, you give him the candy, and your child stops crying. *Your* behavior (giving the candy) is negatively reinforced by the fact that your child has stopped crying (cessation of the unpleasant event): you may be more likely to give your child candy in the future to stop his crying in the same situation. In the process, you also reinforce your child's crying by giving him candy: he will be more likely, in the future, to cry for candy when standing in line at the grocery store.

Here's another example: Suppose your child is sitting in your TV room with a sibling and they are watching the sibling's favorite TV program. Your child becomes very upset because his favorite show is on at the same time and he wants to watch it. He begins to make such a fuss that the sibling walks away. Once your child is able to watch his TV show, he is content and the fussing stops. The sibling's walking-away behavior is negatively reinforced by the fact that his brother stopped crying: in the future he will be more likely to leave the TV room in order to keep the peace. In addition, your child's fussing behavior is reinforced when he gets to watch his favorite TV program.

Using Reinforcement Appropriately and Effectively

Listed below are several guidelines that you can follow in order to use reinforcement appropriately:

- Especially when you are beginning to teach new skills, you need to provide reinforcement *immediately* after your child engages in the desired behavior. If you wait, the reinforcer quickly loses its beneficial effect.

- Reinforcers should not be given away for free. In order to increase performance of a specific skill, you should give the reinforcer only *after* the desired behavior occurs. This means that your child must perform the desired behavior in order to receive reinforcement.

- When teaching a new behavior, you should give reinforcement each time the behavior occurs.

- When your child begins to catch on to a new skill during the teaching process, it is important to gradually give reinforcement less often. Gradually decreasing the frequency of reinforcement is important because it will help you ensure that your child does not come to depend on continuous reinforcement in order to perform. You can accomplish this in a number of ways. When using the massed practice format, instead of reinforcing every correct response, you could begin to reinforce every other correct response. If the rate of correct responses remains high, you could then begin to reinforce every third (and then every fourth, and then every fifth) correct response as long as the rate of correct responding remains high. If you are reinforcing duration of activity, you can gradually increase the amount of time that your child participates in a given task before reinforcing "on-task behavior" (for example, he sits at the dinner table for five minutes, then ten minutes, and so on until he is reinforced for the targeted duration).

- When possible, use naturally occurring reinforcers—that is, those that occur within the context of the natural environment. In the above example of the child who stays at the dinner table, a naturally occurring reinforcer would be having dessert with the family.

- Always pair social reinforcement with other types of reinforcers. By consistently pairing social reinforcers with tangible or activity reinforcers, you help the social consequences to take on the reinforcing value. The goal is to make the social consequences sufficiently reinforcing that they maintain newly learned behavior. In other words, when you always give your child a sticker *and* a hug in response to his positive behavior, pretty soon he will come to see the hug as a reward and will repeat the positive behavior in order to receive it.

Extinction

The term *extinction* refers to the process of decreasing behavior by removing reinforcement. Extinction can affect both wanted and unwanted behaviors. That is, if your child has learned a positive skill and you stop offering reinforcement when your child performs the skill, the frequency of the behavior will decrease. Over time, if the skill is ignored, your child could stop performing the behavior altogether. Let's suppose that you teach your child to occupy his free time by playing appropriately with toys in the family room while you are preparing dinner. After the teaching program is successfully completed, you continue to schedule this playtime, but because you are busy with dinner preparation, you forget to reinforce your child for playing appropriately. Over the course of several days, your child begins to leave the designated play area and start getting into other things. What happened? By abruptly removing reinforcement for appropriate play behavior, your child's behavior was "extinguished."

The same applies to unwanted behaviors that are not reinforced. For example, Elsie had a tendency to scream when her mother was on the telephone, when her parents were spending time with their other children, and when her parents were interacting with company. Her screaming tended to stop as soon as her parents stopped engaging with others and interacted with her. We concluded that Elsie's behavior was being maintained by the social attention she got as a result of screaming. Her parents were then able to gradually reduce her screaming by consistently ignoring it when it occurred.

Pairing Reinforcement and Extinction to Change Behavior: Differential Reinforcement

Differential reinforcement is a very powerful tool in the process of behavior change. It involves ignoring the unwanted behavior and simultaneously reinforcing a socially appropriate alternative behavior. The effect is that appropriate behaviors are strengthened (they increase in frequency) and unwanted behaviors are weakened (they decrease in frequency). Two types of differential reinforcement will be discussed below.

Differential Reinforcement of "Other" Behavior

In the above example, the extinction program that Elsie's parents used could have been paired with a technique designed to teach Elsie a socially appropriate means of getting adult attention (known as "other" behavior). Each time that Elsie screamed, her parents would ignore the screaming, thereby removing all reinforcement of the behavior (extinction). They would also introduce a more appropriate way of getting her parents' attention—saying "Excuse me" and then waiting appropriately—and consistently reinforce this behavior. As a result, Elsie would scream less often and she would use more appropriate ways of getting her parents' attention more often. The graph below shows the expected effect when differential reinforcement and extinction are combined. The dark circles represent Elsie's screaming and the dark squares represent her saying, "Excuse me." As you can see, as Elsie's instances of saying "Excuse me" increase, her screaming decreases. When extinction and differential reinforcement are used together, the effect can be powerful.

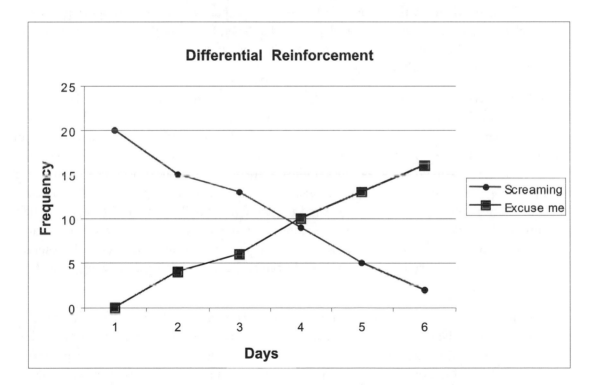

The section you have just read provided you with information about how to use consequences effectively to promote behavior change. We reviewed basic principles of reinforcement, extinction, and differential reinforcement and provided examples of ways you can use these principles when developing your own teaching programs. Before continuing with the next section, which focuses on the use of prompts to expedite learning, we suggest that you practice using the principle of positive reinforcement: reinforce your own efforts thus far by taking a break. Indulge in a preferred activity!

HOW TO PROVIDE CUES (PROMPTS) THAT HELP YOUR CHILD LEARN

In the language of applied behavior analysis, cues that help your child produce the desired response are called *prompts*. Prompts can be verbal (for example, you might give your child a verbal direction, provide part of the verbal response required, or emphasize the critical information in a verbal direction), physical (hand-over-hand guidance that demonstrates a specific action or gets the child started with a movement that enables him to complete the desired response), nonverbal (gestures such as pointing or demonstrating), or visual (written cues, picture cues, signs, highlighted letters or other cues in printed materials that help your child decipher printed material). Four general principles for using prompts follow:

- Prompts should be used in the early stages of teaching a new task to help your child respond correctly. The idea is to prevent your child from making errors. Repetitive errors can interfere with the learning process as your child may be making the wrong connections (associating an incorrect response with a particular stimulus).

- The use of prompts should be decreased as soon as possible so that your child does not become dependent on the prompts. Overuse of prompts can lead to prompt dependence, which, in turn, can impede the development of independent, functional skill repertoires. In other words, children come to rely upon adult cuing and are therefore unable to perform skills without the adult's assistance.

- There are two general strategies for using prompts: "most to least" and "least to most." In the most-to-least method, more assistance is given in the early stages of teaching. As the teaching program progresses, the amount of support is systematically reduced so that your child gradually does more of the work. In contrast, the least-to-most method allows your child to try to make the response independently. If he does not succeed, you add increasingly more helpful prompts (for example, first a verbal prompt, followed by a verbal prompt and demonstration of the desired response, and finally a physical prompt) to help your child perform the skill. Two advantages of the most-to-least method are that it provides more opportunities for the child to make correct responses (albeit prompted responses), which result in increased reinforcement, and that it prevents your child from making errors.

- Research has shown that prompts and cues that do not rely on the presence of a parent or teacher tend to be easier to systematically reduce than those requiring a parent or teacher. These prompts include visual prompts that are embedded in the stimuli, and picture or written cues. In the example below, size cues embedded in the stimulus array were used to teach a student the meaning of a "poison" symbol. Size cues were used as prompts for making the correct response (the correct response was enlarged) when teaching started; over time, the response options became more similar in size as teaching progressed. In the last step of the teaching program, the child was required to identify the correct response without any cues.

Put an "X" on the correct response.		
poison	Don't touch	Touch
poison	Touch	Don't touch
poison	Don't touch	Touch
poison	Don't touch	Touch

Two other examples of using "easy to fade prompts" include the use of tape recorded instructions and the use of written directions or cues.

As indicated above, it is important that you systematically decrease the use of prompts in order to help your child perform the skill independently. The process of systematically reducing prompts, or making gradual changes to the stimulus, is referred to as *fading*. This means that when you use a fading technique, you will make a change in the part of the stimulus-response-consequence model that comes before the response, but the response itself remains unchanged. For example, suppose you are teaching your child to follow simple directions. You could use a strategy similar to the one below:

Say your child's name and present the stimulus, in this case the verbal direction "Bring the tissues to your father," while walking your child over to get the specific item needed for the task and escorting him seven-eighths of the way toward his dad (the physical prompt), who is in the living room. Once your child has mastered this step of the teaching program, you could say your child's name and present the same verbal stimulus while walking your child over to get the specific item needed for the task and escorting him half of the way toward his dad in the living room.

In this example, the environmental events that set the stage for the response change, but the response—bringing dad the tissues—remains the same. The goal is to systematically reinforce the child's response as you change the environmental events so that they gradually resemble the environmental events that he will encounter in the natural environment.

There are several things that you should know in order to help you use fading effectively. First, fading involves changing the environmental events that set the stage for responding (the *stimulus control*). Second, when using a fading procedure, you change the dimensions of specific elements of the stimulus complex (characteristics that can be measured), such as volume, intensity of visual cues, number of prompts, pressure of teacher's hand while guiding a child's response, complexity of the environment, and so on, so that they more closely approximate stimuli in the natural environment that will elicit the response. Third, fading techniques can also be applied when making gradual changes in the complexity of settings in which you want your child to perform specific skills. Again, the stimulus conditions change (for example, the physical dimensions of the classroom and the teacher-student ratio), while the child's response remains the same (for example, paying attention, completing independent work, controlling his emotions).

HOW TO TEACH THE APPROPRIATE TIME AND PLACE FOR SPECIFIC BEHAVIORS

Sometimes you may want to change one of your child's behaviors so that it only occurs at certain times or places, or in the presence of very specific cues. Take, for example, a young child who has just learned to say the word "mommy." The child learns very quickly that every time she says "mommy," she receives a tremendous amount of hugs, kisses, and praise. Initially, the child calls all women "mommy." However, not all women react as positively toward her as her mother does when she says "mommy." As a result, she learns over time to say "mommy" only when referring to her mother.

In another example, children can be taught that it is fine to run and shout outside during recess but that these behaviors are not allowed in the school building or in the classroom. The mechanism at work when children make these kinds of discriminations is stimulus control. Several procedures contribute to children's ability to learn to behave in expected ways when certain stimulus conditions are present. One is to make the rules for the setting explicit. This can be done verbally, by reviewing the rules, or by reviewing pictures that depict the rules. Another is to make the specific stimulus conditions more salient (as when preschool children put mats down on the floor for rest time). Finally, consistently reinforcing situation-appropriate behavior increases the likelihood that children will learn the rules of conduct. Over time, the stimulus conditions should be sufficient to cue appropriate behavior.

This chapter covered a lot of important information related to selecting and prioritizing goals for your child and your family. You also received a crash course in some of the basic terminology and concepts needed when you're developing teaching strategies, and you had the opportunity to apply them in the exercises contained in the chapter. The information you have just learned will make it easier for you to understand and put to use other suggestions and strategies included in the remainder of the book.

Now that you have many of the tools to help you get started on developing effective interventions at home, we want to be sure that you have access to the supports and resources that can help you implement behavior change programs and still have time to devote to other personal and family needs. The next chapter focuses on the issue of utilizing available resources.

6

Getting the Help You Need

As you already know, parenting a child with autism spectrum disorder is exhausting and stressful. And one of the most challenging aspects of raising a child with ASD is the limited range of resources to assist parents and provide them with the support they so greatly need. Unfortunately, the current economic climate has only led to a decrease in the already deficient range of supports available. The situation becomes even more dire the farther you live from major population centers. Thus, rural families face even greater challenges than city-dwelling families when they begin to search for adequate child care (whether from individuals with experience with children with ASD, respite care, after-school programs, or recreational activities that will accommodate children with special needs).

What can you do to increase the amount of support for parents of children with ASD? Well, for starters, you can advocate in the political arena for more services. Affiliating with local and national advocacy groups is a powerful way to join forces with others to make the needs of parents of children with ASD known to those in influential positions. However, while getting involved in politics is great way to help make things better for everyone in the future, it certainly will not provide you with support or relief right now. For quicker results, consider looking at the resources that are currently available to you—if you use your creativity to maximize the impact of these resources in your life, you may be able to improve your situation and get some relief.

Of course, having access to resources is only part of the solution. In order for the supports to be beneficial to you and your family, your child will need to have whatever skills are necessary for participation in the program, class, or other service. For example, in order to participate in a gymnastics class, your child will need to be able to follow some basic directions, wait for assistance, tolerate turn taking, and display some athletic ability. In addition, we have found that even when specific resources are available, ASD-related problems with rigidity, need for sameness, noncompliance, and other difficult-to-manage symptoms may prevent children with ASD from joining or staying in programs that might be helpful to them.

One important potential impediment to your success in utilizing available supports is *you*. Now, at first glance, this idea may seem absurd—*you're* not preventing yourself from getting help, are you? Well, perhaps your responses to the questions below will make our point clear.

Do you ever reject offers from family members when they volunteer to give you a night off?

Do you make excuses explaining why your child cannot participate in available programs?

Do you believe that if other caregivers do not exactly match your caregiving style, your child will have a negative reaction that may have long-term consequences?

Do you find that you cannot relax when others are caring for your child?

Do you receive comments from other people saying that you are too critical of those who provide respite care for your child?

MAXIMIZING USE OF AVAILABLE RESOURCES

The first step toward getting the help you need is to make a list of all of the possible sources of support you can think of. Following are some ideas to get you started:

- Explore getting assistance with child care from family members living at home, extended family members, or neighbors (particularly those with responsible high-school- or college-age children).

- Contact local agencies to inquire about services offered and whether or not your child qualifies for those services. For instance, if your child has also been diagnosed with mental retardation, he may be eligible for services through your local Association for Retarded Children program.

- Get information about community activities such as scouting, sports, and programs such as swimming classes, music groups, story groups, and so on. Your local Autism Society of America chapter may be able to direct you to ASD-friendly services.

- Talk to school personnel (your child's teachers, chairpersons of special education committees, and others) and identify services that might be available within your school district. Find out whether your child's teacher is willing to help you address specific skills in the areas of self-control, self-care, and socialization if these have not already been specified on your child's Individualized Educational Plan (a formal list of instructional goals that will be addressed during each school year). For example, in our school program, we explicitly target goals that affect family life, such as toileting, delaying gratification, taking walks, watching movies or TV, following schedules, tolerating changes in schedules, asking permission to engage in particular activities, remaining in a designated area (such a playground), complying with adult requests, waiting, and taking turns. The benefit of having the school teach your child needed skills is that you do not have to tackle these challenging behaviors on your own. If your child's teachers can identify effective teaching strategies and begin the teaching process, you can then use the same strategies to transfer the newly learned skills to the home setting and to other settings in the community.

THE RESOURCE-CHILD MATCH: WHAT DOES IT TAKE TO MAKE IT WORK?

In the table below, make a list of the resources in your community. Next, for each resource, indicate how likely it is that you'll be able to use it (in other words, ask yourself, "Is this resource a possible source of support?"). Then try to generate a list of skills that your child would need if you were to use the resource successfully. We have provided five sample entries below and have left blank spaces for your entries.

Resource	Possible to use this resource for support?	Skills your child would need for inclusion/successful participation
The child's immediate family members (biological and stepparents; teenage, young-adult, or adult siblings)	Very likely	Compliance, greater independence with self-care skills, ability to follow a picture schedule and occupy time productively and safely
Babysitter	Maybe	Ability to tolerate separation from parents, follow directions, behave appropriately, play with toys, follow activity schedule, show more independence with self-care skills to decrease caregiver burden, go to bed when asked to do so by people other than parents, and eat meals for people other than parents
Scouts and similar organizations	Maybe	Ability to follows adult directions, take turns, work in small groups, adhere to behavioral limits, tolerate group activity for approximately ninety minutes, learn skills needed for participation ahead of time, and refrain from interrupting
After-school programs	Yes	Possibly none, if the program is geared toward children with ASD
Grandparents	Yes	Ability to tolerate separation from parents, follow directions, play with toys, follow activity schedule, go to bed when asked to do so by people other than parents, tolerate assistance with brushing teeth, dressing, and toileting, and eat meals for people other than parents

UTILIZING YOUR IMMEDIATE FAMILY AS A RESOURCE

A partner who shares in child care responsibilities is, of course, a tremendous source of support. Unfortunately, not all parents are fortunate enough to have a partner who is able or willing to ease the child-care burden. In this case, immediate family members who are old enough and mature enough to take on child-care responsibilities may be a valuable source of support. While older, responsible siblings can constitute the best "pool" of potential caregivers, it is important not to place too heavy a burden on siblings (see chapters 4 and 7 for more on involving siblings in child care).

We will illustrate how families can equitably share the caregiving responsibilities by way of example. Several years ago, one of our city-dwelling parents, Mrs. Ames, was informed by the police that they would have to alert Child Protective Services if they found her nine-year-old son, Charlie, wandering around the downtown area again. During our numerous conversations with Mrs. Ames, it became apparent that, even though the family members were doing their best to keep an eye on Charlie, he would get bored and quietly slip out for a walk, putting himself in potentially dangerous situations. We devised an intervention plan to help the family that included the following:

- A schedule for child supervision

- A picture schedule to organize Charlie's time free time at home

- A reinforcement program to motivate Charlie to follow his schedule

Taking supervised walks was incorporated into Charlie's schedule, since this was one of his favorite activities. The schedule was also used to keep track of the family members' child-care responsibilities so that everyone could do their share to keep Charlie safe. A segment from his weekend schedule is presented below:

Time	Activity	With whom?
9:00	Eat breakfast	Mom
9:30	Dress and brush teeth	James (brother)
10:00	Take a walk	Mary (sister)

UTILIZING OTHER CAREGIVERS AS A RESOURCE

Chances are that even if everyone in your family helps out, you'll still need some help from outside sources, whether a babysitter or after-school program. If your child is not accustomed to spending time with different caregivers, this kind of change can be very upsetting to him. And if he doesn't have the necessary skills, both he and the caregiver may be in for a tough time. However, there are many ways that you can prepare your child to be cared for by others, and we'll discuss these options in the pages that follow.

How Can Your Child's School Help?

As we mentioned previously, your child's school may be able to help teach skills that can increase your child's readiness to tolerate child care from others or skills that are needed for participation in structured community programs. Talking with classroom teachers, school psychologists, and support service personnel (such as speech pathologists and occupational and physical therapists) can help you identify goals that can be included in your child's educational plan. Here is a list of some of the skills that can be taught at school:

- Compliance with adult requests

- Staying with the group when moving from one classroom to another or when taking walks outside

- Toileting and hygiene skills

- Waiting

- Occupying free time appropriately

- Following schedules (picture and/or written schedules)

- Making transitions without incident

- Tolerating changes in schedules

- Expressing wants and needs

- Playing sports

- Working appropriately on group projects

- Asking for help

- Working or spending time with different teachers at school

- Refusing politely

Once the child has learned the targeted skills at school, ask school personnel for advice on how to transfer the skills to the home setting. Some of the strategies we have found to be effective include the following:

- Have parents observe in the school setting

- Have parents work with their child at school on the targeted skills until the child has mastered them, and then transfer them to home

- Have parents work on active school programs at home, but lessen the demand in order to ensure success. One way of doing this is to start the home teaching program one or two steps behind the child's current level of performance at school.

Childproofing Your Home to Minimize Risk

Safety is, without question, always a concern, and it becomes even more important when others assist you in caring for your child. Before your caregiver starts work, you'll want to make your home as safe as possible. The list below can be used as a checklist for eliminating dangers in your home.

- ☐ Keep sharp items out of reach.

- ☐ Keep medications in a safe, inaccessible place.

- ☐ Keep valuable personal items locked away.

- ☐ Keep toxic materials locked up or out of reach.

- ☐ Keep cabinets that contain messy foods (for example, flour and sugar) locked.

- ☐ Install covers for electrical outlets.

- ☐ Anchor tall furniture like dressers and bookcases to the wall so that they cannot be pulled down. (Inexpensive anchoring devices are easily found at baby-gear stores.)

☐ Cover stove burners and dials.

☐ Conceal wiring for all electronics and appliances.

☐ Secure furniture and lamps that may be unsafe.

Some children with ASD who like to be outdoors will leave the house when no one is watching. Knowing that your child may be wandering around neighborhoods or urban areas is very upsetting. Prevention is the key here. Many of the families we work with have used the preventative measures below to keep their child from wandering off.

☐ Make sure that your child cannot easily open or unlock doors that lead outside. Placing a hook and eye latch on the door (out of your child's reach), adding locks that require use of an inside key, installing doorknob covers, or placing locks or security bars on sliding doors or windows may be helpful. However, be aware of the importance of teaching other family members how to use these devices so that they could escape in an emergency.

☐ Put chimes on doors so that you hear your child leaving.

☐ Lock windows if your child has a history of climbing out of windows.

☐ If your child has a history of breaking windows, replace window panes with nonbreakable glass.

☐ Install a door alarm system that signals exit and entry or have your child wear a monitoring device so you will be alerted if your child has exceeded a preset distance from you. Monitoring devices can also help pinpoint your child's whereabouts if he moves out of your sight. Although these products are more expensive than the other solutions listed above, they may be worth the investment if they keep your child safe.

☐ Have your child wear an identification bracelet and a medical alert bracelet (if needed) in the event that he does get lost.

Increasing Your Child's Tolerance for Being Supervised by Others

Now that you've prepared your child, made your home safe, and found a caregiver, you face the challenge of actually leaving your child with that person, a major transition that can cause anxiety or stress for both you and your child. To manage this stress, you can use shaping to gradually increase his tolerance for spending time with a caregiver, as outlined below.

1. Begin by having someone provide care for your child in your home while you occupy yourself with at-home activities that keep you out of your child's sight. Be sure to review safety concerns (e.g., keeping cleaning-supply cabinets and front and back doors locked) with the caregiver beforehand. Also, explain your child's method of communication so that the caregiver will understand his attempts to communicate his needs and wants. During this phase, you can supervise potentially difficult interactions and provide the caregiver with guidance regarding how to manage these situations.

2. Spend brief chunks of time out of the house and away from your child. Leave him with a trusted caregiver and take a walk around the block.

3. Once your child demonstrates the ability to tolerate your absence, gradually increase the time that you spend away from home. For example, make a quick trip to the grocery store to pick up food for dinner.

4. As your child develops his ability to handle your absence for short periods of time, increase your time spent away from home in small intervals until you are able do things like attend a parent-teacher meeting, work out at the gym, or shop for groceries for the week.

Other potentially helpful strategies include the following:

- Prior to leaving your child with a caregiver, allow your child to get to know the caregiver, and create opportunities for them to have some fun together.

- Also, before you leave home, take care of any tasks that may cause your child stress (for example, give him his lunch beforehand if eating is problematic, or give him his bath if he typically has tantrums at bath time). Don't expect the caregiver to complete tasks that are difficult for you to do with your child.

- Restrict access to some of his favorite activities (specific movies, books, or toys) for a few hours or days before your caregiver arrives and make them available only while the caregiver is in charge.

- Leave plenty of his favorite snacks (ideally the healthy ones) and activities for the caregiver, and pull them out when the caregiver arrives.

- If your child is accustomed to using picture schedules, make a schedule of activities and place a picture of Mom and Dad at the bottom of the schedule, showing that you will return after he completes the activities. Review the schedule with your child before the caregiver arrives.

- If you are using a program to reinforce good behavior, spend some time reviewing the procedure with your child-care provider and, if possible, schedule some time in advance when the care provider can actually put it into practice under your guidance. Sticking to your child's usual schedule and reinforcement routine will help to minimize problems that may arise while you're gone.

- Be sure to provide your caregiver with telephone numbers for backup support and emergency interventions (see box).

EMERGENCY AND CRITICAL INFORMATION

You already leave emergency information for care providers anytime you go out, but you may want to approach this task in a slightly different manner, especially if one of your goals is to carve out some personal time for yourself. First, specify what constitutes an emergency and whom, other than you, the caregiver can call with minor issues or procedural questions. Before you leave, of course, make sure that the people on your list will be available to your care provider. A sample emergency procedure and telephone number list is presented below. When you create your own list, feel free to add information that is relevant to you and your child.

Ambulance: 911 Fire: 911 Hospital: 555-2408 Physician: Dr. Brown, 555-3905	Whom to call	What to do while you are waiting for assistance	How the issue was resolved (this is to be completed by the caregiver is assistance is needed).
Emergencies	■ 911 ■ Me at 555-8765	■ Follow standard safety protocol. ■ Talk to Sammy in a calm and soothing voice. ■ Explain the situation to Sammy in simple terms and tell him his mommy is coming. ■ Play soft music.	Called 911 and Sammy's mom. Kept Sammy calm by singing.
Procedural questions (For example, Sammy has diarrhea and has soiled his pants but is refusing to let his caregiver change his clothing.)	☐ Sammy's dad (555-6045) ☐ Sammy's grandmother (555-7641)	■ Try to keep Sammy calm. ■ Try to engage him in a preferred activity. ■ Try to minimize mess. ■ Try to minimize Sammy's discomfort.	Called grandmother for advice on changing soiled clothes. She recommended setting up picture schedule to show Sammy that I would change his clothes and then he could go in the backyard to play. Worked like a charm!
Behavior problems/concerns (For example, Sammy keeps trying to leave the house; or Sammy is crying and can't calm down.)	☐ Sammy's dad (555-6045) ☐ Sammy's grandmother (555-7641)	■ Review rules for behavior and remind Sammy about the rewards for compliance. ■ Make Sammy's communication book available to help him "tell" you what's wrong. ■ During calmer moments, offer him choices (2 pictures at a time from his communication book) to help him tell you what's wrong or what he wants.	Reviewed rules and showed Sammy the rewards available if he followed the rules. He was fine after that!
Permission to engage in specific activities	☐ Sammy's grandmother (555-7641)	Keep Sammy occupied with activities on his schedule.	

In addition to emergency telephone numbers, a critical information sheet that you can review with care providers can be beneficial and make you feel more at ease. After you go over the information with the caregiver, post the sheet in a visible spot. A sample critical information sheet is provided below.

Critical information sheet			
Area of concern	Status	Suggestions	Parent expectations
Allergies	Allergic to milk products and chocolate	Offer other treats. When you give Johnny a choice of two different snacks, he is usually content.	Johnny will have no milk or chocolate products.
Toileting	Needs cues/reminders to use the bathroom (generally every ninety minutes). Bowel movements usually occur after lunch.	Johnny sits when urinating. He sometimes likes to take a book into the bathroom with him. This is fine. Watch fluid intake, as Johnny will drink continuously if allowed to. Restrict fluids after dinner.	Johnny will remain dry and unsoiled during the day.
Eating pattern	Johnny tends to eat little at meal time, but he likes to snack. He should be required to eat at the kitchen table.	Limit snacking. Only one snack between meals.	Johnny will eat at least a bowl of cereal and a piece of fruit for breakfast, half a sandwich and a piece of fruit for lunch, and a small serving of dinner.
Bedtime routine	Current routine: toilet, wash hands and face, read book, listen to music with lights out (he is allowed only one exit from bedroom after "lights out")	Use picture schedule for bedtime routine. Remind Johnny that he can earn points for following his schedule.	Johnny will complete all activities on his schedule and will be in bed no later than one hour after designated bedtime.

USING COMMUNITY ACTIVITIES AS A RESOURCE

Before signing your child up for participation in a community activity, it is important to identify what skills are required and determine whether your child has at least the basics in his repertoire. Before you make a decision, talk to the teachers or coaches who will be leading the activity and actually observe the activity in progress to find out what your child will need in order to participate. Once you have this information, complete the worksheet that appears below. The sample worksheet shown here assesses a seven-year-old's ability to participate in a soccer league with typical peers. A blank worksheet is provided for your use.

Community activity readiness worksheet				
Activity: _Soccer_ **Duration of the activity:** _90 minutes_				
Current ability level (relative to other participants)				
Skills required	**No skill**	**Some skill**	**Adequate skill**	**Excellent skill**
Running				X
Ball handling			X	
Passing and teamwork		X		
Following directions		X		
Accepting feedback	X			
Displays good sportsmanship (handles losing)	X			
Getting along with others		X		
Coping with physical contact during play	X			

Community activity readiness worksheet				
Activity: _____ **Duration of the activity:** _____				
Current ability level (relative to other participants)				
Skills required	**No skill**	**Some skill**	**Adequate skill**	**Excellent skill**

After you have completed the assessment of your child's ability, you should take the following actions:

- Share your assessment with the coaches/teachers to find out whether they would be willing to coach your child. In your discussions, address the following issues:

  - Would they allow you to come to practices to help with coaching, provide support for your child, and troubleshoot problems?

  - Would they be willing to provide you with drills and teaching strategies so that you can begin training with your child well before the season starts?

  - Even if your child doesn't join the activity now, would they allow him to come to some of the practices to begin developing the skills in preparation for later years?

- Develop teaching programs that address your child's weak areas. In the case of soccer, for example, you would want to teach your child to follow instructions, accept feedback, be a good sport, and handle physical contact during play.

Remember, the goal is not just participation, but successful participation. The last thing children with ASD need is more experience with failure.

In this chapter we have talked about how you can utilize existing resources to help get you the help you need as you strive to raise a child with ASD. Even though the support services in your community may be limited, thinking creatively may enable you to identify new sources of support. In the next chapter, we will address skills you can teach your child that will decrease stress at home.

Teaching Family-Friendly Skills

Despite the many ways that ASD presents in children and the need for individual teaching programs, there are specific skills you can teach your child that will have a positive impact on your family life and your ability to meet your family's needs, no matter what symptoms you're dealing with. In this chapter we target four "family friendly" skills that frequently appear on parents' wish lists: compliance (following directions), waiting, respecting personal and physical boundaries, and staying with an adult in public places. The first part of this chapter will provide you with guidelines for developing these skills.

In the second part of the chapter, we will provide you with guidelines for how to apply problem-solving strategies to overcome other obstacles to family need fulfillment. The topics will include empowering siblings, setting limits and consistency, and implementing house rules that all siblings must abide by.

COMPLIANCE

When you're constantly worrying about your child's safety, it can be close to impossible to get anything done. Teaching your child to follow directions is a good investment, since you will likely receive a high rate of return for your efforts. While your quality of life would undoubtedly be improved if your child learned to follow *all* directions, you can teach him to follow some specific directions that can help you prevent harm to your child, other children, and property, and as a result spend less time worrying about keeping your child safe. Think for a few minutes about specific instructions that, if followed consistently, would have a positive impact on your family's life. Write them in the spaces provided below:

_____

_____

_____

We'll be using these instructions later in the chapter. But first, let's look at a few instructions that many families find useful: "Come here," "Stop," "Sit down," "Hands down," and "Talk quietly" or "Use your indoor voice." What is the benefit of teaching your child to respond to these directions? Teaching your child to consistently respond to such directions can be helpful when you're trying to finish a task, manage your child's behavior, and protect him.

"Come here": If your child is able to consistently follow this instruction when you need to get him dressed, ready for bed, ready to go out, ready for dinner, or ready for a bath, you will save time, energy, and hassle, and you will eliminate the need to go and get your child and escort him to the bathroom, bedroom, or dining table. Similarly, when you're out in public, your child's ability to consistently follow the direction "Come here" can be a lifesaver if he starts to wander too far away from you.

"Stop" and "Sit down": Many children become playful and act as if they want to be chased, or sometimes just become impulsive, in settings where this behavior is not safe, such as near streets or roads, in parking lots, in playgrounds (where the child might not be aware of dangers like swings in motion), and near bodies of water. When children have learned to respond to specific directions like "Stop," this may give parents an opportunity to get to the child and keep them from danger.

"Hands down": This is another instruction that can be used to prevent harmful outcomes. Many years ago, we were working with a child who engaged in a lot of self-stimulatory behavior. Over the course of many teaching sessions, as a way of managing his self-stimulation, he learned to respond to the instruction "Hands down." One day, during a play session, the child suddenly jumped up, darted across the classroom, and reached up to pull on the cord of a television set that was mounted to the wall. The teacher, fearful that she would not be able to get to the child in time to avert a potential accident, said, "Hands down," as she ran over to him. The child immediately put his hands down. This short reprieve gave the teacher enough time to reach the child and move him to another area of the classroom.

"Talk quietly" or "Use your indoor voice": Making vocal sounds, singing, and repeating dialogue from movies or books are common behaviors seen in children with ASD. Many children with ASD are also insensitive to the effect that these and other sounds (like talking loudly) have on the people around them. The behaviors themselves are not necessarily bad. What causes problems is the disruptive effect that these behaviors have on others. We have found that it is easier to teach children to decrease their volume than to eliminate the behaviors altogether, using the instruction "Talk quietly" or "Use your indoor voice."

Teaching Your Child to Follow Instructions

"Come Here"

The text below outlines a strategy for teaching your child to consistently respond to the instruction "Come here" in a variety of situations (including at home, outside in the yard, at the park, when hiking, and at the grocery store). You can apply similar teaching strategies in order to teach your child to follow the other directions mentioned above (such as "Sit down," "Stop," and "Hands down"). Before you start, consider the following factors:

- In the beginning stages of teaching, it is most helpful to have two responsible people involved in teaching, because one can prompt and cue while the other acts as the target to be reached.

- Begin teaching in a quiet setting where you can provide multiple teaching trials and where you will have the fewest distractions.

■ Change to a slightly more complex setting after your child demonstrates competence in the first setting. For example, in your house, begin with your child ten feet away from you. Then increase to a distance of twenty feet. Then call to your child from another room. Next, while he is playing outside, call your child from a distance of ten feet, then twenty feet, and then thirty feet.

Now you're ready to start the teaching sequence:

Step 1. Adult #1 brings your child to within three feet of you (adult #2). In a clear voice, say your child's name and the words "Come here." Adult #1 gives your child a gentle nudge (a prompt) to move him in your direction. If your child walks the remaining distance to you, give him hugs and tickles, high fives, or other forms of social reinforcement. If he does not walk to you or he wanders off in another direction, adult #1 brings him back to the starting point, repeats the direction, and escorts your child to you, saying "*This* is coming here." Then adult #1 walks your child back to the three-foot mark, you give the direction again, and adult #1 gives your child a gentle nudge. Continue this routine until your child responds to the prompt by walking to you on nine out of ten occasions.

Step 2. Repeat the procedure, with adult #1 bringing your child to a point within five feet of you.

Step 3. Repeat the procedure, with adult #1 bringing your child to a point within ten feet of you.

Step 4. Repeat the procedure, with adult #1 bringing your child to a point within fifteen feet of you.

Step 5. Repeat the procedure, with adult #1 bringing your child to a point within twenty feet of you.

Step 6. Call your child when he is engaged in an activity anywhere in your home. Wait ten seconds. If he responds by coming to you, give him plenty of social reinforcement. If not, go and get him, bring him to the spot where you called from, and say, "*This* is coming when I call you." Continue until your child comes to you when you call him.

Step 7. Repeat the procedure in other settings (for example, outdoors and at the grocery store). If at any point your child does not respond to your request, especially in a dangerous situation, go back to steps 2 through 6. If you have to do this on more than one occasion, reevaluate your child's readiness to learn this skill. If your child continues to engage in behavior that puts him at risk, you may want to delay teaching this skill outdoors or in community settings until he has mastered the skill in environments with less potential danger.

Below we have outlined some additional prompting strategies that you might find useful, along with instructions on how to fade the prompts. Remember that it is important to fade prompts as soon as possible so that your child will be able to respond to your instructions independently (that is, without cues or guidance from you). As *always, if safety is a concern, maintain close supervision and vigilance.*

"Stop"

As in the example above, it is wise to start this multiple-step teaching program in a setting that is safe and has minimal risk (such as a fenced-in backyard). The prompting procedure used in this teaching sequence uses a most-to-least format. As your child's competence grows, so can the environments in which you do your teaching. Once you and your child have mastered this skill in a safe environment, you may venture out into slightly less-confined areas (such a small, fenced-in area at a playground or school yard). Each time you begin teaching in a new, less-restricted environment, bring another adult with you to keep your child safe in case he runs off, and to assist with the prompting procedures.

Prompt 1. At a moment when your child is moving away from you, say "Stop." When you say "Stop," go over to him and place both hands firmly on your child's shoulders to increase the likelihood that he will stop. Reinforce his compliance and say, "I like the way you stopped" or "You stopped! Good job." Once your child is no longer moving in a forward direction or pulling to free himself of your grip, reinforce his behavior with a favorite snack, points that can be exchanged for a reward at a later date, or an appealing activity.

If your child does not respond to your request, bring him back to the original location and go through the procedure again. Place both hands firmly on his shoulders, while saying "Stop."

Because of the importance of this task, you should be sure that your child achieves mastery of this step of the program before moving on to later steps. Setting a fairly conservative mastery criteria—for example, appropriate responding on fifteen consecutive occasions on three separate days—can increase your confidence that your child is ready for the next step in the program. Note that the teaching opportunities do not have to be done in a massed practice format. The teaching trials can be conducted within the natural environment. However, each time you provide a teaching opportunity, you should keep track of your child's responses. See the record sheet below.

"Stop" teaching program														
(criteria for continuation = 15 consecutive correct responses)														
Circle correct responses that are consecutive (with no incorrect responses between correct ones). If your child makes an incorrect response, begin recording on a new line.														
1	2	3	4	5	6	7	8	9	10	11	12	13	14	15
1	2	3	4	5	6	7	8	9	10	11	12	13	14	15
1	2	3	4	5	6	7	8	9	10	11	12	13	14	15
1	2	3	4	5	6	7	8	9	10	11	12	13	14	15
1	2	3	4	5	6	7	8	9	10	11	12	13	14	15
1	2	3	4	5	6	7	8	9	10	11	12	13	14	15
1	2	3	4	5	6	7	8	9	10	11	12	13	14	15
1	2	3	4	5	6	7	8	9	10	11	12	13	14	15

Prompt 2. Follow the same procedure as with prompt 1, but place only one hand on your child's shoulder when you say "Stop." Continue until your child responds by stopping fifteen times in a row.

Prompt 3. Follow the same procedure as with prompt 1, but only touch your child's arm when you say "Stop." Continue until your child responds by stopping fifteen times in a row.

Now that your child has mastered the skill of stopping with just a partial physical prompt, it's time for you to teach him to stop when he hears you say "Stop," with no physical contact. In order for this skill to be functional, you need to gradually increase the distance between you and your child as you practice. You can follow the distance-increasing pattern used in the example for teaching "Come here," if you like. However, as you increase the distance between you and your child, you increase the risk of having your child run off. During these teaching sessions, have another person with you so that you can keep him safe.

Another way of motivating your child to comply with your requests to "Stop," particularly if your child has had experience with symbolic reinforcement, is to explain that when he earns a specific number of points, he will be ready to participate in a community activity that he has wanted to attend but has not been allowed to because of safety concerns. A chart for keeping track of the points he has earned, along with a picture of the activity that he is working to earn, can be effective visual reminders of the reinforcer. *If your child often resists prompts or behaves in a manner that places him at risk, immediately stop this teaching program and seek assistance from a professional trained in applied behavior analysis.*

"Sit Down, Please"

As with the "Stop" program, you should begin teaching in a safe environment that has physical boundaries, and progress to less-controlled environments *only* when your child has mastered the earlier steps of the teaching program. Again, having the help of a second person will be extremely helpful to you in the initial stages of teaching this skill.

Prompt 1. As you say "Sit down, please," model sitting down on the floor. Then say "You do it." If your child responds by imitating your actions, reinforce his behavior and say "I like the way you sat down" or "Good job sitting." In order to receive reinforcement, your child must sit for at least five seconds. If he does this, reinforce his behavior by giving him a favorite snack, points that can be exchanged for a reward at a later date, or a preferred activity. If your child gets up before five seconds have passed, take his hand and say "Sit down, please." Have the second adult provide a physical prompt (gently pushing behind his knees and assisting him to the ground) if he does not comply. Continue presenting your child with opportunities until he responds correctly fifteen times in a row on three separate days.

Prompt 2. Follow the same procedure as in prompt 1, but only touch the child lightly at the back of the knees while saying "Sit down, please." If your child does not respond to the prompt, follow with the full prompt. Continue presenting your child with opportunities until he gives fifteen consecutive correct responses. When your child meets these criteria, continue with prompt 3.

Prompt 3. Follow the same procedure as in prompt 1, but only touch your child's leg when you say, "Sit down, please." Continue presenting your child with opportunities until he gives fifteen consecutive correct responses. Then remove the prompts altogether but continue to give him plenty of positive reinforcement when he follows your direction to sit down.

Transitioning this skill to situations outside of your home may increase the risk to your child because of the increase in distractions (such as noise and visually stimulating objects and events) and the wide range of hazards that exist in community settings (traffic, crowds, animals, and so on). For this reason, move gradually to less-restricted areas as your child increases in competence. As in the examples above, we strongly advise you to have another person with you so that you are able to reach your child if he starts to run away. *If your child often resists prompts or behaves in a manner that places him at risk, immediately stop this teaching program and seek assistance from a professional trained in applied behavior analysis.*

Teaching Compliance with General Requests

In the preceding pages, we have shown you how to teach compliance, with a focus on safety. However, increasing your child's ability to comply with routine requests can also make a positive difference in everyday family life. Remember the instructions you wrote down at the beginning of this chapter? Below are some guidelines to help you teach your child to follow these and other routine requests:

- If your child has demonstrated the ability to follow a specific direction but does not do it consistently, use reinforcement to increase your child's motivation to comply. Offer reinforcers such as favorite snacks or drinks, activities, and tokens, depending on which will be more effective. Always pair verbal praise with other, tangible reinforcers, since ultimately you'll use verbal praise to reward compliance.

- In the early phases of teaching, you will likely choose to reinforce your child's behavior every time he does what you ask him to do. However, remember that once your child is responding consistently you'll need to reduce the frequency of the reinforcement so that your child does not become dependent on the reinforcement. Fading the reinforcement can be done in several ways, including the two described below:

  - Instead of reinforcing every correct response, reinforce every second or third correct response, using both verbal and tangible reinforcement.

  - If your child is able to wait to receive reinforcement, you can keep track of how often your child complies with your requests and tally the results halfway through the day or in the evening, and then give him reinforcement based on his overall performance for the morning or the day. If he met your goals, perhaps complying seven out of ten times, then he would receive the reinforcement.

- It is often wise to start your teaching program with a limited number of requests and gradually add to the pool as your child learns to respond to them consistently. This approach limits the demands placed on your child at any one time. The general rule of thumb is to teach each instruction until the child masters the response, and then add the next instruction in that set. If you were following the first example in the table below, once your child had mastered his response to "Get out of bed when asked," you would continue to reinforce this behavior while also teaching him to respond to "Brush teeth." Once he had mastered brushing his teeth upon request, you would then require him to both get out of bed when asked *and* brush his teeth in order to receive the reinforcement. When he had mastered this sequence, you would teach him to respond to "Get dressed." In the final step of this teaching program, you would require your child to complete all three tasks in order to receive the reinforcement.

- It is also important to measure your child's progress so that you can determine whether your teaching program is effective (your child is learning) or ineffective (there is little behavior change). An example of a performance record sheet follows. To use this form, place a mark in the column every time you make a request. Then place a mark in the column that describes your child's response. If you are working on general compliance with directions throughout the day, you may need to use a separate record form each day. Alternatively, if you are working on a few specific requests, you could use a form, like the one below, for a longer period of time (say, one week) and evaluate progress on a weekly basis.

If the percentage of correct responses increases steadily, you'll know that you are on the right track. If it decreases or stays the same as it was before you started teaching, you will need to make some changes in your teaching program.

Compliance record form				
Date: _____ (Or week of: _____)				
Specific directions	Number of requests	Correct responses	Incorrect responses	% correct (number of correct responses divided by total requests)
"Put your toys away."				
"Dinner time! Come to the table."				

Three other examples of instructions designed to make completion of daily routines easier are outlined in the table below. You can apply the same strategies outlined above in your teaching program.

Teaching compliance with instructions to make daily routines easier		
Set 1 Morning routine	Set 2 Bath time	Set 3 Preparing to catch the bus
1. Get out of bed when asked.	1. Go to the bathroom to take a bath.	1. Get your coat.
2. Brush your teeth.	2. Put on your pajamas.	2. Get your backpack.
3. Get dressed.	3. Go to bed.	3. Go to the bus stop.

Of course, the actual number of requests that you include in any teaching set will depend largely on your child's ability and how quickly he learns new information.

- If your child has difficulty comprehending verbal language, pair your verbal instructions with pictures or signs.

- In the initial stages of teaching, use full prompts so that your child quickly learns what is expected. As quickly as possible, begin to gradually fade out the prompts so that your child does not become dependent upon your prompts for performance. You might reduce your prompts by following the progression below:

    1. Full physical prompt

2. Partial physical prompt

3. Gestural prompt

4. Verbal prompt

5. Picture cue

■   When you feel that your child is ready to perform these tasks independently, you can use the strategies described in chapter 9 that involve using picture schedules and checklists.

WAITING

Children with ASD often have a difficult time when their parents take them on errands in the community, largely because these activities simply do not interest them. Although these children may enjoy the car ride, problems often arise when they have to wait for any length of time (for example, waiting for a sibling to finish sports practice, waiting in line with Mom at the dry cleaner's, or being patient while Mom or Dad shops for the family's groceries).

The methods we use to teach children to wait appropriately are often variations on a simple strategy: teaching the child how to occupy waiting time with satisfying activities.

Complete the following steps to develop a waiting program for your child:

1. Make a list of your child's favorite toys and activities.

2. Highlight those toys and materials that are small, portable, quiet, and safe (no sharp edges and not so heavy that they would hurt someone if they were thrown). If you are coming up empty, here are some suggestions: books, coloring books, workbooks (such as the dot-to-dot variety), a CD or tape player with headphones, electronic games, no-spill bubbles, a miniature Etch A Sketch, or a Magna Doodle.

3. You can assess your child's ability to occupy himself appropriately with toys in the "waiting bag" either in the natural environment or at home. Find a relatively quiet area where you and your child can sit either at home or in one of the settings in the community where you would like your child to wait. Using a timer, track the amount of time your child can play appropriately with these toys. Do this on several occasions to get an average duration of play (add the number of minutes of all of the play sessions put together, then divide that total by the number of play sessions—three if there were three sessions—to get your average).

4. Draw outlines of your child's feet on paper and tape them to the floor in an area where you want your child to stay while playing with toys. In doing so, you will emphasize the idea of staying in a specific location while playing and occupying the waiting period appropriately.

5. When you are ready to start teaching your child to wait appropriately, start with the shortest time you think your child will tolerate. When he shows that he can wait that long without any trouble, add a minute. When he meets that goal, add two minutes, and so on, until he can handle lengths of time of up to fifteen minutes. Use the forms below to keep track of your child's progress. (We've filled in the first row to give you an idea of how to use the table.)

Preferred activities/toys (list the toys and activities that you will put in your child's "waiting bag")	Determine the starting duration time (see step 3, above)	Decide on the play interval lengths that you will expect at each step of your teaching program
Toys to go in "waiting bag": Magna Doodle, coloring books and crayons, listening to music and stories on tape	Time 1: __1 minute__ Time 2: __1.25 minutes__ Time 3: __.75 minute__ **Average:** __1 minute__	Step 1: 1 minute Step 2: 2 minutes Step 3: 4 minutes Step 4: 6 minutes Step 5: 10 minutes Step 6: 15 minutes
Toys to go in "waiting bag": _____ _____ _____ _____ _____	Time 1: _____ Time 2: _____ Time 3: _____ **Average:** _____	Step 1: ___ minutes Step 2: ___ minutes Step 3: ___ minutes Step 4: ___ minutes Step 5: ___ minutes Step 6: ___ minutes

Use the record form below to track your child's progress on this program. Again, before you begin to conduct this teaching program, you should decide the level and stability of performance that you will expect before you move to more challenging steps (for example, "90 percent correct responses" or "plays appropriately for the expected duration on five consecutive occasions").

Teaching opportunities	Expected length of constructive "waiting time"	Record a "+" if your child stays in the designated area and occupies himself appropriately and a "–" if he does not	Did your child reach mastery of the teaching step? If yes, increase the amount of time you expect your child to occupy himself; if no, continue at the current step
1.			
2.			
3.			
4.			
5.			
6.			
7.			
8.			
9.			
10.			

6. When you go on an outing, bring along your materials. Find a relatively quiet area where you and your child can sit, and mark the designated area. Present the clear instruction by saying "We have to wait. Let's see what's in your waiting bag."

    a. If needed, take out a few of the toys and model how your child should use the toys to help him get started. Once your child begins to manipulate the toys, set the timer for the expected duration.

    b. In many cases, the toys themselves function as reinforcers that maintain the play behavior. However, when you start this teaching program, your child may need some additional reinforcement (such as a preferred snack) to motivate him.

    c. If your child does not play with the toys, physically prompt toy use.

    d. Some children benefit from having an activity schedule that helps them use all of the toys or activities in the bag. When the timer rings, reinforce your child with praise, tickles, hugs, and a snack (if you have decided to use food reinforcement). Then engage your child in another activity (such as taking a walk or reading him a story).

    e. Gradually fade use of prompts to encourage more independent toy use. Increase the duration of productive waiting *only* when your child is consistently able to occupy himself for the initial duration specified.

Occupying Unstructured Time with Minimal Supervision

You can use similar procedures to teach your child to occupy his time productively with minimal supervision:

1. Identify several of your child's favorite activities that involve materials that are safe and cannot be used for property destruction. For example, avoid activities that require the use of scissors, paints, or crayons if your child has a habit on writing on nonpaper surfaces, and other items that can potentially damage household fixtures or furnishings.

2. Place these materials in a large bin or in separate bins labeled with pictures.

3. Designate and mark off a play area.

4. Identify realistic starting points for duration of play using the sampling technique described above (that is, taking the average time of at least three samples of independent play behavior). These may range from as little as ten seconds to as much as thirty (or even sixty) minutes.

5. Outline a progression of time increments (such as thirty seconds, one minute, two minutes, five minutes, and so on).

6. Specify performance criteria that let you know when to move on to the next phase of the teaching program.

7. Identify a reinforcer. This could be a special play activity that you and your child could engage in after the allotted time.

8. Inform your child that it time to play. Bring him to the play area and open up the bin or bins where materials are stored.

9. Set a kitchen timer for the appropriate amount of time.

10. If your child stops playing or leaves the designated play area, redirect his activity.

11. Give reinforcements to your child if he occupies himself appropriately for the entire time period.

12. Be sure to celebrate even small changes in behavior.

RESPECTING BOUNDARIES

As we've mentioned previously, your child's intrusion into other family members' "space" can be a major issue at home, especially for siblings of all ages who value their possessions and want to keep them intact. How can you help prevent these intrusions from occurring? There are several different approaches that you can consider. You may find that using a combination of these strategies works best for your family.

One strategy is preventative: making physical changes in the environment to physically prevent the child from having access to other people's personal belongings. Here are some actions you can take:

- Provide siblings with lockable cabinets so they can store their most prized possessions. Make sure that these cabinets are secured to the wall and cannot be toppled—determined children can be very inventive.

- Permit older siblings to lock their rooms.

- Encourage siblings to clean up and put important things away in safe and inaccessible places.

- Place door chimes on doors that are closed but not locked to alert you when someone is entering a room that has been designated "limited access."

The second strategy involves teaching. In helping families deal with these issues, we have used several different teaching programs, most of them involving teaching the child with ASD to discriminate between rooms that are accessible and inaccessible. An example of how the Black family managed this issue follows.

Mr. and Mrs. Black taught their five-year-old daughter, Arlene, to discriminate between "red light" (no access) and "green light" (free access). At the time we initiated the teaching program, Arlene was able to consistently identify a wide variety of objects, point to pictures of many familiar objects on request, and point to primary colors on request. Her parents began by teaching her that green means "go" and red means "stop" by using a variation of the children's game "red light, green light." The steps included in their teaching program are listed below.

1. One parent (parent #1) stood with Arlene approximately ten feet away from the other parent (parent #2). Parent #2 held up a green circle and said, "Green light, go!" Parent #1 prompted Arlene to go over to the other parent, where she received reinforcement for following the direction.

2. When Arlene had followed the directions five times in a row, parent #1 began to fade the prompt as parent #2 provided the direction. They kept practicing until Arlene responded accurately 90 percent of the time (with at least ten opportunities in a day).

3. When parent #2 held up the red circle and said, "Red light, stop," parent #1 put out his arm to block Arlene's passage. When Arlene had stayed put five times in a row, parent #1 discontinued use of the prompt. The Blacks continued in this way until Arlene responded accurately 90 percent of the time (with at least ten opportunities per day).

4. The parents next alternated between red and green circles, reinforcing correct responses and providing feedback when Arlene made mistakes. They continued with this step until Arlene responded accurately 90 percent of the time on three consecutive teaching sessions that consisted of ten trials each.

5. Next, the Blacks began to apply the concept to doors in the home by putting either a red or green circle on each bedroom or bathroom door. Several times a day they walked through the house with Arlene and pointed to each sign, asking Arlene, "What does this mean?" If Arlene read the sign correctly and behaved in a way that was consistent with its message (for example, walked away, or stopped and did not enter, when the sign was red), she received reinforcement. If Arlene responded incorrectly, the parents prompted her with cues to help her read the

sign accurately or modeled the appropriate behavioral response to the sign. Before ending the teaching interaction, the Blacks would ask Arlene what the sign meant and what she was supposed to do. They continued teaching until Arlene responded accurately on 90 percent of the trials included on three consecutive teaching sessions that consisted of ten trials each.

6. The Blacks continued to reinforce Arlene's positive behavior with verbal praise when they saw her observing the signs on closed doors. They also gave her reinforcement for getting through the day without intrusions.

Remember, the program above is just an example. You will need to modify the basic outline to meet your child's needs. For example, if your child can read words or comprehend universal signs, you can use written words or symbols instead of colors.

STAYING WITH AN ADULT IN PUBLIC PLACES

Parents are often unable to enjoy themselves at recreational or community-based events because they are concerned about their child running off, "getting into things," or being injured. This is one of the main reasons that families avoid such activities. For this reason, you may want to teach your child to stay with you in public places. Because this type of teaching program has many variables, it's not possible for us to provide an example of an actual program. However, here are some components of this kind of program that you might want to consider when developing your teaching method.

Consistent with the methods already discussed, the first thing to consider is what skills your child already has in his repertoire that can make this skill easier to teach. Prior mastery of the skills listed below can be extremely useful, as these skills can be included in a functional skill cluster that addresses behavior in public settings. If these skills are not in your child's repertoire, you should consider teaching them before developing your "community outing" program.

- Complies with basic requests

- Keeps volume of verbalizations/vocalizations within a reasonable range

- Follows an activity schedule (using pictures or words)

- Exhibits low levels of inappropriate behavior when appropriate behavior is being reinforced

- Has some capacity to delay reinforcement; that is, your child is able to maintain appropriate behavior for time intervals that are manageable during your outing (for example, reinforcement for appropriate behavior is not needed more frequently than every ten minutes)

You should also have a plan for what you will do if behavior goes awry. Some common strategies include the following:

- Having consequences for inappropriate behavior (such as returning to the car with one parent while the other stays with other family members)

- Recognizing when your child is becoming overly aroused and giving him a brief break from activities (or a calm-down period, if needed) followed by an opportunity to resume participation

Use the techniques discussed earlier in the chapter to custom design your own program for teaching your child to stay with you when you go out.

EMPOWERING SIBLINGS

As discussed earlier in the book, empowering siblings is important for good family functioning, especially when the child with ASD is learning new skills that will improve your family life. The list below identifies different ways that you can help your children feel that they understand and can manage their sibling's ASD.

- ☐ Keep siblings apprised of the skills that your child has learned and tell them what techniques seem to help the child stay in control.

- ☐ Tell siblings how to handle specific problematic situations with their sibling with ASD (such as giving corrective feedback, remaining calm, asking nicely, and seeking help from an adult if their efforts do not resolve the problem).

- ☐ Teach siblings how to have positive play interactions with their sibling with ASD.

- ☐ Involve siblings in teaching if they express an interest. Teach them how to prompt and cue responses. However, be careful that you do not make young siblings primary therapists for your child and do not overburden older siblings.

HELPFUL HINTS FOR CONSISTENT, SUCCESSFUL TEACHING

Consistency is paramount in the process of behavior change. It applies not only to incorporating behavioral expectations into ongoing activities but also to the use of consequences for both wanted and unwanted behaviors. If you implement your teaching programs or enforce behavioral expectations only intermittently, your child will have a difficult time understanding what he is required to do under specific stimulus conditions. Thus, his ability to learn new stimulus-response-consequence relationships will be compromised, as will his ability to maintain the changes you have achieved. As you become more comfortable with implementing the strategies in this book and you see benefits from them, they should become a routine part of many of your interactions with your child, beyond the times you dedicate to goal-focused teaching. In the same way that effective parenting of a typically developing child involves identifying and taking advantage of teaching moments during naturally occurring activities, providing opportunities for learning and reinforcing previous learning should be woven through all waking hours. This is not to say that if you miss an occasional behavior or consequence you're doomed for failure. The point is that increased consistency can lead to more rapid learning and better maintenance and generalization of acquired skills.

In order to maximize your ability to be consistent with your new expectations and procedures, we recommend the following guidelines:

- ■ Consider how many skills you can realistically teach at once. While many of the skills you will want to teach are easily incorporated into everyday self-care skills and activities (for example, communication goals like requesting, telling about events, and conversational exchanges; and social goals like sharing experiences, playing appropriately with toys, and managing emotions), it may be too stressful to address them all at once.

- Your teaching will be more effective if you select fewer goals that are consistently addressed than if you select too many goals and address them inconsistently.

- Apply the shaping principles discussed in chapter 5 to your own behavior. Specifically, establish a teaching plan so you can gradually and systematically increase the new skills that you are teaching and the acquired skills that you are maintaining. Remember, behavior change is gradual, and this fact applies to you as well.

- Develop reinforcement programs for teaching and maintaining acquired skills since these programs can also serve as reminders for you to attend to and reinforce appropriate behaviors. Having tangible or visible cues (for use as symbolic reinforcers, such as tokens, pennies, stickers, or points on a reinforcement chart) can provide you with feedback regarding how well you are tracking behavior. In our own teaching experiences, these types of programs have been invaluable. On one occasion, at the end of a teaching session during which "on task" behavior was being rewarded with pennies, one of the authors still had a pocketful of pennies despite the fact that the child had generally been "on task." This alerted the author to the fact that she had not been consistent in reinforcing the target behavior.

Rules and Consequences for All

As your child becomes better able to understand and comply with behavioral expectations, you may want to consider establishing "house rules" that all children in the family are required to follow. Although the house rules may have to be fairly generic at first (so that you have some latitude to individualize the particulars for each of your children), a public listing can have several benefits, as follows:

- Typically developing children may start to view their sibling with ASD as less "special" or privileged because he now has rules and expectations, too.

- Symbolic reinforcement programs that reward all siblings for compliance with house rules help siblings to feel included and provide a structure for maintaining sibling compliance.

- Establishing house rules reinforces your family's values and also reinforces the concept of your family as a team (discussed in chapter 3), in which everyone is contributing to improve family life.

This chapter focused mainly on strategies for increasing compliance to ensure your child's safety and to help you teach him to consistently follow directions. We also discussed the importance of setting limits and being consistent with your responses to your child's behavior. Increasing your child's compliance with your requests can have a significant impact on family functioning, helping you complete daily routines more efficiently, prepare your child to participate in family outings, decrease sibling complaints of differential and unfair treatment, and decrease overall levels of stress at home. We also addressed the benefits of being consistent in your use of behavioral expectations, limits, and rules. Not only does consistency in these areas expedite learning for your child with ASD, but it also levels the playing field with respect to rules and expectations for all siblings.

In the next chapter, we will discuss issues related to teaching communication skills and applying the teaching strategies you have learned to the improvement of your child's communication.

Strategies for Increasing Your Child's Communication Skills

More often than not, improving communication skills appears at the top of parents' wish lists. This is not surprising, since all children diagnosed with ASD have difficulty with some aspect(s) of communication, ranging from severe to mild. Language development is a complex phenomenon, and children can be skilled in some aspects of language, but not others. It is also important to understand that the language deficits in ASD are often both expressive and receptive—your child may have difficulty producing language (expressive language) and understanding language (receptive language).

One problem associated with severe language deficits is minimal speech that is compensated for by limited use of nonverbal communication (gestures or signs). When speech is present, it may be meaningless and repetitive (such as parrotlike repetition of dialogue from movies, commercial jingles, or phrases). The child may repeat sentences that he has heard previously (either immediately or some time after the sentence is heard) and that may not make sense in the context of verbal exchanges with others. Other problems at this level of severity include the limited use of spontaneous (self-initiated) speech even when the child has a substantial speaking vocabulary. Children may speak too slowly, too quickly, or in a sing-song tone, or they may phrase statements in the form of a question (for example, saying "Do you want a cookie?" when he wants a cookie). It is also common for children with ASD to have difficulty understanding more lengthy or abstract information contained in various phrases or sentences (such as directions, explanations, and stories that are presented in verbal or nonverbal formats). For example, when given the direction "Go straight through the traffic light," we understand the message to be "Continue walking or driving straight when you approach the intersection," but an individual with ASD may not easily understand this, possibly interpreting the direction differently. Therefore, giving and understanding directions may be difficult for a child with ASD.

Even when a child with ASD has developed language skills in a fairly typical manner, he may lack the ability to engage in meaningful conversational exchanges with others—a mismatch of skills that can be confusing to parents and others. Problems at higher levels of language competence include a tendency to interpret language in an inappropriate, literal, or very rigid way. While these children may be very good at understanding familiar phrases or sentences, slight changes in the vocabulary or the sentence structure may make the message unintelligible to them. Children with ASD also tend to have limited comprehension of the subtleties and nuances that we routinely use in our communication. These deficits contribute to their inability to recognize and appreciate jokes (or humorous situations in general) and detect sarcasm and teasing. Thus, they may interpret innocuous comments as mean and insulting but not understand or respond to comments that are meant to be insulting or derogatory. Limited ability to interpret facial expressions, emotional reactions, and body language, in addition to poor understanding of abstract verbal concepts (such as metaphors and proverbs), can make social interactions difficult. Children with ASD may also have trouble using multiple pieces of information to draw conclusions about an event or situation.

Children with ASD may have difficulty with *pragmatics*, a term used by professionals to describe the *use* of language as opposed to its structure. Problems exhibited by children with ASD include difficulty initiating and ending conversations, understanding the rules of turn taking in conversations, and speaking too loudly or too softly. Children with ASD also tend to assume that their conversational partners have the same information they do about specific personal interests; that is, they neglect to provide the listener with the background information needed to understand what they are talking about. As a result of this lack of appreciation of the other's point of view, the listener interprets the child's attempts at conversational exchanges as odd.

The restricted range of interests exhibited by children with ASD can also affect their ability to carry on ordinary conversations in several ways. First, a child with ASD tends to talk exclusively about topics that interest him, often in a repetitive manner, without any sensitivity to the listener's reactions. Second, a child with ASD may not enjoy listening to others sharing information about their own personal interests, activities, and experiences, especially if the child has no specific interest in these topics. All of these limitations make it difficult for children with ASD to have age-appropriate conversations.

HOW TEACHING COMMUNICATION SKILLS CAN IMPROVE FAMILY INTERACTIONS

Teaching communication skills to your child with ASD can be helpful to your family in a number of ways, including the following:

■ Improving communication about preferences and needs or wants can make it easier to address the child's needs and anticipate his desires.

■ Improving expressive communication can help family members feel more connected.

■ Improving expressive communication can increase opportunities to share information.

■ Improving comprehension of language can make learning of new concepts, information, and procedures easier. In addition, broadening your child's receptive vocabulary can be helpful when you are trying to teach him limits for safety purposes, and it can be helpful when you are working to set limits and manage unwanted behaviors.

■ Improving language comprehension can play a big role in helping your child understand simple game rules. In this way, receptive language skills can indirectly affect your child's ability to participate in fun social interactions with other family members.

■ Improving your child's understanding of the nonverbal aspects of communication, such as gestures, body language, eye contact, and facial expressions, will lead to better social interactions with others. Understanding nonverbal aspects of social interactions will also help your child regulate his emotions and behavior in social situations.

■ Improving your child's ability to ask questions can enrich the quality of his social interactions, since it can enable him to find out information that might be important to him and receive feedback from social partners.

BEFORE YOU START

Did you know that approximately 50 percent of children with ASD are nonverbal (that is, they do not have verbal speech)? Of course, if your child is nonverbal, this does not mean that he will not be able to communicate with you or that your child will not learn to use spoken language. What this does mean is that you may have to use alternative methods of communication in order to get started. And the sooner your child learns to use any form of communication, the better, since having a communication system increases opportunities to interact with others in appropriate and satisfying ways.

A number of possible alternatives to verbal communication are available. These include pictures, signs, gestures, written words, symbols, miniature objects (representations of real objects), or a voice output system (a rather sophisticated electronic device that produces vocalization when children select pictures or type in words). Which one you choose depends, in large part, on your child's skill repertoire and what form of communication is easiest for him to learn and use. You may also find, as is often the case with nonverbal children, that using more than one communication method (a "multimodal approach") produces the best results. For example, by pairing a nonverbal form of communication with spoken language, you may achieve two goals: First, you are providing your child with a more immediate method of communication (assuming that the nonverbal form of communication can be learned more quickly than speech). Second, you are continuing to provide instruction in spoken language. This multimodal approach is exemplified in the case of Susie, below.

Susie, a four-year-old girl diagnosed with pervasive developmental disorder not otherwise specified, produced a variety of speech sounds (for example, "buh," "ah," and "tuh") spontaneously and had good verbal and nonverbal imitative skills. However, she did not use any of her speech sounds to communicate her wants or needs, state preferences, or label objects or events, even though her parents tried to motivate her to use her speech in this way. Susie did show relative strength in the area of visual discrimination (that is, she had strong matching and sorting skills and recognized many pictures of objects and actions). Because she was having such a hard time using her verbal language to express her needs, we decided to use a picture communication system to get her started. However, since Susie demonstrated good potential for developing verbal communication, we did not want to give up on this possibility for her. Therefore, we required Susie to produce both a verbal response and a nonverbal response (also called a *picture exchange response*) each time she requested an item or activity. (In a picture exchange response, the child shows, points to, or gives you a picture of what they wish to communicate. For example, if a child wanted to read a book, he would find the picture of a book in his picture communication binder and give it to you. Several picture communication systems are available; for more information, please consult a speech language pathologist or board certified behavior analyst.) Early in the teaching process, we only required her to produce approximations of words (for example, "buh" for "book," "at" for "hat," and "ike" for "ice cream"). Over time, we required her to produce closer approximations of the names of items and activities that she was requesting in order to receive the item she wanted. Within a short period, we were able to discontinue the use of picture communication, since Susie had learned to communicate basic needs verbally.

For children like Susie, whose skills are at the entry level of communication development, priority should be placed on such skills as requesting highly desired objects or activities (specific foods and special toys or games), sharing information about ongoing activities (by pointing, gesturing, or saying "Look"), answering yes or no questions to express preferences, expressing needs (such as toileting, asking for help to get an item that is out of reach, and telling parents when they are hurt, injured, or ill), and following simple directions. Remember, the key to teaching basic communication is to focus on *functional* communication—the communication skills that are most useful during everyday activities. At more advanced levels of language development, emphasis should be placed on increasing the child's ability to share information (for example, providing information related to his school day or discussing a movie with others), developing the ability to engage in conversational exchanges, knowing how to begin and end conversations appropriately, reading nonverbal cues, and sustaining conversations on topics of interest to others.

Modifications May Be Needed in the Early Stages of Teaching

Sometimes you will need to modify the signs, symbols, or verbal responses that you are expecting your child to use in order to increase the speed of your child's learning. For example, if you are going to use a standard communication system, like American Sign Language, you may find it helpful to simplify some parts of the system so that your child can use them, such as modifying a sign to make it easier for him to produce if he has difficulty with fine motor skills. As long as each sign is distinctly different from other signs in his repertoire, you will be able to understand his messages. When you make these kinds of changes, make sure that others know about the modified sign so the child will be able to effectively communicate with others. If others do not understand the new sign, then they may not respond to your child's efforts to communicate, and after a while he may stop using that sign.

A second example of modifications involves the picture exchange system. Your child may learn to use some pictures more quickly than others. For some children, using very simple black-and-white or color pictures of everyday objects works best in the early stages of teaching, while others do better with photographs because these are more realistic. More complex pictures, such as detailed photographs and images containing abstract symbols such as letters, numbers, or words, may be more difficult to learn. The specific type of picture that will be easiest for your child to use depends upon his ability to learn what the pictures represent and how well your child can discriminate between the pictures. Determining the type of picture to use is not always an easy task. If you find that you need assistance in this area, please consult a professional.

BASICS FOR TEACHING COMMUNICATION TO YOUR CHILD

When you are in the early stages of teaching language, it is important for you to understand the various functions that language serves. We will discuss four types of language functions below (manding, tacting, sharing, and questioning), since these are areas that you may want to teach your child.

Manding

A *mand* is a request, direction, or command. An example of a mand is a child's request for affection: "Hug me, please." Children are generally highly motivated to use mands since they receive instant reinforcement—they make the request and (usually) immediately receive the item or activity requested.

Tacting

A *tact* is a label for a item or event. When you look at an apple and say "apple," you are using a tact. Typically, tacting is taught after manding. The reason for this, as explained by experts in the field of verbal behavior, is that a mand is easier for children to learn because they are more motivated to ask for things they want than they are to label items or events in the environment.

Sharing

Sharing of information, such as talking about one's likes and dislikes, is another function of language. Sharing can also involve information about one's environment, one's personal experiences (past and present), and one's feelings, as well as factual information about events and other people. The important aspect of sharing is its social quality. Information is being exchanged: the speaker gives information to a recipient. Sharing of information can eventually evolve into more complex conversational exchanges in which both parties exchange information.

Questioning

Asking questions—who, what, where, when, and why—is an entirely different skill. People ask questions for many different reasons, some of which are listed below:

- To get functional or practical information ("Where is my coat?")

- To get social information ("How are you?" "Have you seen the new Harry Potter movie?")

- To get explanations ("How do I do this math problem?")

- To get factual information ("What does *irritable* mean?" "What is ASD?")

- To get abstract information ("What do you think would happen if . . . ?")

ASSESSING YOUR CHILD'S LANGUAGE SKILLS AND DECIDING WHAT TO TEACH

The table below is designed to help you identify specific communication skills that you may wish to teach your child. As you may notice, the skills are organized according to the language functions we discussed above. Place a check mark in the far left column next to each skill that you would like your child to learn.

Next, indicate whether you are planning to teach your child to communicate using a verbal or nonverbal approach (that is, whether you will be teaching verbal responses or gestures, pictures, or sign language).

In the "prerequisite skills" column, put a check mark if your child has the skills he or she will need to have before you begin teaching a new verbal or nonverbal communication skill.

In the "language comprehension" column, place a check mark if your child is able to understand another person's use of expressive language, both verbal and nonverbal. For example, does your child fully understand when you ask him to stop doing something? Does he actually understand when you nod your head to indicate that it is okay to have a cookie or draw with crayons? If you believe that he does, examine the reasons for this belief. Make sure he *consistently* responds in an appropriate way to verbal or nonverbal messages, because when teaching language skills you must build new skills on a sturdy foundation. All too often, we have seen parents and educators become frustrated when their children are unable to progress to more complex forms of communication. In many cases, they thought that their children already had important prerequisite skills in their repertoires; however, when we conducted more formal assessments to try to figure out why these children were not making progress, we found that their grasp of foundation skills taught earlier was at best inconsistent. Therefore, expecting the child to be able to understand and use more complex language structures was unrealistic. As with a house of cards, when the demand exceeds the strength of the foundation, the structure crashes.

Communication assessment worksheet				
Expressive language skills	Verbal	Nonverbal	Prerequisite skills	Language comprehension
Manding				
Asking for something to eat or drink				
Asking for affection				
Indicating yes (saying "yes," nodding head)				
Indicating no (saying "no," shaking head)				
Requesting to stop something				
Understanding yes				
Understanding no				
Bringing something (a toy or object) to you to fix				
Tacting				
Indicating he or she is feeling hurt, sad, or angry				
Indicating he or she is feeling happy or surprised				
Indicating he or she is feeling sick or ill				
Relaying information				

	Sharing an experience (for example, what happened at school today)				
	Greeting others				
	Responding to greetings				
	Sticking to the current topic of conversation				
	Commenting on things in the environment				
	Sharing				
	Pointing to something in a room that he or she is interested in				
	Shifting gaze to share experiences (alternating attention between you and an interesting object or person, for the purpose of sharing with you)				
	Bringing something to share				
	Questioning				
	Asking who, what, where, when, and why questions				
	Asking how questions				
	Asking for help				
	Asking for permission				

By now you should have a relatively clear idea of what types of language skills your child has and what skills you would like to teach your child. (You may want to return to this worksheet periodically to assess your child's language development over time.)

Now that you have identified the skills that you would like to teach, use the table below to help you develop teaching sequences. The table is designed to help you figure out which communication skills to address first. In the left-hand column, some communication areas are listed. The column on the right provides a sequence of skills that correspond to the communication area. Please note that the sequence of skills listed is not the only order used for teaching language. However, it does provide a general teaching sequence for each communication area. Within the two categories of expressive language and language comprehension, all types of communication methods can be used. As we described earlier in the chapter, this simply means that your child may be using a picture communication system to express himself, but he may also be able to understand verbal speech from others. It is important that you have a good understanding of your child's current expressive language and language comprehension abilities. To use this table, decide which area of communication you want to work on—reciprocity, for example. Look in the Receptive language skill sequence column and note the progression from simple to complex. Then identify specific skills that you want to teach.

Communication area	Possible skill sequence
Speech (verbal language)	1. Making vocalizations 2. Imitating single sounds and blended sounds 3. Imitating words 4. Using sound combinations to label objects, people, and events ("ma-ma," "da-da") 5. Articulating (from specific sounds to sounds within words, to words within phrases or sentences) 6. Using correct speech quality (rhythm, volume, inflection)
Reciprocity	1. Looking from object to person 2. Looking from object to person and back to object 3. Engaging in reciprocal play 4. Verbalizing, gesturing to effect change in environment 5. Taking turns
Receptive language	1. Following simple directions (first one direction, then two directions, and so on) 2. Following complex directions, such as those involving more than one action (e.g., "tie your shoes and put your coat on," or "get ready to go outside") 3. Pointing to objects, people, and other things 4. Differentiating objects, people, and pictures 5. Differentiating objects by function 6. Responding to questions (nonverbally) 7. Answering questions based on information given in a short story or description of another's personal experience

Expressive language	1. Making self-initiated vocalizations, using gestures and mands
	2. Labeling objects and people with single words, then two words, and so on
	3. Labeling objects, people, and events using sentences
	4. Responding to questions
	5. Using adjectives, adjective-noun combinations, adverbs, and prepositional phrases
	6. Asking questions to request items, obtain information, initiate interactions
	7. Telling simple stories, relating experiences
	8. Engaging in a short conversation with others (one exchange)

* Table adapted from *Individualized Goal Selection Curriculum* (Romanczyk, Lockshin, and Matey 1996).

BASIC STRATEGIES FOR TEACHING LANGUAGE: HOW TO TEACH

In this section, we will provide examples of how to use six basic teaching strategies to teach language/communication skills to your child or expand your child's language/communication repertoire. These approaches, some of which were explained in chapter 5, include the following: shaping, prompting, fading, modeling, incidental teaching, and social scripts. Please note that these strategies can be adapted to other alternative communication methods, such as using miniature objects (representations of real objects) and using a voice output system.

Shaping

As we described earlier in the book, shaping is a teaching strategy you can use when your child is not performing a behavior or skill that you would like him to perform. In other words, shaping is used to teach a new behavior. In shaping, you at first reinforce behaviors that resemble the skill you trying to teach. As your child begins to perform that behavior more frequently, you start to request, and reward, a closer approximation of the desired behavior, no longer reinforcing the first approximation. When you continue to reward closer and closer approximations of the desired behavior, your child will soon learn to perform the desired behavior itself. The table below provides you with basic strategies for teaching different communication skills using shaping.

Shaping		
Use of tacts and mands		
What do you want to teach?	**How do you do it?**	**Example**
How to make words using sounds that the child already has	First reward your child for saying any single sound after you give the direction "Let's talk" or tell him to say a particular word. Once he consistently makes a sound after your direction, ask for a specific sound. Only reward the production of that specific sound if it follows your direction. Next, ask for two sounds, following the same teaching pattern. As your child begins to acquire two or more single sounds, begin to teach your child to say partial words (for example, "bo" for "boat") or sound combinations using these acquired sounds. You may use a picture or object as a visual cue when teaching as well. This helps to teach the association between the sound and the object or picture. Continue using the same shaping procedure to teach your child to imitate words.	Jimmy said "mm" frequently. 1. Jimmy's mom rewarded all sounds when she asked Jimmy to say "mm." 2. She only rewarded sounds that sounded like "mm" (such as "mm" and "nn") in the presence of objects or people whose names began with the "mm" sound. 3. She rewarded only "mm" sounds as a label for objects or people. 4. She added the "ah" sound to "mm," rewarding only "mah" sounds. 5. She added "m" at end of "mah" to make "mom." When Jimmy said "mom," she rewarded him with a special prize. *Where to go next:* Teach more sound combinations and shape these combinations into labels. Require your child to use the combination or label in many different settings or activities to generalize your child's ability to use the sound combinations or labels in multiple places and with multiple people. You can also use the same shaping strategy to teach your child to use more words and longer sentences when he speaks. (Start by requiring one word, then two words, and so on; for example, "book" becomes "book, please," and then "I want book, please.")

Shaping appropriate social distance during conversation		
What do you want to teach?	**How do you do it?**	**Example**
How to avoid standing too close when speaking to others (personal space)	Reward your child for approximating maintaining appropriate social distance during conversations until he consistently maintains a comfortable distance from the social partner when conversing (approximately 2 to 3 feet away).	Initially, Lucy's family members reinforced her behavior when she was at least 6 inches away from her social partner when talking. Once Lucy was consistently maintaining this distance, they only reinforced her behavior if she was at least 12 inches from her social partner. The distance required for reinforcement was gradually increased (18 inches, 24 inches, 30 inches, and then 36 inches) until Lucy was consistently engaging in conversations without invading the personal space of others. In an effort to generalize this skill to new settings, Lucy's family taught her to use arm length as a guide for appropriate social distance. They told her that if her hand could touch the other person when her arm was straight, she was too close and needed to move back. Then the family had Lucy practice using this gauge in different rooms in the house. Lucy's parents then taught her to imagine stretching her arm out while having a conversation with others at an appropriate distance.
How to avoid standing too far away when speaking to others	Use the same method, but simply reward your child for gradually standing closer to the conversation partner.	Chris's family followed the same approach as Lucy's family did, except that they focused on systematically rewarding Chris for decreasing the distance from his social partner.

Shaping appropriate voice volume for situation		
What do you want to teach?	**How do you do it?**	**Example**
To speak with an appropriate conversational tone (child whispers or speaks too loudly)	First, determine your child's typical voice volume in different settings, or with different people. Rank the volumes from most appropriate to least appropriate for the setting. Start with the setting where your child uses the voice volume that is most appropriate to the situation. Provide a cue (prompt), giving feedback to your child about being too loud or too soft (for example, using a hand gesture, showing her a picture, or saying "Speak up" or "That's too loud; speak a little softer"). As your child learns to speak with a more appropriate tone in the first setting, use the same procedure in the next setting on your ranked list and so on.	(Below, write an example of how you might teach this skill using shaping.)

Prompting

Prompting involves providing a cue to your child to help him perform a desired or requested behavior. Prompts, or cues, can be verbal (telling your child what to do), gestural (making a gesture such as shaking your head, waving for the child to come to you, and so on), written or pictorial (showing your child a word or picture), or physical (providing physical help for your child to complete a behavior or task).

Prompting		
Some common ways to use prompts to teach communication: Tacts		
What do you want to teach?	How do you do it?	Example
New sign-language words	Most-to-least prompting might be used in this case. When first teaching your child the new sign, you might physically assist him to make the sign. As a result, your child at first will always get the sign correct because you will be helping him. After a certain amount of time, test your child's ability to form the sign independently (no prompts). This will tell you how much you still need to prompt. Because it's best to fade your physical prompt out as soon as possible, you will gradually provide less and less physical prompting, until you are only modeling the correct sign or showing how to start making the sign. Continue to gradually fade the modeling prompt until he only needs a verbal prompt.	Joanna uses sign language as a form of communication with her family. Joanna's father, Ian, wanted to teach Joanna new functional signs for use at home. Due to Joanna's fine-motor difficulties, she could not learn some signs, so Ian taught Joanna to use simpler versions of the signs. For example, when teaching the American Sign Language sign for "hat" (a tap on the top of the head), Ian chose to teach Joanna to touch anywhere on her head. Ian held up a hat and asked Joanna to sign for hat by saying "Joanna, what is this?" Since Joanna did not make any sign, Ian prompted by pointing to the hat and saying "Joanna, this is hat." Then he gently took her hand and moved it to her head, while he said, "hat." Ian continued to fade the physical prompt as follows: 1. He raised Joanna's hand three-quarters of the way to her head. 2. He raised Joanna's hand halfway to her head. 3. He raised Joanna's hand one-quarter of the way to her head. 4. He gave her wrist a gentle push in the direction of her head. 5. He didn't give her any physical prompt at all.

Naming (tacting)	Least-to-most prompting: Verbally give the initial sound of the word you are trying to teach. Only provide the remaining part of the word if your child is unable to provide the label when you tell him the first part (cue) of the word. You want to start by giving the smallest amount of help in order for your child to respond correctly. By giving your child the least information, you encourage an independent response. Most-to-least prompting: Start by giving the full prompt (the full word). Once he's mastered saying the full word after you've given him the full prompt, begin to prompt him with only the first sound of the word, then with no prompt.	(Below, write an example of how you might teach this skill using prompting.)

Fading

For all children, independence in their ability to communicate with others is essential. However, it's easy to slip into helping too much, especially when they're taking a long time to finish a word or when we think we know what they are saying. Even though helping is done with good intentions, it prevents children from learning how to communicate on their own. Therefore, it is important to keep the number of cues you use to a minimum and watch how long you use each cue.

As your child learns to use a communication method, you should begin to fade out some of the cues (pictures, signs, and so on) so that the child does not learn to depend on them. For example, if you are teaching your child to use pictures for communication, at first you might have to physically assist your child in taking the picture off of the picture board or book and handing it to you. This physical assistance should be faded out quickly, since your goal is that your child be able to independently find a picture of what he wishes to communicate and give it to you on his own.

One way to test whether your child is ready to leave a cue behind is to do an assessment. If he succeeds most of the time, you may be able to move to the next step in eliminating the cue and see how he does. If your child gets it right 75 percent of the time, then it may be time to get rid of that cue. If your child's performance decreases to less than 75 percent, then you may want to continue to use the cue, or look for a cue that is little less salient. The table below provides you with some ways to use fading to teach communication skills.

Fading		
Fading of prompts		
What do you want to teach?	**How do you do it?**	**Example**
To initiate conversations with others	Use a picture schedule that shows your child the steps for starting a conversation (e.g., look at the person, wave hello, say hello, and ask a question, whether verbally, in writing, or in sign language). Praise your child's use of each step.	Tommy had difficulty starting and maintaining conversations with others. He would greet the other person, but he then did not know what to say. To assist Tommy with selecting a topic to discuss, his dad made a wallet-size visual prompt with three pictures representing topics Tommy enjoyed talking about. This prompt was not terribly intrusive or noticeable to others, since it was kept in Tommy's pocket. When Tommy began to use the prompt more reliably, Tommy's dad replaced the card with one that had no pictures, so that only the card remained as a prompt for Tommy. The card reminded him of the pictures and the conversational topics they had represented. Eventually, Tommy no longer needed the card to maintain conversations.
Fading of prompts to teach differentiation		
What do you want to teach?	**How do you do it?**	**Example**
To discriminate between objects, pictures, spoken words, and so on (receptive language)	Take one object that you want to teach first (this object is called the target stimulus) and first make it more noticeable or more different from the other objects around it. In order to assess whether or not the child recognizes a specific item or picture by name, you need to demonstrate that he can consistently pick this item out of an array. Then you gradually make the item increasingly less noticeable.	Fading an auditory prompt: The parent first says the target word or sound loudly. Then, as the child begins to learn the word or sound, the parent fades or lowers his or her volume to a normal conversational level. Fading a picture prompt: The parent makes the target picture larger than the distraction or other picture(s). As the child responds correctly more often, the parent makes the target picture smaller and smaller until it is the same size as the other items.

Modeling

In modeling, an individual is shown the behavior that he or she needs to perform. In essence, when you model behavior, you are showing your child how you want him to act or behave. Imagine that you are showing your child how to throw a ball. If it is your child's first time playing toss and catch, you will first show your child how to throw (model the throwing action) before asking him to do the same thing. If your child is able to imitate your actions, then modeling can be a very powerful teaching strategy.

Modeling		
Common modeling strategies		
What do you want to teach?	**How do you do it?**	**Example**
To appropriately ask for items he wants (manding)	First make desirable items inaccessible to your child. Then model the appropriate way to ask for the desirable item (by using words, handing you a picture, or producing a sign). If he imitates the correct behavior you have modeled, reward your child with the item he requested.	Dewayne's parents set up a toy box with all of his favorite toys inside. Before this, Dewayne's parents had taught Dewayne the picture symbols for many of those toys. Now, they wanted to teach Dewayne how to ask for specific toys. On the locked toy box, Dewayne's parents put a picture board that displayed all of the toys contained therein. Dewayne's parents would accompany him to the toy box when it was time to play and ask him what toy he would like to play with. If Dewayne did not choose a picture, then one of his parents would show him (model) taking off a picture and then receiving the toy that was on the picture. The parents would then close the toy box and ask Dewayne to choose a toy to play with. If he pointed to or handed a parent a picture at any time, he was allowed to play with that toy.
To use social language appropriately when ordering food in a restaurant (manding)	In social situations, have siblings or parents model appropriate responses for the child with ASD.	In a restaurant, each person in the family decides what food he or she is going to order. The child with ASD orders last in order to have several appropriate models of how to order his meal. This type of modeling is not noticeable to others (e.g., the server), yet it provides ample instruction opportunities. In this example, the reward is getting to eat the meal the child wants.

| To improve articulation of words, phrases or sentences | Repeat aloud, with emphasis on the part of the word that the child is not articulating properly. You may want to provide repetitive practice during teaching or throughout the day. | A dialogue in which a mother is using modeling to teach her daughter to pronounce the word *zipper* correctly might look like this:

Phuong: Dipper stuck.

Mom: *[points to zipper on jacket]* Phuong, say "z."

Phuong: Z.

Mom: Good, now say "zipper."

Phuong: Dipper.

Mom: Good try. Say "zipper. Z-z-zipper."

Phuong: Zipper.

Mom: Great job! Zipper! Your zipper is stuck.

Phuong: Zipper stuck! |

Incidental Teaching

So far, we have discussed what to teach and how to teach. Now, let's consider where to teach. For any skill, teaching can occur in a number of different settings, but you'll want to choose the right location for the skill you're working on. Sometimes it may be best to teach a skill while seated at a desk or table, to enhance your child's focus and ability to concentrate on learning. For example, homework is often done at your child's desk or the kitchen table, rather than in front of the TV. However, teaching exclusively at a desk or table can be limiting. For instance, it is usually difficult to teach a child how to make a sandwich or ask for a particular food when you're away from the kitchen. However, this is not to say that teaching your child to recognize and label objects or pictures in a focused environment is a problem in itself. In fact, some children learn best when a new skill is first taught in such an environment and then moved to a more natural setting. For example, you can teach a child to recognize pictures of food items at a table or desk, and then move your teaching sessions to the kitchen, the dining room table, a grocery store, a restaurant, and so on. Incidental teaching or naturalistic instruction involves arranging the environment in order to provide opportunities for language and consequences to arise naturally. Below is a list of just a few common strategies to use incidental teaching methods.

- By *hiding a desired object*, especially one that your child frequently requests, you set up a situation in which you can teach him how to ask for the desired item or how to ask where questions.

- By *placing an item in an out-of-reach (but visible) location*, you set up another situation that is ideally suited for teaching how to ask appropriately for items. You can also use this strategy to teach your child to initiate social conversation (in order to get the item).

- By *asking a question or making a comment that requires a response from your child*, you set up a situation that is just right for teaching social interaction and use of social language teaching tasks. (Remember, your child should be able to answer the question that is asked.)

Social Scripts

Typically, social scripts are used for teaching higher level language skills, such as maintaining a conversation or learning to incorporate social skills into language (as in inviting another child to play). Using a social script involves describing (using either written words or pictures) the steps a child needs to follow in order to utilize their language skills within a social context. Typically, a child might use a social script to learn a specific skill. As a child learns the script, variations of the script can be taught so that the child doesn't use the same sentence each time he greets a peer, for example ("Hi, Joey," "Hey, Joey," "Hello, Joey," and others). As the child learns the script, fade the use of it as soon as possible.

Social scripts		
What do you want to teach?	**How do you do it?**	**Example**
How to ask another child to play	Start by teaching your child to choose a peer to ask to play. Next, have your child ask the peer to play with him. Finally, teach your child to respond appropriately to the peer's acceptance or rejection of the invitation.	Sample social script:* 1. Go over to a friend. 2. Look at friend. 3. Say "Do you want to play with me?" 4. If friend says yes, say "Let's play!" 5. If friend says no, say "Okay. Maybe next time." 6. Go to next friend. * Have a list of friends to use when starting this social script.
How to greet others	The first step is to teach your child how to greet others. Next, teach your child appropriate ways to greet adults versus peers. To prevent your child from using only one greeting, provide him with two or three ways to greet another person.	Below, write a social script for greeting others:
How to express displeasure in an appropriate manner	Provide your child with at least two or three ways to say "No, thank you" or "I do not like this."	(Below, write a social script for expressing displeasure.)

Repetitive Practice

In order to teach effectively, you will need to create opportunities for learning. There are two main ways of doing so; one is *naturalistic instruction* and the other is *repetitive practice*. Naturalistic instruction is similar to incidental teaching in that you are choreographing opportunities for language instruction in an environment where your child would typically use the skill you are trying to teach. Experts still don't know which method is best for teaching language to children with ASD, although most agree that a combination of naturalistic instruction and repetitive practice, based on the child's individual communication and language needs, is most effective. So, if you use repetitive practice, it is imperative that you do so using naturalistic instruction—this allows the child to generalize the new skills to his everyday environment. Typically, repetitive practice is used for teaching beginning language skills (learning sounds, recognizing pictures, matching pictures to objects) that are then generalized to the environment using naturalistic instruction. Let's look at an example of what repetitive practice might look like for a child learning how to say the word *cat*.

Parent: Say "cat."

Child: [*No response. Parent waits five seconds for a response.*]

Parent: Cat. Say "cat."

Child: Ca.

Parent: Good try. Cat. Say "cat" [emphasizing the "t" sound].

Child: Cat.

Parent: Great job! You said "cat"! I loved the way you said "cat."

Parent: [*The process repeats.*] Say "cat."

Teaching communication is difficult. And, for most families, it is also a top priority. When you find yourself and your family members feeling frustrated, your child is showing little or no improvement, or you feel that the communication or language skill you would like to teach is too complex for the child, consult a professional.

PUTTING IT ALL TOGETHER

Up to this point, you have read about the importance of working together as a family to address family issues, you've learned some ways of teaching your child, and now you've learned some aspects of communication skills. We hope that you can begin to use some of the teaching strategies provided in this chapter to help improve your child's communication skills. Below are examples of how two different families assessed their child's strengths and weaknesses in communication, some of the family issues that were brought up during family meetings, and the teaching tasks that the families came up with as a team.

Child's name: Seth	
Strengths	**Weaknesses**
■ Has a good vocabulary and primarily uses speech to communicate	■ Has difficulty initiating conversations with others
■ Has excellent comprehension skills	■ Has difficulty staying on topic of conversation
■ Is motivated to engage in social situations with others	■ Does not recognize nonverbal cues to end conversations or change topics

Family issues
Seth always talks about the same topic, which frequently leads to frustration on the part of other family members. (Family needs: sense of belonging; support)
Seth's siblings feel embarrassed when they go on family outings because of Seth's difficulty maintaining appropriate conversations with others. (Family needs: acceptance; leisure and recreation)

Teaching tasks
■ Attend fully to speaker ■ Ask simple social questions ■ Hold a conversation for a five-minute period ■ Initiate conversations with others ■ Spontaneously request information about an ongoing activity ■ Listen to an experience related by another person and relate his own relevant feelings or experiences

Possible teaching strategies
■ Attend fully to speaker: Shaping the amount of time Seth has to attend to the speaker. ■ Ask simple social questions: Using social scripts to increase questions Seth can ask. ■ Hold a conversation for a five-minute period: Shaping the amount of time engaged in a conversation. It might be helpful to use a fading procedure here. Seth's parents could use a digital timer that makes a noise to provide Seth a prompt letting him know how long he has to stay in the conversation. Over time, the noise can be faded and the digital timer can be removed. ■ Initiate conversations with others: Modeling and prompting could be used here. ■ Spontaneously request information about an ongoing activity: The use of social scripts and incidental teaching might be helpful for teaching this task. ■ Listen to an experience related by another person and relate his own relevant feelings or experiences: Modeling could be used to show Seth how to let others know you are listening (maintaining eye contact, nodding head, staying oriented to the person talking). Social scripts may also be beneficial. Clearly, this skill would be taught after some of the prerequisite skills listed above are achieved.

Child's name: Anita	
Strengths	**Weaknesses**
■ Has excellent eye contact (responds when she hears her name called)	■ Has difficulty learning new things quickly
■ Is able to discriminate between photographs (is starting a picture-communication system with photographs)	■ Only interacts with family members when she needs something
■ Loves all types of stickers	■ Has difficulty occupying herself for long periods of time (fifteen minutes or more)

Family issues
Anita wanders around her house a lot, which causes stress for her parents, since they frequently have to check on her to make sure she's not getting into trouble. (Family needs: autonomy; support)
Anita's lack of social interaction with family members makes it difficult for siblings to play with her. (Family need: sense of belonging)

Teaching tasks
■ Greet family members and identify family members by name or picture ■ Invite family member to participate in an activity ■ Follow functional directions (such as "Anita, come here") ■ Occupy self for more than fifteen minutes ■ Play simple games with adult ■ Help out with chores (using picture schedule for chore sequence)

Possible teaching strategies
Can you think of some possible teaching strategies for the above teaching tasks? (When doing this for your child, remember to assess your child's current ability level, the desired skill level for your child, the teaching strategy, and how it would be used to teach a specific skill.) How would you teach her to greet family members and identify family members by name or picture?

Many families find it easy to summarize information in this way, especially during (family) meetings. You and your family (including your child with ASD) can use the blank chart below to identify problems and goals, so you can be on your way toward improving your child's communication and your family's life.

Child's name:	
Strengths	**Weaknesses**
▪	▪
▪	▪
▪	▪
Family issues	
Teaching tasks	
▪	
▪	
▪	
▪	
Possible teaching strategies	

9

Strategies for Increasing Your Child's Self-Control

What is self-control? *Self-control* is often defined as the ability to regulate one's behavior and emotional reactions in a way that matches parental, community, and societal values as well as that person's image of how they would like to manage their feelings and behavior. This definition suggests that the expectations, standards, and consequences set by parents, the community, and society at large play a large role in establishing what behavior and emotional reactions are acceptable.

In typical children, the development of self-control is a process that begins at birth and continues into adulthood. Self-control is learned during innumerable interactions, observations, and experiences in which the child tests the limits of acceptability and learns about the consequences of their behavior and their choices. In infancy and early childhood, children learn the basics of self-control when they learn which behaviors their parents like and which their parents don't like. At first, children require reminders to regulate their behavior (from parents, teachers, clergy, and other authority figures). However, as they get older they begin to do this for themselves. As parents, we can only hope that as our children mature they will begin to recognize upsetting situations, think of ways to keep themselves under control, and make decisions that solve the problem without negative consequences.

While the above discussion highlights some important aspects of self-control, it does not talk about the social nature of the development of self-control. Learning to behave in ways that please others requires social awareness and connectedness, as well as perspective taking ("If I were my mom, I would be so happy if my son apologized for breaking that dish."). It also involves the capacity to learn rules (sometimes, fairly complex rules) about what behaviors are acceptable in which settings, and the ability to use past experiences to find solutions that are likely to work in the present situation. In addition, self-control includes the capacity to identify one's own and others' emotional reactions and the ability to use coping strategies so that you can stay calm enough to examine your options and make good choices. In this way, insight and prediction are also significant skills in self-control.

Not surprisingly, children diagnosed with ASD are not very good at self-control. This is in part because from birth onward the learning histories of children with ASD are extremely different from those of typically developing children. Problems with language, social development, and inflexibility prevent them from having the early learning experiences that typically serve as the basis for the development of self-control.

Whether or not your child will learn to independently regulate his feeling and behavior is difficult to predict. You will be in a better position to evaluate his ability to engage in self-control after he begins to follow rules and accept limits, anticipate the consequences of his behavior, recognize his own emotional reactions and link them to events, and use coping and problem-solving skills to maintain or regain control. It is important to remember that learning self-control, even in typically developing children, is a process, and that even if your child does not learn to independently manage his behavior and emotional reactions, his ability to do this with guidance from others will certainly be a major accomplishment.

COMMON ISSUES FACING FAMILIES

If your young child has trouble with self-control, you may be seeing some of the following behaviors and characteristics:

- Poor regulation of activity levels

- Inability to manage affect (emotional reactions)

- Limited safety awareness

- Limited capacity to delay gratification

- Tantrums and excessive noise

These behaviors can disrupt family activities and generally cause stress. For example, your child's lack of safety awareness may prevent your family from socializing with friends or participating in activities, since he may need constant vigilance in order to keep him safe. Or, if your child engages in obsessive, compulsive, ritualistic, or sensory-seeking behaviors, or tantrums and angry outbursts, these may be a source of embarrassment for you and your other children. As a result you may end up feeling isolated because you are reluctant to invite friends over and may avoid participating in family and community events. Moreover, your child's difficult behaviors may prevent him from participating in age-appropriate activities.

As children with ASD approach adolescence, the behavioral issues that existed during childhood may become more complicated. Increases in size and strength (as well as other physical changes), increased irritability associated with hormonal changes, heightened sexual urges without an understanding of how to manage these new feelings, and an increased desire for independence can present new challenges for families. Moreover, others' expectations of self-control tend to be higher for adolescents than for children, and some of the more unruly or challenging behaviors that might have been tolerated in childhood are now considered entirely unacceptable. For example, if one form of a child's self-stimulatory behavior involved touching his genitals, in adolescence this behavior not only would be seen as odd but might even be considered sexual misconduct, particularly if the behavior occurs in public places.

PROBLEM BEHAVIORS THAT MAY HAVE FUNCTIONAL VALUE FOR YOUR CHILD

When you watch your child as he is having a tantrum or behaving in other destructive ways—which may seem to be completely random—you probably find it difficult to imagine that these behaviors may actually be serving a purpose for your child. We, like other experts, believe that most behavior, including that of children with ASD, has functional value; that is, most behavior is predictable if we understand what triggers and maintains the behavior.

Of course, there are some triggers, those related to physiological factors (such as neurochemical or hormonal changes), that we can't observe directly and therefore can't reliably anticipate the resulting behavior(s) or describe the relationship between the physiological change and behavior with certainty. But when triggers and consequences associated with specific behaviors are observable, research tell us that, in many cases, these problem behaviors can, in fact, serve a purpose for children with ASD. Knowing about the function of the behaviors can help you to develop effective ways to decrease them, since you may then be able to teach your child to satisfy the need in a more socially acceptable way.

The research on challenging behaviors has shown that they can serve four functions: communication, escape from nonpreferred activities, attention, and self-stimulation. Let's look at each of these now.

- *Communication.* When infants are tired, hungry, or not feeling well, they communicate that they are in need even though they do not yet have language skills. The same is true of non-verbal children with ASD. Thus, tantrums and other disruptive behaviors can serve as a method of communication for nonverbal children. The behaviors can become an effective means of saying "I'm hungry," "I want more of that activity," and so on.

- *Escape from nonpreferred tasks.* When a child, or even an adult, wants to get away from something (such as a task, a person, a sensation, or a situation), he or she may engage in what is called "escape behavior." Most of us will try to escape from things we do not enjoy or like. For example, when an ambulance or fire truck drives by with its sirens on, we cover our ears to escape from the loud noise. If an individual dislikes having his picture taken, he might put his head down and walk in the opposite direction when he sees a photographer. By doing this he escapes from the photographer; so, when he encounters a photographer in the future, he will be even more likely to engage in the same behavior. In children with ASD, behaviors like crying or hitting (either themselves or others) could function as escape behaviors if others react by terminating the unpleasant event (such as ending a teaching session or toilet training session). Therefore, in a case where the behavior serves an escape function, tantrums and other disruptive behaviors provide the child with a way to get away from a situation that he considers unpleasant.

- *Attention.* When you were in school, was there a class clown in any of your classes? This child knew what all attention-seeking children know: engaging in unwanted behaviors is a surefire way of getting attention, from both adults and peers. These clowning behaviors were maintained by the attention they attracted from peers.

- *Self-stimulation.* Individuals with ASD may engage in several types of self-stimulatory behaviors: visual self-stimulatory behaviors (such as staring at lights or windows, waving hands in front of eyes, and spinning an object), auditory self-stimulatory behaviors (such as humming, repeating words or sentences, and screaming for no apparent reason), oral self-stimulatory behaviors (such as licking objects, biting or chewing on clothes, and biting self or others), and internal and vestibuar self-stimulatory behavior (such as spinning, rocking, pinching, and rubbing).

Self-stimulation is perhaps the most difficult function of behavior to determine. Why? Because sometimes we jump to this as an explanation for a behavior, when in fact we are mistaken. For example, think about a typical person biting his or her nails: we would probaby attribute this behavior to that person being nervous or anxious. But if a child with ASD bites his nails, we sometimes assume that this is self-stimulatory behavior and that the child needs other types of self-stimulation. This may be true, but the child could also simply be nervous or anxious. If anxiety is the source of the problem and the behavior is not due to a need for self-stimulation, a different type of intervention would be warranted. Therefore, a careful analysis of self-stimulatory behavior is needed, since the function is usually difficult to determine at first glance.

STRENGTHENING APPROPRIATE SKILLS TO DECREASE UNWANTED BEHAVIORS

Because determining the function of a behavior is not always simple, careful observation and recording of the child's behavior and surrounding events throughout the day for several days is necessary. Then, a more complex analysis is typically completed to provide the information needed to make educated guesses about what might be triggering or maintaining the behavior. The only way to determine whether or not your guess is right is to develop an intervention plan based on your assumption. To see how this might work, let's look at the following example:

A child makes silly faces during class, making the other children laugh, and upsetting the teacher. What is the function of this behavior? Here are two possible functions:

- To upset the teacher (this would mean that getting the teacher's reaction is reinforcing to the child)

- To entertain classmates (this would mean that the peer attention is reinforcing to the child)

If the child's behavior serves its function (that is, he is rewarded with scolding from the teacher or laughter from peers), then he is more likely to continue to behave in the same way to get attention. (On the surface, determining the function of a behavior seems simple; however, trust us, it is much more complex than it seems. Unfortunately, the issue is larger than we can cover in this book. For more information on this complicated topic, consult the Resources section.)

Determining the function of a behavior will sometimes be easy and sometimes be difficult. But if you keep track of the information about the behavior when it happens, you will be much closer to understanding the function of the behavior than if you had simply guessed. Let's take a look at an example:

What was the behavior (e.g., hitting, spinning, yelling, or other behavior)?	When did the behavior occur?	What happened just before the behavior occurred?	What happened just after the behavior occurred?	Where was the child when the behavior occurred, and what was going on at the time?
The child started to sing a song off-key.	In the hallway	Students were walking down the hall.	Other students laughed.	Transitioning from the classroom to music class
The child started jumping up and down in his chair.	In the classroom	The teacher walked away from the child to help another student.	Teacher stopped helping another student and went over to the child.	At his desk during the class "quiet work time"

Now, look at the times when the behavior occurs most often: do certain events occur just before or just after? Once you identify situations in which the behavior does occur, you will also need to find out about the situations where the behavior does not occur. What is different about the situations in which the behavior does not occur? Having this information may help you determine what elicits the behavior, and also what might be an alternative behavior to teach your child.

Once you determine the function of the behavior, you can identify an alternative behavior that is more socially appropriate. Keep in mind that teaching alternative behaviors is about providing your child with more skills to be able to cope better with situations that are difficult for him.

Use the table below to jot down your observations each time the behavior happens.

What was the behavior (e.g., hitting, spinning, yelling, or other behavior)?	When did the behavior occur?	What happened just before the behavior occurred?	What happened just after the behavior occurred?	Where was the child when the behavior occurred, and what was going on at the time?

The table below illustrates the types of socially acceptable alternative behaviors that you might teach for each function of behavior.

Function of behavior	Alternative behaviors
Communication	Using socially appropriate alternative means of communication (pictures, signs, words, and so on)
Escape from nonpreferred activities	Asking for a break (using whatever communication method is appropriate for your child)
Attention	Using socially appropriate ways to obtain attention (such as tapping on the person's shoulder, showing a picture, using social scripts)
Self-stimulation	Squeezing a stress ball, using relaxation strategies

Utilize Your Child's Strengths to Find Solutions

Children with ASD often have a relative strength in the processing of visual information. Therefore, it is common to use picture communication devices to assist with communication skills, and to use pictures to assist a child with other tasks, such as following a schedule. This section describes some uses of a picture schedule for increasing your child's self-control.

Capitalize on Preference for Structure—Use Picture Schedules

Picture schedules, often used to organize and structure behavior, can be employed in teaching children to tolerate changes in their schedules and to smoothly move from one activity to another.

Below is an example of a picture schedule, which you'll notice includes written words. Picture schedules do not always need a written equivalent of the scheduled task; however, for some children who can read or are learning to read, adding the written word may assist them in learning simple sight vocabulary words (which are words the child can recognize by sight, without having to sound them out). Additionally, for children who can read and write, a written schedule (with no pictures) may be better, since it more closely resembles the daily and weekly schedules adults create for themselves.

Time	Activity	Activity
7:15 A.M.		Eat breakfast
8:00 A.M.		Go to school
3:00 P.M.		Go home
3:30 P.M.		Have a snack
4:00 P.M.		Read and do homework

A picture schedule will help your child with ASD understand when activities will change, and what the behavioral expectations will be for each activity. However, all too often unpredictable events occur, requiring us to be flexible and change the other activities we had scheduled for that day. Children with ASD have difficulty being flexible, and so flexibility is an important skill for these children to learn in order to increase their self-control. Teaching flexibility involves sometimes providing choices and sometimes not providing choices for your child. When you provide choices, you are teaching your child that, within each activity, he can be flexible when dealing with the specific aspects of that activity. Take breakfast, for example. When you offer choices for breakfast, it means that breakfast can look different each day, and that the child can accept these changes. However, in addition to teaching flexibility, you are teaching how to deal with unpredictability. What if there are no more eggs in the refrigerator? When your child learns to handle choices, he can gradually learn to handle unpredictable events. Picture schedules are a wonderful medium for teaching flexibility and coping with unpredictability. Look at the picture schedule below:

Time	Activity	Activity
7:15 A.M.		Egg Sausage Waffle Cereal and milk
8:00 A.M.		Wait for bus outside with sister. Wait for bus inside. Take blue coat. Take green coat.
3:00 P.M.	My house Grandma's house	Go to my house. Go to Grandma's house.
3:30 P.M.	?	Make bed, pick up toys, ride bike, or play toss and catch.
4:00 P.M.		Do science homework. Do math homework. Do English homework. (Child can choose order of homework.)

Notice that at 3:30 P.M., a question mark appears, indicating that the activity for that time varies from day to day. Looking at the right-hand column, you can determine that the child may have to complete a chore (making the bed or picking up toys) one day and may engage in an enjoyable activity (riding a bike or playing toss and catch) on another day. Rewarding your child for accepting these types of changes in schedule and for being flexible will help him continue to be flexible for future events.

What Can My Child Do When He's Upset?

Have you ever started to feel nervous or anxious just before giving a public speech? What did people tell you to do? Probably something like "Take a deep breath and relax, and your speech will go just fine." You might have even said to yourself, "I have practiced this speech. I know it well. Everything will be okay." Can you remember what you did just before confronting someone you were angry at? You probably took a deep breath to relax yourself. What you were doing was engaging in effective coping strategies to relax your body and mind so that you could think clearly and stay in control. You probably did not want to feel embarrassed by running offstage in fright, and you certainly did not want to hurt the person you were mad at, and so you practiced coping techniques to keep yourself from doing something you might regret.

Now, think of the many types of situations that may be anxiety provoking for a typical child, such as meeting students in a new school, trying out for a baseball team, being bullied on the playground, playing a solo in a music school recital, or taking a test in a challenging subject. Depending on the amount of experience a child has had with these kinds of experiences, he may choose good or bad coping strategies. When under stress, some children may get into fights, while other children are able to relax themselves appropriately, and still others may not know how to react and simply run away from the situation. For individuals with ASD, learning and utilizing coping skills is an even greater challenge. One of the most difficult challenges is learning when to use coping strategies. If you look at what goes into learning and using coping skills, you'll see that these are quite complex:

- Learning individual coping skills

    - Deep breathing

    - Relaxation

    - Self-talk

- Learning what thoughts or bodily sensations signal when a coping skill is needed

    - Sweaty palms

    - Shortness of breath

    - Tensing of muscles

    - Clenching jaw

    - Feeling "hot" inside

- Identifying situations in which coping skills should be used

- Ways to learn coping skills (for more information see *The Coping Cat* in Resources.)

    - Finger counting (using your fingers to count to 10)

    - Relaxation techniques

    - Deep breathing

    - Use of coping card (with written or picture cues or both)

The coping card below provides a child with coping strategies that he can use if he becomes sad or upset when he receives a poor grade. By having the thoughts and statements in written form, the child does not have to remember his coping strategies; he can just take out his coping card and read it. When a child first begins to use a coping card, he may need reminders or prompts by his teacher or parent to use the coping card at appropriate times. Reinforcing the child for using the coping card and engaging in a coping strategy is important to help the child use the coping card more independently. Over time the child might be able to remember the coping statements on his own.

Coping with my grades in school
Helpful thoughts
■ It's only one low grade; otherwise I get good grades.
■ This grade is only a small part of my overall average.
■ If I work hard, I can raise my average.
Coping statements
■ It's okay.
■ I get lots of good grades.
■ If I find out what I did wrong, I won't make the same mistakes again. I can learn from my errors.
■ I can always ask my teachers what I can do to make up the grade.

When teaching coping skills to your child with ASD, you may have to provide concrete cues regarding situations or feelings that call for a coping skill. For example, you may want to write down things people might say or do that might elicit a negative reaction and require a coping skill. Also, identifying specific situations, such as playing games, waiting in line, and other scenarios that often cause stress, might be useful. So, if your child often becomes agitated or frustrated when waiting in line, you might teach him that when he is waiting in line, he should take a deep breath with every step forward. Or, if he is able to visualize images, teach him to imagine he is somewhere that is relaxing and pleasant. Sometimes this means practicing the coping skills first in non-anxiety-provoking situations. Once he has learned the skill, go wait in lines—first short ones, and then longer ones. What teaching strategy would you use here? Shaping! Reinforce your child for using his coping skills in these situations.

Teaching coping skills is an extremely challenging task. Just think of how difficult it is for you to use coping skills in different contexts. It's even more difficult for your child with ASD. So take it easy with him. Your expectations for your child as he learns to use coping skills effectively should take into careful consideration his level of functioning, ability to identify physical symptoms of anxiety, ability to perform and learn the coping skill itself, and ability to communicate with you about whether the coping skill is helping relieve some of his anxiety, frustration, anger, or agitation.

In this chapter we have provided you with several strategies for teaching your child self-control. We cannot emphasize enough that children with ASD have a wide range of ability to achieve self-control; however, sometimes it takes professional assistance in order to make the steps toward increased self-control. Some children may simply take longer than others to reach each stage.

As you go about teaching your child the valuable skill of self-control, it is extremely important to differentiate between management of behavior (teaching limits and boundaries, and acceptance of consequences), prompted and cued control of behavior, and self-control. We briefly covered each of these topics in this chapter. The diagram below depicts these three main stages of achieving self-control. Where is your child on this continuum? What level of self-control can you realistically expect your child to reach?

Management of Behavior	Prompted and Cued Control of Behavior	Self-Control

We hope this chapter has helped you answer these questions and provided you with strategies to help your child reach his potential.

10

Strategies for Increasing Your Child's Independence

Like many other parents of children with ASD, you may have limited your expectations regarding how much your child can do for himself. You may be reluctant to place additional demands on the child with ASD for several reasons:

■ You want to minimize stress for your child. Your child deals with demands all day at school, and so when your child is at home you may want him to have some downtime.

■ Your child may have reacted negatively when you tried to place demands on him in the past, perhaps acting defiant or having tantrums. Because these reactions are so upsetting to parents, it is common for them to stop making demands. Unfortunately, while it is understandable, this course of action can develop into a long-term pattern of dependence and caregiving that is difficult to change.

■ It is often easier and quicker for you to take charge and just get things done, since your child's resistance or possibly tantrums can make everything take longer, and because teaching new skills can be a tedious and time-intensive endeavor.

These issues, in addition to concerns about your child's safety, can certainly dampen your enthusiasm about letting him do anything without supervision.

HOW THESE ISSUES AFFECT FAMILY NEEDS

Taking care of a child with ASD can be a twenty-four-hour-a-day job. In comparison to some typical children, who are able to play safely in their rooms for hours at a time, children with ASD may tend to get themselves into precarious situations if left alone for more than thirty seconds. Some parents don't even get uninterrupted sleep, since their children may wake up and get into trouble at all hours of the night. If you feel that you or another responsible adult must watch your child at all times, you are probably experiencing an increased amount of stress. In some families, this situation may mean that the parents are less available to the other family members, and less involved in their children's and partner's lives. Below, write down your thoughts about how your family is being affected by this need for vigilance and the resultant stress.

_____

_____

For some parents, this situation may mean decreased personal flexibility, decreased free time, decreased sense of control of their time, and increased stress. What does this situation mean for you, personally?

_____

_____

How These Issues Affect Your Child with ASD

Taking responsibility for all of your child's personal care needs can be viewed in two very different ways. By attempting to minimize the demands on your child and the stress he experiences in certain situations, you may be either a "good parent" or a "too-good parent." The long-term consequences of being a "too-good parent" can be counterproductive: if you have no specific plan for how you are going to increase your child's ability to function independently in a variety of home and community settings, full-time caregiving may become a lifetime responsibility for you.

Furthermore, if only one person is primarily responsible for meeting your child's needs, you may be inadvertently establishing a rigid pattern of behavior in the child, encouraging him to refuse to let anyone other than that person help with daily caregiving tasks. Clearly, this places unnecessary stress on the caregiver and other family members, and it limits your options for utilizing other types of child care.

In summary, teaching your child to function more independently and participate in family activities is very important. Teaching independence and participation to your child will likely:

- Decrease stress related to caregiving

- Change your child's role within the family, from a dependent to a contributing family member

- Decrease siblings' perception of unfair treatment or expectations in comparison with those of the child with ASD

- Teach your child with ASD personal responsibility (there is no time like the present to begin this important task)

- Start preparing for your child for more independent living

- Integrate your child into family activities

RETHINKING HOW YOU USE YOUR TIME

Is caregiving a time-consuming activity for you or your family members? Use the table below to see how much of your time throughout the week is spent caring for your child with ASD. (Depending on how you schedule your and your family's day, you may want to change the time intervals to hour long blocks, two-hour blocks, or whatever works for you.) Place a check mark in each box representing a block of time when you usually take care of your child (regardless of the activity).

Time	Sun.	Mon.	Tues.	Wed.	Thu.	Fri.	Sat.
6:30–7:00							
7:00–7:30							
7:30–8:00							
8:00–8:30							
8:30–9:00							
9:00–9:30							
9:30–10:00							
10:00–10:30							
10:30–11:00							
11:00–11:30							
11:30–12:00							
12:00–12:30							
12:30–1:00							
1:00–1:30							
1:30–2:00							
2:00–2:30							
2:30–3:00							
3:00–3:30							
3:30–4:00							
4:00–4:30							
4:30–5:00							
5:00–5:30							

5:30–6:00							
6:00–6:30							
6:30–7:00							
7:00–7:30							
7:30–8:00							
8:00–8:30							
8:30–9:00							
9:00–9:30							
9:30–10:00							
10:00–10:30							
10:30–11:00							

By completing this table, you have an estimate of the proportion of time you spend in a caretaking role. The significance of this amount of time depends on several things:

On days when you spend a large amount of time taking care of your child with ASD, do you experience more or less stress? _____

Do your caregiving responsibilities cause you to miss important events and activities in your and your relatives' lives? _____

How are you affected by having to miss out on these events and activities? _____

_____

How are your family members affected by your need to miss out on these events and activities? _____

_____

Who else can assist with taking care of your child with ASD? _____

_____

These are important questions to ask, since they may highlight the sheer amount of time you devote to taking care of your child with ASD instead of completing other necessary household or personal tasks. Of course, we do not mean that you should give up your caregiving role. Rather, we mean that examining how you spend your day may make you more aware of times when others could be helping out with your child's care. On the other hand, you may also realize that the amount of time you spend on caregiving is not all that much. Or you may realize that even though you do not spend an excessive amount of time caring for your child with ASD, the time that you do spend in that role is stressful for you.

So what do you do now? After you have completed the above table, there are a few strategies you can use:

■ Continue your current pattern of caregiving.

■ Recruit assistance from others to help complete activities of daily living (for example, brushing hair, getting dressed, and making a lunch).

■ Now that you have identified the specific times of day that you spend in caregiving activities, you could shift the focus of your energies during those times: instead of *doing* for your child, you could be *teaching*. By completing the table above, not only have you identified the many times during the day when you care for your child, but you have also identified many times when you could be teaching your child skills to help him increase his independence.

But, you may be wondering, where do I start? One method of generating lists of possible teaching tasks is to identify the activities you might be doing if your child with ASD had more skills in the area of independence. First, look at the times you have filled in on the table above. Then, in the table below, write in the activity that you would like to do or are already trying to do during each time slot. Would you be able to incorporate teaching into these activities? For example, if you spend Monday mornings watching your son with ASD while trying to make lunches for your other children, would it be possible to teach your son to help by putting the sandwiches, fruit, juice boxes, and crackers into the lunch bags?

Ways to incorporate teaching independence into daily activities							
Time	Sun.	Mon.	Tues.	Wed.	Thu.	Fri.	Sat.
6:30–7:00							
7:00–7:30							
7:30–8:00							
8:00–8:30							
8:30–9:00							
9:00–9:30							
9:30–10:00							
10:00–10:30							
10:30–11:00							
11:00–11:30							
11:30–12:00							
12:00–12:30							
12:30–1:00							
1:00–1:30							
1:30–2:00							

2:00–2:30							
2:30–3:00							
3:00–3:30							
3:30–4:00							
4:00–4:30							
4:30–5:00							
5:00–5:30							
5:30–6:00							
6:00–6:30							
6:30–7:00							
7:00–7:30							
7:30–8:00							
8:00–8:30							
8:30–9:00							
9:00–9:30							
9:30–10:00							
10:00–10:30							
10:30–11:00							

Now review the table and think about the following questions:

☐   Are there any tasks that your child could help with, provided that the task is in no way dangerous and he could learn the skills needed? Examples include helping with simple food preparation, cleaning the house, setting the table, sorting laundry, and putting laundry away.

☐   Are there tasks that you could teach your child that are compatible with the activity you would like to complete? For example, you might be able to teach your child to listen to a book on tape while you read, color or listen to music while you prepare dinner, or exercise with you by following directions on an audio- or videotape.

IDENTIFYING SKILLS TO TEACH FOR INCREASED INDEPENDENCE

Using the table of activities you created above is an excellent starting point for identifying specific self-care, recreational, and daily living skills that you can teach your child. When thinking about skills to teach, be sure to think about the age-appropriateness of the skills (that is, whether other children of the same age routinely perform similar tasks) and the developmental appropriateness (that is, whether children of the same developmental level perform similar tasks). For example, you would not expect a typical six-year-old child to plan and cook an entire meal, but you might expect him to help set the table. And you would not expect a child with a *developmental level* of two years old to be able to play outside in the backyard without adult supervision (even if his chronological age is nine).

Look back at the previous table "Ways to incorporate teaching independence into daily activities" and choose a few activities you'd like to accomplish in your daily life. Write these in the left-hand column in the table below. Several examples are included to help you get started.

Activity you want to do	Compatible child activity	Skills to teach
Exercise	Exercise	Following the directions on a videotape while you are working out on the treadmill
Do laundry	Sort clothing before laundering	Sorting by color
Work in garden	Pick weeds or play in the sandbox	Matching samples of weeds to plants in the ground, or playing safely and independently in the sandbox

Since planning and teaching new skills to your child can be very time intensive, the best way to approach this is to choose skills that your child already has, at least partially. For example, if your child can get one arm in his coat, but he has difficulty putting the other arm in and zipping up, then this might be a great place to start. If he doesn't even know how to start putting on his coat, then trying to teach him how to tie his shoes is probably not a good idea.

You'll probably find that planning—identifying skills you would like to teach and determining at what level you should start teaching—is usually the most time-consuming aspect of teaching any skill. The actual teaching does not have to take a lot of time. Since you probably do the target activities at least once a day, you can incorporate carefully planned teaching sessions into these activities as you do them. For instance, when you are helping your child get dressed in the morning, you can take the opportunity to teach him the steps involved in putting on a shirt.

HOW TO TEACH SKILLS TO INCREASE INDEPENDENCE

Numerous skills in many areas can be taught to increase your child's level of independence. We have chosen to demonstrate teaching strategies for three important skills in the domain of self-care: self-dressing, grooming, and household chores. The teaching strategies we will be using are *chaining procedures* (forward and backward), *picture schedules*, and *token economy procedures*.

Self-Dressing

When teaching the child to dress himself, chaining is often effective. Chaining is a teaching procedure in which you first break a skill into its components, then teach each component, and then teach the components in a sequenced order, until the child learns the full skill. If you are *forward chaining*, you are teaching the steps in the order they naturally occur. If you are *backward chaining*, you are teaching the steps from the end to the beginning. Backward chaining has a built-in advantage: when your child completes part of the chain, the reinforcer is the completion of the task. The chart below, which reads from top to bottom, provides a few examples of backward chaining.

Putting on pull-on pants	Putting on shirt
1. Place pants over feet and bring pants to child's waist. Say "Put on your pants." If your child completes task, reinforce. If not, prompt you child by physically assisting him.	1. Put shirt on child (over head, arms through sleeves) and pull down to just above belly. Say "Put on your shirt." If your child completes task, reinforce. If not, prompt your child by physically assisting him.
2. Place pants over feet and bring pants to child's hip. Say "Put on your pants." If your child completes task, reinforce. If not, prompt.	2. Put shirt on child (over head, arms through sleeves) down to underarms. Say "Put on your shirt." If your child completes task, reinforce. If not, prompt.
3. Place pants over feet and bring pants to child's thigh. Say "Put on your pants." If your child completes task, reinforce. If not, prompt.	3. Put arms through sleeves only. Say "Put on your shirt." If your child completes task, reinforce. If not, prompt.
4. Place pants over feet and bring pants to child's calf. Say. "Put on your pants." If your child completes task, reinforce. If not, prompt.	4. Put shirt above child's head. Say "Put on your shirt." If your child completes task, reinforce. If not, prompt.
5. Place one foot in pant leg. Say "Put on your pants." If child puts other foot in and pulls up pants, reinforce. If not, prompt.	5. Hand child the shirt. Say "Put on your shirt." If your child completes task, reinforce. If not, prompt.
6. Help child put on all other clothing items. Point to pants and say "Put on your pants." Reinforce or prompt as necessary.	6. Help child put on all other clothing items. Point to shirt and say "Put on your shirt." Reinforce or prompt as necessary.

Now that you have read the backward chaining procedures for putting on pants and shirt, try to write the sequence for putting on shoes. Before you get started, you'll want to ask the following questions:

- *What shoes do I use to start teaching?* Choose shoes that are easy to put on and not too tight. Shoes that have laces are best avoided at this point. Remember, you want to be able to reward your child for putting the shoe on. If the shoe is too difficult to put on without help, then you should try an easier shoe (such as moccasin slippers versus lace-up sneakers).

- *What are the steps for putting the shoes on?* List them below.

1. _____

2. _____

3. _____

4. _____

5. _____

6. _____

- *How will I reward my child for achieving each step in the chain?*

- *How long will I teach a step in the chain before moving to the next step?* This depends on your child's skill level. Some children will move quickly through the steps, while others will take more time. The rule of thumb is that your child should be able to perform the skill in the chain independently several times before moving to the next step. Moving on too soon, before he has learned the current step, may lead to frustration for your child, because he is not yet ready to learn the next step. On the other hand, moving too slowly may lead your child to get bored. Simply do your best to move at a pace that is appropriate to your child's ability.

Chaining Procedures

To use chaining as a general teaching method, you must first decide the skill you will "chain"—washing hands, for example. Take the skill and break it down into its components (turning on faucet, rinsing hands, putting soap on hands, rubbing hands together to create suds, rinsing soap off hands, turning off faucet, and drying hands). Next, establish the sequence of the components or the chain. Start with one end of the chain (either the first or the last step). Now it is important to decide on the criteria you will use to determine when it is time to move on to the next part of the chain. For example, you might decide that when your child performs the component skill correctly nine times out of ten on two consecutive days, he has mastered that skill and it is time to begin teaching the next component skill in the chain. Your child will have the best chance of learning skills through chaining if he gets to practice them when opportunities arise naturally during the day. For most of the tasks you will be teaching to your child, you may find that backward chaining is preferable, since your child will experience a larger number of opportunities for more immediate rewards and a sense of completion. However, research supports both forward and backward chaining procedures.

Grooming

Completing grooming tasks independently involves the ability to perform fairly complex chains of behavior, and it may be difficult for your child to remember all of the steps and to sequence them in an efficient manner. Although you could provide your child with prompts and cues to get him through the sequences, you run the risk of teaching your child to become dependent on you for task completion. An alternative strategy is to use picture schedules that provide a visual display that tells your child how to get the job done. There are many advantages of using picture schedules when you are teaching grooming skills. Two of the biggest advantages follow:

- Using picture schedules in your teaching program makes it easier to foster independence, because you can fade out your assistance and guidance by teaching your child to rely on the prompts and cues embedded in the schedule (the pictures).

- The picture schedule is portable and your child can learn to use the schedule to complete tasks even when you are absent (for example, with other caregivers or at school).

Using Picture Schedules

Use of picture schedules can be applied across a variety of ability levels and many types of tasks. For example, you could use a picture schedule to teach the steps for a single grooming skill (such as brushing one's teeth or washing one's hands) or you could use a picture schedule to outline a sequence of tasks after your child has mastered the individual skills (like a checklist). Below is a list of the kinds of pictures you could use to teach the skill of hand washing. The pictures can be photos you take or photos from magazines or commercial resources, e.g. www.difflearn.com.

Washing hands	
1	Sink
2	Water
3	Soap
4	Water
5	Towel

This single skill, washing hands, is incorporated as a step in the next multistep picture schedule, which shows all the steps involved in using the bathroom. If your child has not yet fully mastered the skill of washing his hands, you can put up the picture schedule for washing hands next to the sink where he will see it. The table below provides a list of the kinds of pictures that you could include on a schedule that targets independent toileting:

Using the bathroom	
I	Bathroom
2	Sit on potty
3	Use toilet paper
4	Flush
5	Wash hands
6	Dry hands

Remember that you can use photographs, colored or black-and-white pictures, or written schedules, if your child is able to read. If your child seems to need motivation to follow the picture schedules, you should consider offering your child a reward when he completes all the individual tasks included in a schedule (an especially helpful tactic to use when you are toilet training your child; see the Resources section of this book for a book that specifically address toilet training children with ASD).

A picture schedule for a more advanced task, such as getting dressed, may involve not only putting on the actual clothes but also choosing clothes to wear, learning how to match colors or patterns, and dressing appropriately for the weather. When your child reaches a particular age, such as adolescence, he may want to choose his own outfit. One way to increase independence in this case is to take photos of his clothing items (individual shirts, pants, shoes, and so on), and let your child use these to put together a "picture" outfit and run it by you. Another way is to provide your child with several mix-and-match outfits; using photos of these items he can put together an outfit entirely on his own. When he puts on the clothes he chooses, he can follow a schedule like the one below:

Dressing independently	
I	Underwear
2	Shirt
3	Socks
4	Pants
5	Belt
6	Shoes

Once your child has learned the necessary individual skills, you can combine them into picture schedules for getting ready for school (listed below), getting ready for bed, and other complex tasks.

Getting ready for school	
1	Use the bathroom
2	Wash hands
3	Wash face
4	Get dressed
5	Eat breakfast
6	Brush teeth
7	Pack lunch
8	Get backpack
9	Wait for bus

DRESSING COMPLETELY USING A PICTURE SCHEDULE

Once your child can complete the individual component skills of dressing, you are ready to teach him to dress independently. A picture schedule can be an effective tool for accomplishing this task. The first thing to do is to find pictures that show the steps in the sequence (see the Resources section of this book for sources of pictures, which can save you an enormous amount of searching time). Be sure that your child recognizes the images in the pictures that you have chosen—you can assess this by having him demonstrate the task shown in the picture. The next thing to do is to arrange the pictures in the order that you want the tasks to be done. Start with a fairly simple picture sequence. As your child learns to dress himself more independently using a picture schedule, add pictures to the schedule.

You can also provide a picture of the item along with a picture of the child (indicating that the child can do the task independently) or with a picture of a parent (indicating that the child needs to have help with this task). Providing a paper or magnetic doll and clothes that correspond to the clothes your child is putting on can help him keep track of his progress: as your child puts an item of clothing on himself, he can put the clothing on the doll, seeing what clothing he still needs to put on.

Using Checklists

Like a picture schedule, a checklist is a tool that can be used to assist your child to become more independent in many areas. Think of a checklist as a to-do list; each time an item is completed, your child can check off the item. To save time and paper, you may choose to laminate your checklists and let your child use dry-erase markers, so you do not have to rewrite the checklist every time. Below is one example of how you could use a checklist to help your child get ready in the morning:

Morning routine checklist
☐ Wake up
☐ Use bathroom
☐ Wash hands
☐ Wash face
☐ Brush teeth
☐ Get dressed
☐ Eat breakfast
☐ Check backpack
☐ Lunch
☐ Homework
☐ Permission slips, etc.
☐ Wait for bus

Another way to use checklists for grooming is to post, beside the mirror in the child's bathroom or bedroom, a list of things your child needs to check. Below the sample checklist, we have listed considerations that would affect a child's ability to complete the task, and prerequisite skills for that task.

☐ Check my hair
☐ Check my teeth
☐ Check my hands

Check my hair:

- Consideration: Having a basket or bin with separate drawers or compartments may be helpful. If the top drawer is designated for hair, you could put a hairbrush or comb inside, along with other hair accessories. Putting a picture of the hairbrush on the outside of the drawer or bin is another helpful cue for your child with ASD.

- Prerequisite skill(s): Teach your child how to brush or comb his hair and teach him to differentiate between messy and neat.

Check my teeth:

- Consideration: Make sure your child knows which toothbrush is his. To prevent injury, encourage your child to brush his teeth instead of picking at them when food gets stuck between teeth.

- Prerequisite skill(s): First, teach the child to look at his teeth and see if food is visible on them. Next, teach the child to brush his teeth (top, bottom, back, sides, and front) for a certain length of time (set a timer) and to spit out toothpaste every few seconds.

Check my face:

- Consideration: Using a designated bin or basket to keep the supplies used for washing your child's face (such as a hand mirror, washcloth, soap, and lotion) might be helpful.

- Prerequisite skill(s): First, teach your child to look in the mirror and identify dirt or food on his face. Next, teach him how to wash his face and, if appropriate, put on moisturizer or lotion.

Household Chores

Most children—even typical children—don't relish doing household chores. In fact, most would rather play or watch TV than make their bed, help set the table, or clean their room, and you may find that you encounter the most resistance when trying to get your child to do these kinds of jobs. However, these are all skills that are important for independence later in life. Using a *token economy*, a method of rewarding desired behavior, can be quite helpful in motivating children to perform these chores, while using strategies like the ones listed above to teach them *how* to do them. In this section we will focus on using token economies to decrease resistance to performing household chores. In the process, you will be increasing your child's independence, since he will be learning to perform the chores without much help from you or others.

The first thing to do is to identify what chores you would like your child to do on a daily or weekly basis. As always, it is important to make sure the chores you give your child are within his abilities and are appropriate for his age. Picking chores that he already knows how to do is easiest, because then you can spend time teaching new chores or skills (such as making the bed). Next, set aside a sufficient number of rewards that your child does not have access to throughout the day or week (for example, watching a movie, going out for ice cream, receiving money). Then, decide how often the chore needs to be completed each day or week and how often will you reward completion of that chore.

If you reward your child on a weekly basis, then you will need to have a system to keep track of how often he has completed his assigned chores. Many parents use a sticker chart, where each time the child completes a chore he earns a sticker and can put it on the chart. At the end of the day or week, if the child has earned a predetermined number of stickers, he receives the reward. In the example below, you can see how a token economy was used for a brother and a sister.

The parents of Mary, a twelve-year-old with ASD, and Josh, an eight-year-old without ASD, have decided to use a star chart to increase Mary's independence when making her bed in the morning. To encourage Josh to do the same and also help set the table, they have decided to use a star chart for Josh as well. Mary needs to earn three stars per week to watch her choice of movie; Josh needs to earn four stars per week to play his favorite video game for forty-five minutes.

Looking at the star chart below, you can see that Mary has earned two stars for this week. In fact, she has only earned two stars three weeks in a row. Her parents, realizing that earning a movie may not be motivating enough for Mary, will ask her if she would like a different reward (for example, picking out a new shade of nail polish). Mary's parents also considered the possibility that her performance was poor because there was too much delay between the time she completed the task and the time she received reinforcement. Although they thought about providing more frequent reinforcement, they opted not to do this because they wanted the reward time to be the same for both Mary and Josh.

As you can see, the star chart is working very well for Josh. When Josh earns four or more stars for two weeks in a row, his parents will increase the demand (that is, he will need to earn five stars in order to earn his reward).

	Monday	Tuesday	Wednesday	Thursday	Friday	Saturday	Sunday
Mary	★			★			
Josh	★	★	★		★		

We could probably write a whole book on promoting independence in children with ASD, since achieving more independence has so many benefits: more participation, more social interactions with others, and greater self-pride. And, as we discussed at the beginning of this chapter, teaching your child these skills will alleviate some of the day-to-day stress that you and your family members might be experiencing as well. Because the child with ASD will be more likely to act as a contributing family member, he can begin to learn the concept of personal responsibility. As a result, siblings may feel less resentful toward him and be more willing to include him in their activities. This could have a number of positive effects in your family, such as more opportunities for your child with ASD to socialize with siblings, decreased stress, and possibly more time for you to get things done or just relax!

As your child begins to become more independent, he will be able to participate in more activities within the family and the community. The next chapter provides you with strategies to increase your child's participation skills.

11

Increasing Your Child's Participation

Increasing your child's participation in school, home, and community activities is a challenging but critical task. In this chapter, we will discuss how your child's limited participation affects your child and your family and provide teaching strategies you can use to promote independence and competence in various settings, leading to more participation.

Having a child with ASD puts considerable limits on the activities that your family can participate in, since your child may need constant supervision, and he may not yet have the skills necessary to attend events outside of the family's home or other familiar places. Limited participation can affect your family in many ways. For example, your family's social ties may decrease; it might be harder for you and family members to maintain friendships or relationships with others because constant supervision is required for your child with ASD or because he is unable to handle being in settings that would allow you and your family to socialize with others (such as family barbecues). This might result in feelings of isolation experienced by you and your family. Further, limited participation reduces opportunities for you and your family to participate in recreational or leisure activities. Over time, decreased participation in family and community activities can hinder the satisfaction of family or individual needs.

As we've just mentioned, ASD can limit a family's ability to socialize at home and in community settings. First, let us consider some of the home-based activities where participation is important, such as playing outside, taking walks, having friends or relatives over for dinner or holidays, and playing board games. Finding ways to have your child with ASD participate in a meaningful way in these activities can at times be difficult, but with some ingenuity, teaching of carefully selected skills, and patience and persistence, the family as a whole can experience success and begin to enjoy activities together.

What are the home-based activities that your family enjoys participating in together?

_____

_____

ASD can also prevent families from participating in community activities, such as going out to eat at restaurants, attending sporting events, and going to the movies. The obvious difference between family activities at home and community events is that community events take place in a public setting, which requires the use of additional skills (such as respecting and interacting with others, dealing with strangers, understanding and adhering to social rules, managing more stimulating and noisy environments, and others).

What community activities does your family enjoy?

_____

_____

_____

_____

One way your family can begin to narrow down which activities your family will participate in is to discuss these at your team meetings. Use the table below to facilitate a discussion of how to increase your family's and your own participation in activities. Photocopy the blank table so that each member of the family can write down and rank the activities he or she wishes to participate in, either individually or as a family. Below is an example of a table filled out by the mother of a family:

New activities for you and your family			
Activity you would like your family to participate in	Rank the activity (1=most desirable)	Activity you, personally, would like to participate in	Rank the activity (1=most desirable)
Going to the movies more often	1	Going out for coffee with friends	3
Playing cards or other games with family members at home	1	Having friends over to the house	1
Eating dinner at a favorite restaurant once a month	2	Watching daughter's swim meet at school	1
Participating in community-held events	3	Going shopping	2

New activities for you and your family			
Activity you would like your family to participate in	Rank the activity (1=most desirable)	Activity you, personally, would like to participate in	Rank the activity (1=most desirable)

After completing the table, and deciding which activities to aim for, you can now focus on how to involve your child with ASD in them. More important, though, you can begin to select skills to teach your child with ASD, so that his participation in the selected activities can be more enjoyable for both your child and your family. Increasing your child's ability to participate will likely enable family members to participate in activities together more often (like attending sister's swimming competition, since the child with ASD can participate as an audience member), thereby decreasing feelings of isolation that you or your family may experience.

Participation may range from simply tolerating certain situations, to engaging in short, simple interactions, and to actively taking part in an activity or task. Participation is inherently social: it involves social demands from others ("Wait your turn," "Watch me," "Pass me the salt"), social interactions (engaging in a conversation with others, sharing, listening), and the ability to begin and end social interactions—all of which incorporate many of the skills that are addressed in chapters 7 through 10. To acquire the social skills needed for participation, your child needs to be able to do the following:

- Play

  - Does your child tolerate others' presence in the same room or area?

  - Is your child able to take turns and share with others (both children and adults)?

  - Is your child able to give and receive help?

  - Is your child able to use a range of toys appropriately?

- Use social communication

  - Does your child greet others?

  - Can your child initiate social interactions with peers and family members?

  - Does your child respond appropriate to social interactions and initiations from others?

  - Can your child carry on a conversation with someone (or, if your child is nonverbal, can he sustain social play interactions)?

- Have self-control in social situations

  - Can your child alter his behavior in response to feedback?

  - Can your child self-monitor his behavior?

  - Can your child recognize when to use coping strategies and then use them effectively?

These questions are geared toward helping you assess the range of skills your child will need for different levels of participation. If you answered yes to all of the above questions, then the level of participation you should expect will be quite different than it would have been you had answered yes to only a few questions. We hope that after you read this chapter you will be able to increase your child's participation in many activities with your family and in the community. The table below illustrates the different levels of your child's participation in several activities. (Note that, in reality, there is a range of levels of participation that is not limited to "basic" and "advanced.") In the blank spaces, write down the names of activities that your family frequently participates in, ways that your child could participate at a basic level, and ways that your child could participate at a more advanced level. We've filled out the first few rows as examples.

Child participation worksheet		
Activity	Basic level of participation	Advanced level of participation
Going to community events (such as the town fair)	Attending the town fair for two hours	Playing two or three games at the fair
Watching movies	Watching a movie at home	Going to the movie theater and sitting for the duration of the movie
Shopping for groceries	Walking with parent through the grocery store during a shopping trip	Finding grocery items on a list with sibling while family is shopping
For your family, write activities in the left-hand column and then write down ways your child with ASD could have a basic and advanced level of participation in those activities.		

HOW TO INCREASE YOUR CHILD'S PARTICIPATION

At this point, you have probably already started to think about the different ways your child with ASD currently participates in family and community events, and how your child might be able to increase his participation. Now is the perfect time to begin to identify specific skills you might want to teach in order to make this goal happen, and determine the prerequisite skills that are necessary for performing the end skill. For example, if your end goal is to have your child with ASD participate in shopping trips with you and your family, you need to figure out what specific skills are involved in going shopping. The table below presents five common family-oriented activities and the prerequisite skills necessary for participating in each activity. The prerequisite skills listed here are not all the possible skills—depending upon your situation, there may be more or fewer prerequisite skills for each activity. For the most part, the skills are listed in order of complexity, so that the basic participatory skills are listed first, and the more complex skills follow.

Examples of sequences of skills to increase participation	
Participating in family games	1. Sustaining attention for duration of activity or game 2. Sharing with others 3. Accepting assistance from others 4. Asking for assistance from others 5. Recalling simple rules of game 6. Taking turns 7. Making comments on game 8. Showing good sportsmanship
Exercising/sports	1. Walking varied distances 2. Riding bicycle 3. Swimming 4. Playing toss and catch 5. Dribbling and shooting basketball 6. Running relay races 7. Playing bowling 8. Playing group games (such as tag, hide-and-seek) 9. Playing team sports that require sustained attention (such as kickball, soccer, and volleyball) 10. Playing sports that require taking turns (such as golf, tennis, badminton)

Dinner with friends and relatives	1.	Sitting appropriately for entire meal
	2.	Opening containers (such as milk cartons, jars)
	3.	Pouring liquids without spilling (into a bowl, cup, or glass)
	4.	Setting table
	5.	Assisting with cleaning up and putting items away
	6.	Serving food to self and others
	7.	Using proper kitchen hygiene (such as washing hands, washing dishes, cleaning counters, keeping hair back, and so on)
	8.	Preparing simple food (such as sandwich)
	9.	Following a recipe
	10.	See all skills under "going to a restaurant"
Going to a restaurant	1.	Sitting appropriately for entire meal
	2.	Waiting appropriately for meal to arrive
	3.	Waiting appropriately in buffet or cafeteria line
	4.	Drinking and eating one mouthful of liquid or food at a time
	5.	Pointing to or requesting items from menu, to parent and to server
	6.	Using the appropriate utensils for different foods
	7.	Using napkin to clean hands and face
	8.	Requesting food that is out of reach
	9.	Excusing self politely from table
	10.	Appropriately obtaining attention of server
Going shopping	1.	Walking beside parent for duration of shopping trip
	2.	Waiting in line appropriately
	3.	Locating items with assistance
	4.	Demonstrating ability to use shopping list

Think about one or more activities that you would like your child with ASD to participate in more. Now, choose one or two activities and write them on the blank lines in the top row of the table below. Next, list his current abilities and participation skills related to this activity. Then, list the skills that are needed to achieve the desired level of participation. Keep in mind, though, that you shouldn't feel obligated to have your child participating to a full extent in every activity. The goal is simply to provide your child with additional social skills so he can increase his participation in family and community activities.

	Activity #1:	Activity #2:
Current skill level (how your child participates now)		
Desired skill level (how you would like your child to participate)		
Skills needed to achieve desired participation		

The next section will provide you with some teaching strategies to increase your child's ability to participate in ways that are more meaningful.

Specific Implementation Strategies

Now that you have considered the prerequisite skills that your child currently has, and the ones your child needs to learn, you can start to think about teaching your child these new skills using the strategies you have learned in this book, so he can participate in activities more fully. When choosing an activity to increase your child's participation skills, first you need to evaluate how realistic the goal is for both the short term and the long term. Generating and answering specific questions that relate to your child's abilities, preferences, and the demands of the task can help you make these important decisions. Let's examine this process using swimming as an example. Answer the following questions:

- Does your child enjoy being in the water?

- Does your child become distressed when water gets in his eyes or ears? (Protective equipment such as ear plugs and goggles can be used to remedy this problem.)

- Does your child know that he should not inhale when he is underwater?

- Does your child tolerate others in close proximity?

- Does your child tolerate being splashed by others?

- Does your child have any swimming ability?

- Does your child follow directions related to safety (such as "Walk, don't run," "Stay on this side of the rope," and so on)?

If the answer to any of these questions is no, then you might want to reconsider the costs and benefits of increasing your child's swimming-related skills in order to participate in a family recreational activity. It just may be too difficult to teach your child to become involved in swimming. This is important information to have in the planning stages, so that if necessary you could select a different sport or activity that the family enjoys and that the child may learn to enjoy more easily than swimming. For each skill you wish to teach your child, you should always assess whether or not the skill is a reasonable one to expect your child to learn.

First, we'll review the basic prerequisite skills involved in swimming as an activity:

1. Watching swimming on TV with family members (this may or may not be considered a prerequisite skill to participating in swimming for your family).

2. Talking about swimming with family members

   a. Learning the terms specific to swimming

   b. Learning about swimming gear

3. Being an audience member at a swimming match

   a. Sitting for the duration of a swim meet

   b. Knowing when to cheer and when to be quiet

   c. Tolerating loud or unusual noises

   d. Staying at a safe distance from the pool

4. Participating in recreational swim

   a. Understanding that when a lifeguard blows a whistle, everyone needs to look and listen to the lifeguard

   b. Leaving the pool area upon request

   c. Taking turns with swim equipment and toys

5. Taking swimming lessons

In the spaces below, write down the important prerequisite skills for taking swimming lessons:

   a. _____

   b. _____

   c. _____

   d. _____

   e. _____

Examine the skills above and note which of them your child already has, and which he could learn. Now, let's look at the possible teaching strategies for a few of these prerequisite skills.

Prerequisite swimming skills	Teaching strategies to increase participation
Watching swimming on TV with family	1. Shaping: Start by reinforcing your child for watching swimming on TV with the family for a short duration. Gradually increase the amount of time your child must watch TV with the family in order to receive reinforcement. For example, you might first start with 5 minutes of TV watching. Next, you might increase the length of time to 10 minutes, then 15 minutes, and so on. 2. Prompting: To increase your child's commenting on the swim meet, you might provide verbal prompts in the form of questions, such as "What did you just watch?" You can also ask your child what he thinks about the swimming. 3. Modeling: You can also increase your child's commenting on the swim meet by modeling making appropriate comments. Reward spontaneous comments made by your child.
Talking about swimming with other family members	To help your child learn the key terms used in swimming, you could play a family game in which players match cards that go together, such as cards printed with the term and its definition or showing a picture of a stroke and the name of the stroke. (This way, you are already increasing his participation by playing a game.) As your child becomes more familiar with the terminology, you can ask him to identify the different strokes, swim gear, and so on. You could use modeling and prompting for both of these approaches.
Being an audience member at a swim meet	1. Modeling: Model appropriate behavior. 2. Shaping: Shape the amount of time you attend an event. Here you can use a strategy referred to as *backward shaping*, wherein you start from the end of a swim meet and gradually increase the amount of time that you stay, arriving earlier and earlier until you are getting there at the start of a swim meet. 3. Differential reinforcement of incompatible behavior: Reinforce your child's behavior when he sits through the meet, makes positive comments during the meet, and does not run at the pool.

Dinner is another common activity that most families participate in. From the preparation of food beforehand to socializing during the meal to cleaning up dishes afterward, dinner offers a wealth of opportunities to increase your child's participation. And on special occasions when guests are at the table, these opportunities only increase. As always, before you determine how your child might participate more and what to start teaching, you should first evaluate whether the goals you are setting are reasonable for your child.

Specific skills to increase participation	Possible teaching strategies
Sitting appropriately for entire meal	1. Shaping: As in the example involving staying at the swim meet, you can also use the strategy of backward shaping. For example, first have your child sit at the table with the group for dessert. Next, have your child sit at the dinner table for ten minutes before dessert. Keep increasing the time (only rewarding your child for sitting appropriately for the entire time you have targeted) until your child can sit for the duration of the meal. 2. Picture schedule: Using a picture schedule may help your child predict the sequence of courses (appetizers, then dinner, then dessert, then done!). You can initially reward your child for following each of the steps in the picture schedule, and eventually reward your child only for finishing the whole picture schedule for dinner.
Setting the table	Modeling and chaining: To teach setting the table you may want to consider teaching skills in the following sequence: 1. Place mats 2. Plates 3. Napkins 4. Forks 5. Spoons 6. Cups/glasses 7. Bread plates 8. Salad bowls (For safety reasons, you or another adult should be in charge of placing the knives on the table.) You may use a different table-setting sequence if you wish, but remember to always use the same sequence when teaching this skill so you do not confuse your child. Use backward chaining so that the table is set when your child completes the last step, giving you and your family a sense of task completion and reward. Incorporate modeling into each step of the shaping sequence, to teach your child what the next step in the sequence is. Additionally, modeling can be a useful prompt if your child makes a mistake.

Preparing simple food: making a peanut butter and jelly sandwich	Pictures can help provide your child with the sequence of how to make a sandwich.	
		Get bread from cabinet.
		Get peanut butter from fridge.
		Get jelly from fridge.
		Ask Mom for knife.
		Take two slices of bread out of package.
		Spread peanut butter on one slice.
		Spread jelly on other slice.
		Clean up.
		Eat!

Once your child learns how to make a peanut butter and jelly sandwich, he can be taught how to make other types of sandwiches using different pictures. Once he learns to make a variety of sandwiches, you can then give him a choice of sandwiches he would like to make.

These are only some examples of the basic strategies that you can use in teaching your child the necessary skills to be able to participate more in family activities. As you begin to add skills to your child's repertoire, you will probably see your child participating more in family and community activities. One of the best ways of evaluating whether or not your teaching strategies are working is to look at whether your family as a whole is participating in more activities together (we will come back to this complex topic in chapter 14). The most important things are to set realistic expectations for both your family and your child with ASD, to teach reasonable tasks, and to remember that a range of participation skills, not just a select few, may have a positive effect on your child and your family. The next chapter assists you with balancing family members' needs as you begin to teach new skills to your child with ASD.

12

Balancing Child and Family Needs

At first glance, this chapter might seem to place an added burden on you. You're already doing so much that having to work to keep balance in your family may seem overwhelming. But, if the truth is to be told, your family's efforts to achieve balance are really no different than any other family's efforts to achieve balance. As we've mentioned before, all families must weigh the needs of the many against the needs of the individual. Your family must do this too. You do have a few extra considerations to deal with, but they differ by amount, not type.

Balancing the individual wants and needs of each family member is also critical to the collective health of the family unit. If one family member is unhappy or in distress, all family members will be affected. However, a family that is happy and functioning well does not allow each person to get his or her own way all of the time. Frustration and compromise are a part of belonging to any group, and this reality must be accepted by all family members. As long as the members see the process of compromise as generally consistent, equitable, and fair, they will be willing to give in at least some of the time.

Have any of your children ever complained to you, "You always let . . ."? This complaint usually means that the sibling is feeling frustrated about what he or she sees as the unfairness of different or "special" rules for the child with ASD rather than the extra care required by that child. We all wish children would understand how complex the process of running a family is, but given their age they can only see the world the way they do, and we must be sensitive to their viewpoint (while gently educating them about others' needs and helping them learn to be flexible). As you know, while sibling relations can be difficult in any family, the difficulties can be more complex when one sibling has ASD. You may feel that you are in a position of always defending decisions you believe are in everyone's best interest. Just remember: *how* a decision is made is just as important as the decision itself.

THE NATURE OF CHOICES

Perhaps there is no greater truism than "Life is all about choices." Choices give us joy and choices give us pain. Because of this, the ability to make good choices is something we all try to instill in our children. We celebrate their good choices and feel pain when they do not choose wisely.

The independence and freedom that make it possible for us to make choices are essential components of well-being and feelings of satisfaction with our life. But for every good thing in life, there is a downside. The adage "Consequences are the children of personal freedom" exemplifies the fact that being free to make choices does not automatically bring happiness, since the consequences of our choices may be unpleasant.

Sometimes we make choices impulsively, based on emotion, need, and immediate circumstance—we simply go with the flow. Impulsive choices can be great fun. Often planned vacations set the stage for such impulsive behavior, and we see no contradiction in planning for the possibility to be spontaneous. Indeed, planned impulsiveness plays an important part in responsible personal behavior. We plan to be impulsive, or modulate our impulsiveness, when we go to a party with a designated driver, or buy something we normally wouldn't. We can enjoy the indulgence of treating ourselves to something and acting in a way that is out of character for us. These choices allow us much-needed relief from stress and the constant responsibility of being a mom or dad—of being responsible for inhibiting the impulsive behavior of our children. Although impulsive choices are not necessarily bad choices, they do seem to have a nasty tendency to result in unexpected, and at times unpleasant, consequences. Such negative consequences can be amplified when our decisions affect others. Impulsively buying an expensive outfit for yourself, then feeling guilty and buying toys for your children, and finally agonizing over bill paying at the end of the month because you didn't stick to your budget is just one common example of the unpleasant consequences that can result from impulsive choices.

MAKING DIFFICULT CHOICES

What are some of the difficult choices and decisions you must make? There are of course the typical choices every family must constantly make about use of resources, work, housing, recreation, schools, and relationships, and the daily mundane choices about what's for dinner and whether there's time to do the laundry, mow the lawn, and help the kids with their homework. In addition to facing this standard set of decisions, parents of children with ASD must deal with some additional issues and problems. Nevertheless, the decision-making tools and processes are the same as they are for other families. Your family needs more complex and specific information than other families do, but the basics remain the same.

No list could encompass all the choices a family will face, but there are core similarities among all families, and we can start there. Some difficult choices your family will face involve the following:

- Social lives of family members.

- Extracurricular activities (amount and type of activities for each child).

- Time allocation among responsibilities. You must come to grips with the concept of "good enough" when you have many responsibilities and limited time. Perfection can be a very harsh goal.

- Family recreation and vacations (who, for how long, where).

- Child care.

- Educational programs for the child with ASD.

- Teaching strategies for the child with ASD.

- Discipline for all children in the family.

- Limit setting for all children in the family.

- Parent involvement in education of all children in the family.

- Organization of day-to-day activities at home (such as schedules, chore assignments, and transportation).

Because of the number of decisions you need to make every day, you need to have a consistent process for making decisions. If family members view each decision as unique and independent of other decisions, then as a group you will end up painting yourselves into a corner and generate a lot of stress for the whole family. In contrast, the consistent use of guidelines in decision making will help everyone accept the process and get on board. To support this family camaraderie, do what you can to share the process and the rationale, and involve each affected family member.

While not every decision requires a "board meeting," there are many decisions that will require group effort. These are the decisions that will directly, and potentially negatively, affect another family member—situations where individual needs are in competition.

Competing Needs

The problem with trying to consider everyone's needs is that often the needs of one individual conflict with the needs of another individual. Have you ever had two children playing in ball games scheduled for the same time on opposite sides of town? How do you solve this kind of dilemma? You know that one child or the other will be disappointed; sometimes disappointment is unavoidable. But you *can* influence how the people involved perceive the disappointment. As we mentioned above, it's particularly critical for siblings to see your decisions as fair and governed by rules, so you can prevent hurt feelings from carrying over to other situations.

Here's an example of a worksheet that you can use to give structure to family discussions about difficult decisions. When you use it routinely, all family members soon learn that they have input, that their concerns are heard, and that decisions are complex. It can also pave the way for family members to make concessions about a specific decision because you have a tangible record of the times when each has gotten his or her way. While it may seem strange to keep score like this, it's actually just a formal way to acknowledge everyone's past contributions and eliminate a common source of many arguments—the human tendency to remember events selectively.

Need					
	Importance of need to each family member (Essential, High, Medium, and Low)	Related needs that are met if primary need is addressed	Related needs that are *not* met if primary need is addressed	What are the consequences if need is not met?	
				Long-term	Short-term
Mom					
Dad					
Child with ASD					
Sibling #1					
Sibling #2					
Sibling #3					
Notes:					

Let's try an example. The issue concerns a monthly family dinner at a restaurant. The intent is to do something special with the kids that is easy for the parents. Charlie and Melissa want to go to their favorite restaurant, Chuck E. Cheese, but Bill (a child with ASD) hates this restaurant. In fact, Bill hates all restaurants and usually expresses that feeling very clearly and physically by having intense temper tantrums when they go out to eat. He would prefer to stay at home, but his parents want him to have more age-appropriate activities and have fun with Charlie and Melissa.

After the family members discuss the situation and they jot down their thoughts, the form might look like the one that follows. You'll notice that the discussion involved layers of issues and that family members had to talk about some uncomfortable emotions. Many of these emotions come out of the "super parent" syndrome, which makes us feel that we have to do everything, and do it perfectly. It's okay and normal to have strong emotions, to feel frustrated, and to experience self-doubt. As always, the important thing is how you deal with those feelings. Remember, trying to bury them never works.

Need: To have some fun out of the house (monthly dinner at pizza parlor)					
	Importance of need to each family member (Essential, High, Medium, and Low)	Related needs that are met if primary need is addressed	Related needs that are *not* met if primary need is addressed	What are the consequences if need is not met?	
				Long-term	Short-term
Mom	Essential	Sense of family cohesion, time to relax, no cooking responsibilities	Provide Bill with positive social and community experiences (This need won't be met because he has terrible temper tantrums that prevent the experience from being positive.)	Feel inadequate because can't meet everyone's needs	Have to manage Bill's behavior
Dad	High	A little dietary self-indulgence, a break in routine, don't have to help with dinner, can show kids "how it's done" on video games	Provide Charlie and Melissa with some special "dad" time (This need won't be met because Dad must help deal with Bill's temper tantrums.)	Feel inadequate because can't meet everyone's needs	Have to deal with siblings' embarrassment about Bill's behavior
Bill with ASD	Low	None (from his perspective)	Maintenance of routine, freedom of movement, and choice of toys and TV	Frustration	Frustration

Charlie	High	Just doin' things, doin' something I want to do.	Social activities, simple play, being involved in family choices (These needs won't be met because Bill's behavior causes them to have to leave.)	Anger at Bill	Frustration
Melissa	High	Don't have to help with dishes, get to play games and run around.	Social activities, simple play, being involved in family choices (These needs won't be met because Bill's behavior causes them to have to leave.)	Anger at Bill	Frustration

Issues: Charlie loves this place, and Melissa likes the variety of things to do. Bill acts up as soon as we enter and wants no part of it, usually throwing a big tantrum. We then leave early and Charlie and Melissa feel cheated out of the special family activity.

So, how did they make a decision? Well, they tried first to find a balance. But because Bill hates eating at restaurants, there seemed little room for compromise—either they all go or they all stay home. What would you do? Fill in your plan before moving on.

After considering everyone's needs, I'd suggest that we solve the problem by:

Here are a few questions about how you came to this decision. Reflect on these questions and fill in your answers before moving on.

In this situation, whose needs were most important?	
In your decision-making process, which child's needs came first?	
Why?	
How many different solutions did you consider?	
What emotion did you feel that was foremost when you were trying to find a solution?	
On a scale of one to ten, how satisfied are you with your solution?	

Keep in mind that there is no one correct answer; there are usually many possible solutions. What makes one solution more or less desirable for a particular family is the specific circumstance of that family. So look at this discussion as a tool for stimulating problem solving, not as *the* answer.

Now let's look at what this family chose. Part of the dilemma was that two very important goals were being juggled, and that was the source of the real problem. Going out with the kids once a month to a place they like is a great idea. It would be a very positive experience for everyone except for Bill. Having Bill participate in ordinary kid activities with the family is also a great idea. It would help his social development—there's no doubt that this is a good thing. But must these two goals necessarily be met at the same time, starting right now?

Let's question the assumptions behind this dilemma. This family came to realize that in their desire to help Bill, they were trying to include him in activities that he really couldn't handle. Going out by themselves and leaving Bill home made them feel guilty for even considering it, so they had brought him along and just toughed it out some months, and they had ended up skipping the outing other months because it was just too much to deal with. Now neither of the goals was really being met.

To solve the problem, they took a long-term approach. First, they hired a babysitter to stay with Bill on the last Saturday of each month and went out together. But even before this, for four weeks they set up practice babysitting sessions for Bill. The babysitter would come for an hour, and the family would go to do shopping. The first time, just Mom went; on the second, Mom and Dad; on the third, Mom,

Dad, and Charlie; and then on the fourth, everyone. This gave Bill some time to acclimate to the new babysitter, who in turn had the support of family members as he became familiar with Bill.

Around the same time, Mom and Dad met with Bill's school program psychologist to ask for help in teaching Bill to deal with eating in restaurants. They developed a complex, long-term plan to address Bill's anxiety, rigid food preferences, and impatience with slow service. This plan was fairly complex, and they knew that it would probably take three or four months of work to accomplish it. They decided that this program would be conducted separately from family dinner night until Bill learned the skills he needed to easily participate in such an outing.

So what was the essential strategy here? Just what our table told us—the need had a different value for each family member, so we had to find a solution that didn't force everyone into the same solution. It was also important to separate the short-term solution from the long-term solution, and learn to accept and enjoy the process of achieving the long-term goal. Rather than dwelling on Bill "spoiling" things or feeling guilty about leaving Bill behind, the family focused on teaching Bill the skills that would allow him to join this activity later and actually enjoy it.

EVALUATING CHOICES: COSTS AND BENEFITS

Using a problem-solving approach to tackle difficult choices involves weighing the pros and cons of the consequences of various options. Too often people self-censor imperfect solutions they come up with because they are looking for the "correct" solution. A better approach is to do a little brainstorming, knowing that some possibilities will be better than others, and that final solutions are usually a combination of the good aspects of several possible solutions. You can use the following worksheet to help you identify those good aspects.

Choice:		
Family member	**Benefits (pros)**	**Costs (cons)**

Let's look at a specific situation in which this worksheet, and this approach, was used. The Kirby family has two children, Meghan (a child with ASD) and Lori. Mom works part-time, and Dad, a landscaper, works long hours, especially when money is short. Lori has to help quite a bit with household responsibilities because there are times when neither parent is home. She would like to have more time for after-school sports activities. Dad's mom, in her sixties, has been living alone on a small pension for a number of years but would prefer more company.

Recently Dad has raised concerns about her and brought up the possibility of having her move in with the family. Here's the cost-benefit comparison the Kirby family came up with:

Choice: Have Grandma move in		
Family member	**Benefits (pros)**	**Costs (cons)**
Meghan	Yes, please! I love Grandma. I want Grandma to live here. She can watch my videos with me.	None expressed.
Lori	Grandma's cool. She's good to talk to. She wants to know what I'm doing. She likes helping me with math and stuff.	None expressed.
Mom	The kids love her. She could help with watching them when we both have to work. It would open the possibility for my husband and me to have some time alone out of the house. She has always been considerate of my feelings.	Ours is a small house, and privacy would be a concern. I have so little time with my husband already, and this might reduce it even more. She and I have conflicts about discipline and limits for the kids. We have different housekeeping standards. I don't have time to discuss things in as much detail as she likes to.
Dad	I'd be less worried about her and feel like I'm taking care of her needs. She could contribute financially and not strain us further.	I'd really be imposing on my wife. Sharing a house can be a strain. My mom does nag me about how the place looks. There would definitely more weekend fix-up chores in store.
Grandma	I just love my Meghan and Lori. I'd feel more involved. I could really help them all since they are working so very hard to make ends meet and raise the kids.	I don't want to be a burden. I'd feel less independent. I like doing things my own way.

And the decision? Well, after several discussions and a lot of talk about openness, roles, and boundaries, they agreed to Grandma's suggestion of a "trial" period, where she stayed with them three days a week for a few weeks. Using this approach, all three adults came to a comfortable understanding, so Grandma moved in. They agreed to chat for fifteen minutes once a week after the kids were in bed just to check in and discuss any issues. The kids of course were very happy with the decision, although a little less so when Grandma kept her part of the bargain with Mom and would let them have dessert only after dinner and only as a special treat.

ACCEPTING CHOICES AND LIMITATIONS

The difficult choices are those where there is a lot riding on the outcome. In an ironic and sometimes very frustrating way, the tendency of professionals and school officials or even other family members to defer to your wishes and emphasize your role as decision maker can put even more pressure on you to make the right decision. This can make these decisions feel like an enormous burden.

However, such decisions should be made like most other important decisions: talk to people who know what they are talking about, weigh the pros and cons, check with trusted friends, and make your decision. Accept that you have made the best possible decision given the situation and the information available to you. For the sake of your emotional well-being, look at your decision-making process and feel good about it—don't allow yourself to give in to feelings of regret and guilt if the outcome turns out not to be what you wanted. These feelings can sap your strength and make you miserable. If we could see into the future and know the outcome of choices before we make them, then it would be a different story. But since we can't, we must make choices, deal with the difficult issues, and keep moving on. By accepting the limitations of our choices and knowing that there are no guarantees in life, you do not weaken and distract yourself with feelings of guilt that are misdirected and not deserved.

In the same vein, it is important, and possibly very painful, to accept the reality of having a child with ASD. We all hope for the best and work very hard to achieve the best outcome for our children. But in this process we must acknowledge that all children are different. All children start with different abilities and deficits. Even though an accurate prognostic measure does not exist, it is true that children with ASD can show the type and severity of symptoms that raise very significant limitations to their development. Ironically, in order to help these children develop, we must accept the reality of these limitations.

Throughout this book we have promoted the careful selection and definition of goals, in order to allow you to achieve these goals in a systematic, but not myopic, manner. We know that no one can achieve unrealistic goals or keep to impossible time schedules. Well-meaning people may tell you to "reach for the sky" and that "nothing is impossible," which sound great emotionally but do not reflect reality or the seriousness of the situation. If you keep pursuing unrealistic goals, you will lose valuable time and opportunity to achieve meaningful, possible goals; you will miss all the wonderful family moments that are there every day for the taking. Too often we see families who come to us having spent years working toward goals that were too complex, too optimistic, and too difficult for their child, and they now must confront the emotionally devastating realization that valuable time has been squandered.

However, accepting limitations doesn't mean that you stop trying. Accepting limitations means critically evaluating the situation and circumstances, being objective, and acting to effect change within the present limitations. Our emphasis promotes neither wishful thinking nor accepting one's lot in life, but rather adopting a strategy and process that allow you to systematically and progressively work to meet meaningful goals. Acceptance is not a passive strategy; it is a tool you can use to meet goals through hard work and perseverance, enjoying and celebrating the incremental successes, and not dwelling on what might have been or should have been.

PERSPECTIVE

Sometimes we must make choices under coercion. Circumstances may dictate our course of action when we are presented with the need to act quickly and no options seem to be available. We feel we have no choice other than to act. This type of decision inevitably leads to feelings of powerlessness, as if someone has taken advantage of us. A good example of this situation is when you purchase something that we need immediately and you can only find one vendor selling the item. You know the price is too high and the salesperson is not treating you well, but you need the item now. You have to act, but acting involves compromising your standards in order to achieve your goal. These feelings tend to devalue the positive aspects of achieving the goal. Because we're looking for the "best" decision, the "best" outcome, anything less than best seems not good enough, and in the process we just make the situation more emotionally negative. There is a big difference between "I should be able to . . ." and "It would have been great if I could have . . . , but this will do fine."

From a psychological perspective, an important type of choice is the informed choice. An informed choice is one where the person was able to gather information relevant to the choice and use this information to weigh the pros and cons of the possible options. It is the opposite of an impulsive or emotionally driven choice. Informed choices are not necessarily easy or always "correct," but this type of process more often than not results in a satisfying outcome. The difficulty with informed choices is that they take preparation, effort, openness, and the sharing of perspective regarding the possible solutions. In order to make informed choices, you must be willing to let others share in the decision-making process by providing input into your deliberations, and in particular you must solicit opinions that may be contrary to your own. While it can be emotionally comfortable to hear relatives, friends, and professionals say, "I'll support you in whatever you decide," you also need to seek advice from people who aren't afraid to tell you what you may not want to hear. Those people are the ones who truly support you and help you find balance and perspective. And that brings us to our next topic—when to seek help.

13

How Do We Know When We're in Trouble?

If you're a fan of old movies, you may remember the famous Clint Eastwood line, "You've got to know your limitations." No matter how capable we are, we all make mistakes, because we all share the same limitation of being human. We are all fallible, and we all need some help at times. It's tempting to expect perfection, but it's more productive to remember that change is a process, and that with successes also come failures. Instead of thinking about the mistakes we've made, we can think about the choices we made that did not lead to the desired outcome. When things don't go the way we want them to, we simply need to experiment or try a different approach. When we learn from this process, we are more likely to have future successes.

As you know, families are complex organizations that grow and change in sometimes unexpected ways. Through most of the ups and downs, the stresses, the surprises, and the frustration, if you use your collective experience, common sense, energy, and some of the tools offered in this book, you'll do just fine. But sometimes your own expertise and abilities may not be enough. It is important to be able to tell the difference between a situation that the family can solve on their own or simply tolerate as an acceptable inconvenience or idiosyncracy and a situation where outside help is needed. The following tables use a simple structure to present how to think about and analyze problem situations. In this first example, we use the table to illustrate a range of possible scenarios concerning the severity of a problem with financial matters that families may face.

Problem situation	Severity	Are you working on it?	Is it improving?	Sources of help
Credit card debt—bad financial planning	High	No	No	Credit bureau, attorney, relatives. You need a plan and a kick in the butt.
Credit card debt—bad financial planning	High	Yes—took another part-time job	Yes	Friends and family for emotional support. You have a plan that's working.
Credit card debt—need to have things that we can't afford	High	No—trying to hide it	No	Psychologist, credit bureau, attorney. There are multiple issues and you need help with each.

Another common problem that families face is negative sibling interaction. Some degree of friction, competition, teasing, and exclusion is normal and expected. It becomes a problem when there are more negative interactions that positive ones. The situation becomes more serious when the fighting becomes physical or highly intense and frequent. The table below, like the table above, illustrates the impact of the severity of the problem and how it affects how this problem can play out in a family, and how the family might make the decision whether or not to seek additional help.

Problem situation	Severity	Are you working on it?	Is it improving?	Sources of help
Older sibling ignores younger sibling.	Moderate	Yes, encouraging him to let his sister join in	Slowly	Perhaps formalizing some structured activities and participating in the activity occasionally.
Kids fight about who rides in front seat with Dad. Lots of yelling.	Moderate	No, let them work it out	No	Use principles in this book and take charge.
Kids fight about who rides in front seat with Dad. Gets very physical. Carrying over to other activities.	High	Yes, encouraging older kids to "grow up" and sit in back	A little	Because it's very physical, is carrying over to other situations, and is perhaps improving only slightly, consult with psychologist or family therapist.

There are, of course, situations where, even though the whole family is affected, the central problem or difficulty lies with a specific family member. While there is wisdom in viewing the family as a whole, sometimes it is more effective to help the specific family member whose difficulty is at the heart of the family's problem. This person's distress becomes a source of distress for the rest of the family. To identify the source of the problem, you need to conduct an assessment, not for the purpose of placing blame, but rather to pinpoint where and what kind of help is needed. The table below provides an example of such an assessment.

Problem situation	Severity	Are you working on it?	Is it improving?	Sources of help
Mom is too tired to get through the day. She tries to spend time with family but can't.	High	Yes, I'm forcing myself to stay awake.	No	Physician, then social services for some respite help.
Dad won't participate with family, is doing poorly at work, stays by himself, and won't talk about it.	High	Yes, I tried talking and giving him space.	No	Psychologist or other mental-health professional. You may need to participate as well.
Dad is despondent over having a child with ASD. He can't see a future or "a way out" and is withdrawing from child emotionally.	Moderate to high	Yes, I'm trying to share perspective on the successes.	No	Since Dad attends regular religious services, enlist help of the cleric. This is perhaps an issue of acceptance. If the problem is reflective of more personal fears, a psychologist may be able to help.
Your child with ASD won't sleep through the night. He wakes up by 3:00 A.M. and awakens everyone, and then he's tired at school, wanting to sleep in the afternoon.	Low for child, high for family	Yes, we tried bedtime routine, increased activity in afternoon, and read up on this problem.	No, the pattern is not changing; it's very consistent.	Because the problem is affecting all family members and threatening employment performance, first consult pediatrician. Explore the medical side, and discuss possible medication to break the cycle. Consult with sleep expert about long-term strategy.
You overhear one of your kids complaining to a friend that his brother "gets all the attention 'cuz of that autism."	Moderate	Yes, we explained some time ago his brother needs extra help.	I guess not—at least at an emotional level.	You probably don't need any. You know how to look at this from a child's point of view. The sibling needs more frequent chats, involvement in activity planning, and the knowledge that you understand it's sometimes frustrating.

In this example the family is clearly under stress, and the needs of each family member need to be addressed. While it may be tempting to look at the situation and think that all would be solved if the child learned to sleep through the night, this interpretation would not include the whole picture. Having a child with ASD can indeed be a stressor for the family, but this may not be the direct cause of all problems. Rather, the stress may be simply amplifying existing relationship issues, and we don't want to focus sole attention on the child with ASD. Clearly, the child's sleeping difficulty is a problem in and of itself that must be dealt with. But all the other family issues are problems that must also be dealt with directly. This is why the table above illustrates the need to provide help for each of the family members.

ASKING FOR HELP

Sometimes you just need some extra help, as difficult as it may be to admit that you need it. At the same time, it is unhealthy to seek help with every decision that needs to be made, since that can lead to dependency and lack of self-confidence. Therefore it is important to differentiate between routine issues that you can effectively cope with and those that are more challenging.

The way to do this is to be able to recognize when trouble is afoot. Most of us recognize the common life events that serve as major stress points: death of a family member, loss of a job, serious illness or injury, legal problem, and so on. During these kinds of crises, most families seek and accept help, whether from family, friends, neighbors, or professionals. However, other problems may be less obvious, and some may simmer quietly for long periods of time before finally exploding into a major crisis. All families experience challenges, minor and major, but having a child with ASD makes things more complex. Normal stressors can be magnified, and other ASD-related stressors can add to the problems you have to deal with.

It may be helpful for you to classify problems so that you can more easily determine what level of support, assistance, or help you will need or want. An important part of this process is identifying the level of distress associated with the problem and also how much the problem and the related distress interfere with everyday functioning. Use the following worksheet to make a list of current important problems that are causing stress in your life. Circle the rating that best describes your level of distress, and do the same for the degree to which the problem interferes your daily life. This worksheet can be completed by each family member, from his or her own point of view.

Type of problem	Level of distress caused by the specific problem					Level of interference with everyday events				
	Low	Mild	Moderate	High	Severe	Low	Mild	Moderate	High	Severe
	Low	Mild	Moderate	High	Severe	Low	Mild	Moderate	High	Severe
	Low	Mild	Moderate	High	Severe	Low	Mild	Moderate	High	Severe
	Low	Mild	Moderate	High	Severe	Low	Mild	Moderate	High	Severe
	Low	Mild	Moderate	High	Severe	Low	Mild	Moderate	High	Severe
	Low	Mild	Moderate	High	Severe	Low	Mild	Moderate	High	Severe
	Low	Mild	Moderate	High	Severe	Low	Mild	Moderate	High	Severe

MONITORING YOUR "STRESSOMETER": DON'T JUST IGNORE IT

Unfortunately, it's common for families to wait so long to ask for help that their problem turns into a crisis. They may have dealt with the problem for some time, and then suddenly, perhaps even after relatively little change, it now exceeds everyone's ability to tolerate it, and the situation can no longer be ignored or denied. Now what? It's usually at that point that people seek professional help in some form. And, as you might expect, waiting until the problem has become an emergency makes it more difficult for the professional to solve it. It's no different than ignoring the warning signs of a physical illness: if you wait until you just can't deny it any longer, then you may be leaving your physician with few options, and most likely unpleasant options, at that.

There is great relevance to the adage "An ounce of prevention is worth a pound of cure." Most of us devote too little of our efforts to prevention. So why do families often wait so long to seek help? It's very understandable. If you are strained and stressed, it's hard to step back, look at the family's situation objectively, and then act proactively. Usually it seems like there just isn't room or time to do even one more thing. And, of course, that's the sign you must look out for: that feeling that "if one more thing goes wrong . . ."

TAKING INVENTORY

While seeking help at a crisis point is necessary and good, it is far better and easier in the long run to seek help before a crisis. But how do you figure out when to seek help? Well, there are some common problems that tend to get worse over time unless specific intervention is made:

- Marital dissatisfaction
- Career dissatisfaction
- Disagreement over child discipline approaches
- Friction with extended family members
- Depression
- Overt sibling jealousy
- Physical violence by or among family members
- Feelings of insecurity
- Child learning problems
- Sleep problems
- Eating problems
- Fears and phobias that last more than six months
- Social withdrawal
- School problems that last more than three months
- Emotional exhaustion

First, take inventory of your current family issues. Reflect on your needs and the family's needs. What problems do you see that really need to be addressed? This next worksheet assists not only in prioritizing the problem situations, but also in taking stock of your efforts and noting where things are headed. Use any of the problems listed above and add your own as well.

Problem situation	Severity	Are you working on it?	Is it improving?	Sources of help

Next, let's examine your list by answering the following questions:

- Which items are immediate problems that are making family members upset or unhappy?

_____

- Are there items missing that are okay now, but may require immediate action in the future? Remember, prevention is key.

_____

- Are you feeling drained by your efforts to work on or solve the problems?

_____

- Are the problems making you feel that there aren't any alternatives?

_____

- Is any of these a serious problem and does it continue to get worse?

_____

We are asking about the details of the problems, but for the purpose of trying to see the whole picture. By looking at both the detail and the big picture, you may conclude that your family does need help with some issues.

Sometimes we hear things like "But if I do this inventory, I'll only feel more depressed and stressed out because it's just too much." However, denial is never a good strategy. It may work for the moment, but it always comes back to bite you. If even the thought of doing an inventory causes stress for you or a family member, then it's clearly time for help.

Our goal here is to help you prevent crises in your family. We want you to get into the prevention mind-set. So hold periodic family discussions, take inventory regularly, and accept the fact that sometimes help will be needed.

SOME PROBLEMS SPECIFIC TO ASD

So what do you do if you've been working at prevention—implementing teaching strategies at home and trying to achieve balance in your family—but it's just not working? The first problem we will discuss is a fundamental issue that even highly skilled and experienced professionals struggle with: how long do you continue a specific teaching program even if progress is not being made?

Unfortunately, there is no one correct answer or set of criteria that you can use to make this determination. If progress is being made, then of course you keep at it—that decision is an easy one. When there is no progress at all, it gets trickier, because you need to examine why there is no progress. But when there is little or inconsistent progress, then it gets even more difficult to decide what to do. It is this type of situation where you need to carefully weigh the pros and cons of a decision. For instance, you might consider moving on to another program, but when you examine the costs and benefits you might see that it could lead to other problems: while it might reduce your child's frustration with a difficult task, by allowing your child to change to another program you may be inadvertently encouraging a poor learning style (when things get hard, switch to something else). Perseverance in learning is a very important characteristic for children to embrace.

In making these kinds of decisions, we need to consider the specific characteristics of children with ASD that affect learning, generalizing, and maintaining skills. These characteristics often act as impediments, but we can use what we know about them through research to assist us in working through a child's learning roadblocks. Some of these characteristics are listed below:

- *Stimulus overselection:* The child may tend to focus only on parts of stimuli, and usually not the most relevant parts. A child might learn the label "chair," but he doesn't learn the whole concept of a chair, labeling only a chair that has a high back or is red as a chair.

- *Difficulty in moving attention:* This is a problem not of the ability to focus attention, but rather of the ability to shift attention when needed. Well-functioning attention alternates between focusing and shifting. Too far one way and we call it distractibility. Too far the other way and we call it obsessive.

- *Motivation:* Many of the social aspects of the teaching environment that are so rewarding for typical children may be absent or weak. The typical social praise, such as "good job," "I'm so proud of you," and "Let's show Mom what you can do," is not at all motivating. Remember, social interactions, a core deficit in children with ASD, are the typical way we motivate children (and even adults) to work hard at difficult tasks. That's why almost-over-the-top enthusiasm on the part of the instructor is often most effective in increasing the child's motivation. This is also where you need to be creative by utilizing things that seem highly motivating for your child and use them as rewards for effort and performance.

- *Impaired language ability:* The child may only respond productively to instructions that are very precise, short, and clear. Too often adults will use a more conversational style when giving instructions instead of a more direct approach.

- *Need for sameness:* Many individuals with ASD seem to have a very strong preference to have things be a certain way and a lack of tolerance for change in the physical and social environment. This presents a significant hurdle, since the essence of teaching is change.

- *Difficulty recognizing emotions in others:* We obtain a great deal of information about people around us by recognizing emotions in others. This is a strong deficit area for many people with ASD.

- *Uneven skill development:* We all have strengths and weaknesses in our learning abilities and skills. But in individuals with ASD, the performance abilities in seemingly related areas, such as being really good at remembering people (faces) but being unable to learn facial expression (emotions), can differ widely.

- *Cognitive deficits:* A significant proportion of individuals with ASD also have cognitive and intellectual deficits, which presents obvious problems in teaching.

- *Stereotyped behavior* (also known, less correctly, as *self-stimulatory behavior*): These specific repetitive behaviors can include hand flapping, finger movements, eye fixations on moving objects or light patterns, rocking, twirling objects, playing with a bit of string, repeating a specific action, and many others. Such behavior can compete with your attempts to get your child's attention, and these behaviors can significantly negatively affect your child's learning.

- *Social interaction:* Because social skills and motivation are often weak, or social interactions may be unpleasant for the child with ASD, great care must be taken to regulate teaching occasions and their respective social interaction aspects. This can be difficult since we all take such interactions for granted, but this can be a factor in child learning. Remember, we are initially trying to adjust to the child's learning preferences, and not immediately requiring the child to learn the way most children do. We must begin at the child's level and gradually increase difficulty of social interaction, or we may end up making learning unpleasant.

Given all of these factors, it would not be unusual or unexpected for you to need some advice if one of your child's teaching programs were to stall. In well-conducted school or clinic programs, staff members constantly consult with each other about these issues. Part of this problem-solving process can include some family members—the situation is like a puzzle that needs to be solved and, as always, help always makes the process go faster. We cannot stress too much that there is no correct answer; rather, this is a process in which we try to determine the best choice at the time, knowing that our choices must always be subject to change based upon the child's progress.

The second problem we will examine is a very important one: how do we evaluate whether behavior problems are serious? Some behaviors can be considered serious because of their possibility of producing significant harm, and these can be included in several broad classes of behavior:

- *Self-injurious behavior:* In some people with ASD this tendency toward self-harm is expressed as head banging, self-biting, self-hitting, throwing oneself onto hard surfaces or against objects, incessant scratching or picking at areas of the body, and many other behaviors.

- *Aggression:* Some degree of aggression is normal in children. We become concerned when it is intense (causing physical injury), frequent (happening several times every week), undifferentiated (directed at anyone, anytime, anywhere), or unpredictable (occurring for no apparent reason).

- *No-fear behavior:* Like self-injurious behavior, this kind of conduct *can* lead to serious consequences, but it may not, depending on luck. A child who runs away from you on a busy street and enters the roadway is at grave risk, but he may not be injured that time. A child who climbs up to dangerous heights may or may not fall. These behaviors are grouped together under the umbrella of poor impulse control and a lack of understanding of safety issues. Like aggression, this behavior is common in children, but we consider it to be a problem when the risks are high and the behavior occurs frequently.

These three classes of behavior, in addition to threatening the child's health and well-being, can severely limit his range of activities and greatly impede development. Potential caregivers, including teachers and other service providers, might understandably be reluctant to take responsibility for your child if any of these behaviors are present. Many schools have a zero-tolerance policy regarding aggression and these policies may greatly restrict the child's interaction opportunities. It is very important that such behavior be dealt with quickly and effectively. In many cases, if you address it as it is emerging, you will be able to deal with it as you would with any child: teach the correct behavior so that the incorrect behaviors fall into disuse.

Most families have different expectations for behavior within the family and behavior in other settings, thus the common instruction "be on your best behavior." For example, perhaps your children like to roughhouse, and at times it may get a little too intense, but you try to let them work it out—a reasonable approach. But a child with ASD may have difficulty making distinctions between roughhousing at home with Dad, who can take a lot of physical interaction, and roughhousing with a classmate at school, and so he may get too rough with his friend. Because of the child's difficulty understanding the different expectations in these two situations, you may fall into the trap of excusing the behavior (it wasn't intentional, there is an explanation for the behavior, and therefore we'll let it go). The fault here is that even if there is an explanation, it's still a problem. A more adaptive approach is to recognize that there is a problem, identify the factors you have contributing to it, and focus efforts on fixing the problem.

So when should you seek help for dangerous behaviors? You'll be glad to know that there are some clear guidelines you can follow: If you have been addressing the problem for perhaps six to eight weeks and relatively rapid progress has not been made, then help is needed immediately. If the behavior is producing injuries that require medical treatment, get help immediately. If you see a pattern of escalation in the problem, get help immediately. It may take some time to find someone with the right expertise to help you, so it's important that you don't wait for a crisis. A general rule of thumb is that the more longstanding the problem, the more difficult it will be to treat it.

FINDING THE RIGHT SOURCE OF HELP

Where and from whom your family gets help will depend on where you live, what existing supports you have, financial matters, the nature of the problem(s), and the urgency of the need. Below is a list of steps you can take when looking for a professional to help you:

- Identify sources of information

- Seek information

- Evaluate

- Make a commitment

- Reevaluate progress on an ongoing basis

The first phase of seeking help involves identifying sources of information. First, seek recommendations from people you already know and trust, and look for a generalist rather than a specialist. A good person to start with would be your child's pediatrician or primary-care physician. He or she may not know what to do to solve the problem but probably can give you some good leads to follow. You might also try your cleric, a human resources coordinator in your workplace, or the local community health department or mental health clinic. If the problem concerns a child's development, then also consulting with your child's teacher or principal is a good idea. The main point here is that you want to get some advice and leads from people who are frequently asked these kinds of questions. Because they work with large numbers of people, they have a chance to see the results of the leads they give. In contrast, if you ask your neighbor who has a niece who has a friend with a child with ASD, then the advice she gives you is based on very limited experience.

Next is the information-seeking phase. Armed with the list of names and numbers you gathered in the first phase, start calling these people. Ask about the services they provide, their costs, and openings in their program or practice, and request any printed materials they can send you. Don't be shy! Any professional who is reluctant to provide such information is someone you do *not* want helping you and your child. You should always know exactly what is required, especially with respect to fees for services.

This is also the time to ask about professional credentials. What is the person's background? What formal training has he or she had? Does he or she have any special credentials or licenses? Don't assume that professionals with a similar title have had similar training. Someone who has a degree in special education may have had only minimal training in ASD, for example. Also, know that experience is not a substitute for training. The fact that someone has been doing the same job for many years doesn't mean he or she is an expert at it—it just means he or she has been doing it a long time.

The evaluation phase is when you start to put the pieces together. Some clinics will set up an initial informal referral meeting so you can ask questions. Now may be a good time for the family to again discuss its options. But don't take too long. Remember, your family has a need that must be addressed with some outside help. You want to get that help as quickly as possible.

We often tell families, "It's easy to cancel an appointment; it's hard to get one scheduled." If you're reasonably sure you want to see a particular person or clinic, get your name on their referral list as soon as possible. It is not uncommon to have to wait months for an appointment. If your circumstances change in the meantime, you can simply cancel the appointment. (As long as you give them a few days' notice, depending on their office policy, canceling will most likely not be a problem.) But if you wait until you're 100 percent sure to schedule the appointment, it will only be longer before you get the help you need.

The next phase is commitment. Once you have met with the service provider and that person has had a chance to speak with everyone involved and get perspective on the problem, he or she will lay out a course of action for you. But to make this course of action work, everyone must be on board. If family members approach this undertaking halfheartedly, saying things like "She has to prove to me that this is going to work," or "Maybe I'll try it," or "I'll come, but only to support you," then these reservations need to be discussed up front. Change is difficult (not impossible, just difficult) unless all members make a commitment to work cooperatively and diligently.

Last comes the ongoing-evaluation phase. This allows you to make sure the service provider is actually helping you and that all family members stay involved. Periodically examine whether everyone is doing their part, and whether the strategies the provider suggests are actually resulting in progress (see chapter 14 for more on measuring results). If this person's suggestions are not working even though your family has been actively participating in the process, then it's time to move on. The lack of efficacy doesn't mean that the person was poorly trained or incompetent—it just means that his or her approach wasn't right for your family, for whatever reason, and you can rest assured that you made the best choice you could at the time. At this point, you can either let the provider know about your concerns and ask him or her to come up with a new plan of attack, or try someone else.

This issue of ongoing evaluation can sometimes be quite difficult when progress is subtle or uneven. To help with evaluating progress, we need to next examine how we set criteria for evaluating change and deciding if the outcome is good, acceptable, or unacceptable.

14

Evaluating Outcomes

Whenever a person or organization is trying to produce any kind of change, a key factor is the ability to measure progress accurately. The way to measure progress is to first set criteria for a successful outcome and then compare your current status to the criteria you set. You've probably heard the expression "You can't know where you are until you know where you have been." Too often you will be given advice that essentially calls for you to trust in the outcome—for example, "Going to a good school will get you a good job," "Working for a good company will get you promotions," and "Getting 'services' for your child with ASD will be beneficial." While this blind-faith method may be adequate for some situations, when it comes to your child's or your family's well-being, you need to take a hard-nosed consumer's perspective. You need to be able to measure the changes in your child and your family, so that you can make sure you are making progress toward your goal.

THE DIFFERENT TYPES OF CHANGE

Sometimes change is subtle, sometimes it is meaningful, and sometimes it is an illusion. For example, while a change in a social-development test score may seem very impressive, it is not necessarily meaningful. This change, although real, may not be producing a positive change in the child's social interaction with his family members. The same can be true when you are seeking specific help services. Feeling more positive about family issues after attending family therapy for several months does not necessarily mean things are getting better—it may simply mean you are feeling better because you had positive expectations and are now perhaps more accepting of the situation. Having such positive expectations is the basis of the placebo (or "sugar pill") effect—you feel better because you were expecting the treatment to help.

Some people mistakenly view the placebo effect as an example of how individuals can be gullible and easily fooled, by themselves or others. A better way to look at it is that the information and experiences we bring to therapy can have very significant, and real, effect. With respect to placebo pills, research has shown that actual physical changes can be observed. Because this type of effect is so common, it is important to understand it and be able to identify it. Why? you might ask. Well, what's wrong with believing something is beneficial even if it's not *really*? Aside from the philosophical question best discussed over a beer on a Saturday afternoon, there are some very critical reasons that directly affect your family.

First, placebo or expectation effects are usually short-lived. The relief or comfort they provide doesn't last long if the underlying problem has not been addressed. But this relief may offer a false sense of progress and in turn delay more effective intervention. Then there's the personal belief of whether an intervention is actually working, which is related to but different from the placebo effect. It's not unusual to see differences of opinion between family members, between different service providers, or between a parent and a service provider over the results of a particular treatment. One reason for this is the subjective influences that affect our decision making. It is a question of perception. Does the treatment somehow tap into our personal needs and beliefs? An intervention for a goal that is enjoyable, feels good, and elicits positive emotion and activity will usually be interpreted as effective, even if it produces no documented positive outcome. That is, you can have a good time but not necessarily be addressing your goal. Having fun is a critical family activity, but it should not be confused as the only measure of whether a goal is being effectively addressed.

When we work to understand different types of change, one important aspect is the identification of exactly who is the consumer and who is evaluating the outcome. When addressing the needs of children, especially the needs of children with ASD, there may be adults involved who are concerned with the outcome, while perhaps the child is not. In fact, a child may state, "I don't like that dumb teacher," because the child would rather not do the extra remedial work needed in order to make up for an academic weakness identified by the teacher. In the short term the work may be unpleasant for the child, but the long-term benefit is clear. For a family to go to weekly counseling may be incredibly disruptive to their already hectic week and may require that some other activity be dropped. But only by getting through the short-term annoyance can long-term benefit be achieved. Thus, in evaluating progress, we always have to consider the different perspectives of the various consumers (adults and children) and providers, as well as the short-term versus long-term impact.

EVALUATING CHILD OUTCOMES

Evaluating outcomes in children always involves decision making by adults. The primary evaluators are parents, but involved professionals and family members can play a large role as well. Involvement of the child is also important, depending on his abilities and maturity. One step that is often overlooked in evaluating outcomes and progress is the initial definition of what will be accepted as progress. Progress is often achieved through a series of many small steps and victories. You must concentrate on the process of change, set reasonable expectations for short-term and long-term goals, and monitor how well you are doing in achieving your goals.

Setting specific goals is an important part of teaching children, because it helps us focus our efforts and monitor progress. It's also critical to examine those goals in order to make sure they're realistic and that everyone involved understands them completely. Two critical questions we ask when we are trying to evaluate outcomes are (1) Can I tell exactly what the goal means? and (2) Can I tell if progress is being made, or is the goal so broad that progress is difficult to track? Think about what happens when parents tell children, "Clean your room." The adult, of course, knows what "clean" means, but the child may not share the same definition. The adult gets annoyed or disappointed because it wasn't done "right," and the child gets upset because he tried to do what his parent wanted but failed. Evaluating a goal is absolutely tied into how specifically the goal is defined, so you'll want to make sure that everyone involved is working with the same definition of the goal.

Progress Components

Evaluating child outcomes has two basic components: absolute progress and relative progress. In this context, *absolute progress* means the amount of change compared to a norm. As an example, we might describe a child's reading comprehension as having "increased to the midyear second-grade level based upon the Woodcock Johnson Test of Reading." *Relative progress* means the amount of learning that has occurred over a relatively brief period of time. We might describe a child's response to a task designed to teach sight vocabulary words by saying, "In the last ten days, fifteen new sight vocabulary words have been learned using flash cards, with a criteria of 90 percent correct on two succeeding days."

The key to evaluation is to measure progress during the course of your teaching sessions. The basics of measurement have been described throughout this book: be precise and objective in defining what you're trying to measure and change. For example, it is very difficult to measure siblings "getting along better." It is a poor goal in that all the people involved will have differing perspectives and definitions of what this means. If you are specific, such as "John will help Sarah put the dishes in the dishwasher after dinner before we have dessert," then all family members will know what is expected and it will be easy to measure how well they do. The key to helping people learn new skills or improve existing skills is to provide them with constructive criticism. The more precisely you define and measure behavior, the easier it is to give feedback and the more helpful it will be. Below are examples of four different teaching programs and the progress that was documented over the course of four weeks of teaching. The progress recorded in the table reflects the average performance during each week of instruction.

Example #	Teaching task	Week 1	Week 2	Week 3	Week 4
1	Bill will play in a group of children with similar toys for 30 minutes.	5 minutes on average	12 minutes on average	17 minutes on average	25 minutes on average
2	Sammy will use his fork to eat solid food 70% of the time at dinner.	0% of the meal	30% of the meal	10% of the meal	10% of the meal
3	Jamie will take turns without prompting when playing a board game at 75% of the available opportunities.	5% of opportunities	30% of opportunities	70% of opportunities	75% of opportunities
4	Beth will make friends, as evidenced by having two playdates each week.	0 play dates	0 play dates	0 play dates	0 play dates

So how do you go about evaluating the outcome of your efforts? Follow the five steps listed below:

1. Look across each row from left to right to see if the behavior you are trying to teach is increasing. In examples 1 and 3, the increase in the behavior from week 1 (baseline) to week 4 is obvious. However, in example 2, some progress was made during the second week, but it leveled out over the next two weeks.

2. Determine whether the rate of progress is acceptable. In other words, is learning occurring at a rate that you would expect or is it happening too slow?

3. If progress is slow, identify possible problems with the teaching task. Looking at the pattern of performance can give you possible clues. For example, Sammy's performance spike in week 2 may indicate that perhaps there is some inconsistency in either measuring performance or in the type or amount of prompts being used. Another possibility is that particular preferred foods were served that week, increasing his motivation to eat.

4. Determine whether you're presenting enough opportunities to teach the task each week. Difficult tasks often require more learning experiences than easy tasks. When learning tasks that are skill based, some concentrated and frequent practice may be necessary.

5. Determine whether your child met the criteria (the performance level) that you had set. In the four examples above, Jamie is the only one who met the performance criteria set by his parents. They may now comfortably move on to another goal that expands on his play-skills repertoire. And while Bill approached the performance criteria, he did not quite achieve it.

Looking at the goals above, do you see that the children showing slower progress were working toward the more complex goals? For instance, Beth's task, in example 4, was to make friends—a very complex task for anyone. Beth's lack of progress on this goal could be due to any number of the following reasons:

- Limited knowledge about how to set up playdates with eligible children

- Limited awareness of who is likely to accept her invitations

- Poor self-control, which discourages others from accepting her invitations

- Poor play skills, which discourage others from accepting her invitations

Beth's lack of progress toward this goal is a red flag to her parents to take another look at the skills she may need in order to successfully arrange visits with friends outside of the school setting. Her parents may have to break the task down into specific pieces and then carefully check progress.

Teaching any skill to children with ASD is a highly technical process. Teaching any form of communication, for example, is an endeavor that has dozens of components. The key to achieving our goals is to use this component-based approach, simplifying each task until it is within the child's reach, and then evaluating consistently to know when to change gears. When parents and other professionals ask us why we put so much emphasis on clarity, breaking things into components, and evaluating, we say, "Our goal is to detect our errors quickly." This statement has become almost a trademark for us. It reflects our belief that no one knows exactly what will be effective in every situation. Therefore it is our obligation to make sure we know precisely how much progress is being made so that we don't waste valuable time on an intervention that looks good and sounds good but really isn't helping.

Because this aspect of evaluation and measurement can be so complex, we advise that you consult additional resources to learn more about the specifics. Two books we like to recommend are *Behavioral Intervention for Young Children with Autism: A Manual for Parents and Professionals* by Maurice, Green, and Luce (1996) and *Autism: Teaching Does Make a Difference* by Scheuerman and Webber (2002). They can provide excellent guidance for both you and your child's service providers.

Now it's time for you to fill in the worksheet below, to set the stage for critically evaluating your progress toward your teaching goals. Write in the names of four specific teaching tasks that you are working on with your child. As you work on the tasks, record your child's progress at the end of each week.

Teaching task	Week 1	Week 2	Week 3	Week 4

After reviewing the information that you entered in the table, complete the following worksheet:

Evaluation of progress	Yes	No
Is your child making adequate progress?		
Is learning occurring at a rate that you would expect?		
Is learning happening at a rate that is too slow?		
Has your child achieved the performance level that you wanted him to achieve?		

Using the information in the worksheet you have just completed, reexamine the goals you chose by asking yourself the following questions:

1. *Is the goal too big?* Is the goal just too complex at this time? Is that why progress seems slow or lacking?

2. *Should we postpone our work toward this goal for now?* This is always an option. It doesn't mean giving up on the goal. It simply acknowledges that progress isn't being made, there are other important goals that also need attention, and it may be more productive to come back to this goal after progress has been made on some other more basic goals.

3. *Does the goal need refinement?* Is the goal itself sound but in need of a little fine-tuning? Perhaps your child's progress is inconsistent or seems to depend on extraneous factors, such as where it is expressed or with whom. In this case you'll need to clarify the goal.

4. *Is more effort needed?* If this task is difficult for your child, learning it may require more time per week. Some goals can only be achieved through concentrated focus.

5. *Is consistent measurement needed?* Is the teacher seeing progress while you aren't? Or is your spouse is seeing progress while you see much less? Are school administrators saying that progress is poor when you know that the child has made big strides in the quality of his inter-actions, eye contact, and attention? This may be because people are measuring with different yardsticks. If you're looking at social functioning in the family, and the school psychologist is looking at a standardized test, in fact you can both be right. But to get accurate results, everyone has to agree on what they are going to measure *and* the tools they'll use to measure it.

6. *Is frequent, regular evaluation needed?* Detecting errors quickly is critical. One of the worst experiences a parent can have is to be told, after a year of school, that the child's progress is poor. You and the service providers need to gather information consistently and frequently in order to make informed decisions.

7. *Is it time for a change?* Evaluate progress and objectively examine your feelings about the situation. If the program isn't working, should you continue on with the current plan or change to something new? This is a tough one, since you want to give a plan a chance to work, but you don't want to put effort into something that is going nowhere. The amount of time needed to meet a goal should be discussed up front, before the program begins. This is where you can rely on your service providers and the information you've gathered from books and articles to provide some guidelines. We'd like to caution you that if the provider tells you that the intervention will take six months or a year, then probably the goal is either too big or poorly defined, or the intervention is too vague. Children change over time on their own, but you want to see more than just this normal change; you want to see specific change based upon your child's program to address goals.

Teaching task	Too big?	Postpone for now?	Needs refinement?	More effort needed?	Better measurement needed?	Better evaluation (daily, weekly, monthly)?	Time for a change?

Now you have the basis for discussions regarding your goals with your service providers, your family, and with the child with ASD, if appropriate. Use this worksheet for periodic evaluation to keep everyone focused.

EVALUATING FAMILY OUTCOMES

You can use the same general issues to evaluate family outcomes. The big difference between evaluating the child's progress and evaluating the family's progress is that the latter is typically done within the family itself (perhaps with the feedback of a family therapist), rather than under the guidance of teachers and specialists outside the family. Your "core constituents" are the family members. The first step in evaluating is to solicit everyone's input on a consistent, periodic basis, just as you do when you're evaluating your child's progress. Remember, our focus is on being proactive, not waiting for crisis and discontent. So, keeping the family's needs in mind, have each family member fill out the worksheet below with the same goals in mind. The purpose is for each family member to examine the same set of goals and how they are being affected by both progress and effort. We want each family member to look at the goals, progress, and effort from the perspective of other family members. This will immediately and simply elicit everyone's feelings and perceptions about the goal's importance, its success, and who is not seeing change.

Goal	Working on it for how long?	How much effort and time goes into working on this goal?	Amount of progress you see	Amount of progress other family members see

This worksheet permits a type of cost-benefit analysis for different family members. Each person can look at the progress and effort involved from their own point of view, which then needs to be shared with all other family members. Each person may have a different opinion, but that doesn't mean that one person is right and another wrong. They are simply evaluating the situation differently, and this difference of opinion can then serve as the basis for discussion, clarification, and decision making.

Now it's time to make the hard decisions. At this stage we ask those seven questions again. The only difference is that these questions apply to specific family members, both adults and children, and not just the child with ASD. Once again, each family member should take a crack at this next worksheet. The emphasis is on trying to find solutions, not just identifying problems. Young children may also take part, but they may need to be asked the questions in a simplified, verbal format. The important thing is that everyone's opinions are elicited and respected.

Goal	Too big?	Postpone for now?	Needs refinement?	More effort needed?	Better measure-ment needed?	Better evaluation (daily, weekly, monthly)?	Time for a change?

Your family's task now is to come to a consensus. This is not always easy, but the process does get smoother with practice. This is not something to be done a couple times a year. Just as is the case in evaluating the child's progress, frequent check-in discussions make the task much easier, because then you can deal with issues and problems while they're still manageable. Especially when you are starting a plan to meet family needs and address problems, having weekly or biweekly meetings would be a good start. Everyone likes making progress, and nothing is more frustrating than identifying and discussing problems that never get resolved because meetings are too short and too infrequent. It's often most productive to meet just a little more frequently than everyone would want—that way, you can make sure that important issues stay at the forefront and don't get forgotten. In order to make the most of this process, family members may need to learn new skills for cooperation, opening up, participating, and sharing. If these skills are particularly problematic for any of the members, then they can become personal and family goals. Families pulling together can do amazing things on their own, but don't hesitate to seek help if you need it (see chapter 13 for a discussion of seeking help).

We have seen so many wonderful families work hard to make tremendous changes in the emotional quality of their life. We wish you the same success as you use the tools in this book to promote your family's growth and happiness.

Resources

It was not long ago that there was almost no information available to parents of children with ASD. The only materials available were publications aimed at professionals in the field of autism treatment and research. This situation has radically changed, but ironically the pendulum has swung just as far in the opposite direction—there is now an ocean of information about ASD available to the average person. At the time of this writing, an Internet search yielded 2,090,000 hits for the term "autism." So now there's plenty of information available, but how much of it is accurate?

When making an important decision such as what treatment to seek for your child's autism, you want to base it on credible, documented research. Yes, the Internet makes it easy to find information, but there's no guarantee that that information is correct: you get both the good and the bad, the accurate and the inaccurate, the experts and the charlatans. One approach to sorting out information is to start with sources that have been around for some time, and avoid the sources that tout "breakthrough" treatments and far-reaching promises. If there really were answers that were that simple and easy, we'd all be using them.

To help navigate this sea of information, we've put together some resources that we consider a good starting point. As you learn more, you will keep adding new sources and become a critical consumer. Families grow and change, and so must your sources of information and strategies. We hope you enjoy and benefit from your journey of growth and change.

WEB SITES

U.S. Surgeon General: Mental health: A report of the Surgeon General (autism), http://www.surgeon general.gov/library/mentalhealth/chapter3/sec6.html#autism.

New York State Department of Health: Early intervention report of the guideline recommendations: Autism/pervasive developmental disorders assessment and intervention for young children (age 0–3 years), http://www.health.state.ny.us/nysdoh/eip/menu.htm.

PERSPECTIVES FOR PARENTS

Harris, S. L., and J. S. Handleman. 2000. *Preschool Education Programs for Children with Autism*. Austin, Tex.: Pro-Ed.

Harris, S. L., and J. S. Handleman. 2004. *Children with Autism: The School-Age Years*. Austin, Tex.: Pro-Ed.

Maurice, C. 1993. *Let Me Hear Your Voice: A Family's Triumph over Autism*. New York: Fawcett Columbia.

Mayerson, G. 2004. *How to Compromise with Your School District without Compromising Your Child*. New York: DRL Books.

Powers, M. 2000. *Children with Autism*. 2nd ed. Bethesda, Md.: Woodbine House.

INTRODUCTION TO EFFECTIVE INTERVENTION

Harris, S. L., and M. J. Weiss. 1998. *Right from the Start*. Bethesda, Md.: Woodbine House.

Weiss, M. J., and S. L. Harris. 2001. *Reaching Out, Joining In: Teaching Social Skills to Young Children with Autism*. Bethesda, Md.: Woodbine House.

BASIC READINGS ON ASD

Attwood, T. (1998). *Asperger's Syndrome: A Guide for Parents and Professionals*. London: Jessica Kingsley.

Baron-Cohen, S., and P. Bolton, P. 1999. *Autism: The Facts*. New York: Oxford University Press.

Gillberg, C. 2002. *A Guide to Asperger Syndrome*. Cambridge: Cambridge University Press.

Howlin, P. 1997. *Autism: Preparing for Adulthood*. London: Routledge.

Kozloff, M. A. 1998. *Reaching the Autistic Child: A Parent Training Program*. Champaign, Ill.: Research Press.

National Research Council. 2001. *Educating Children with Autism*. Washington, D.C.: National Academy Press. (This book can be purchased online at the National Academies Press Web site, http://www.nap.edu/catalog/10017.html.)

Powers, M., and J. Poland. 2002. *Asperger Syndrome and Your Child: A Parent's Guide*. New York: HarperCollins Publishers, Inc.

Scheuerman, B., and J. Webber. 2002. *Autism: Teaching Does Make a Difference*. Belmont, Calif.: Wadsworth Press.

Zager, D. 2004. *Autism: Identification, Education, and Treatment*. Hillsdale, N.J.: Lawrence Erlbaum Associates.

TEACHING AND INTERVENTION STRATEGIES

Azrin, H., and R. M. Fox. 1989. *Toilet Training in Less than a Day*. New York: Pocket Books.

Baker, L., and A. J. Brightman. 1989. *Steps to Independence*. Baltimore, Md.: Paul H. Brookes.

Gray, C. 1994. *Comic Strip Conversations*. Arlington, Tex.: Future Horizons.

Kendall, P. C. 1992. *Coping Cat Workbook*. Ardmore, Penn.: Workbook Pub Inc.

Koegel, R. L., and L. K. Koegel. 1995. *Teaching Children with Autism: Strategies for Initiating Positive Interactions and Improving Learning Opportunities*. Baltimore, Md.: Paul H. Brookes.

Lockshin, S., J. Gillis, and R. G. Romanczyk. 2004. *Defying Autism: Keeping Your Sanity and Taking Control*. New York: DRL Books.

Lovaas, O. I. 1981. *Teaching Developmentally Disabled Children: The Me Book*. Austin, Tex.: Pro-Ed.

Maurice, C., G. Green, and R. Foxx. 2001. *Making a Difference: Behavioral Intervention for Autism*. Austin, Tex.: Pro-Ed.

Maurice, C., G. Green, and S. C. Luce, eds. 1996. *Behavioral Intervention for Young Children with Autism: A Manual for Parents and Professionals*. Austin, Tex.: Pro-Ed.

McClannahan, L., and P. J. Krantz. 1998. *Activity Schedules for Children with Autism: Teaching Independent Behavior*. Bethesda, Md.: Woodbine House.

CURRICULA

Romanczyk, R. G., S. B. Lockshin, and L. Matey. 2000. *Individualized Goal Selection Curriculum*. Apalachin, N.Y.: CBT Associates. (The *IGS Curriculum* can be ordered at http://www.diff learn.com.)

Smith, M. J. 2001. *Teaching Playskills to Children with Autistic Spectrum Disorder*. New York: DRL Books.

Sundberg, M. L., and J. W. Partington. 1998. *Teaching Language to Children with Autism or Other Developmental Disabilities*. Pleasant Hill, Calif.: Behavior Analysts, Inc.

SIBLING ISSUES

Harris, S., and B. Glasser. 2003. *Siblings of Children with Autism: A Guide for Families*. 2nd ed. Rockville, Md.: Woodbine House.

Siegel, B., and C. Silverstein. 1994. *What About Me? Growing Up with a Developmentally Disabled Sibling*. New York: Plenum Publishing Company.

SUPPLIES, DEVICES, AND MATERIALS

Angel Alert Child Distance Monitor: http://www.angelalert.net

Different Roads to Learning: http://www.difflearn.com

Mayer-Johnson LLC: http://www.mayer-johnson.com

TRL Systems Kid Sentry: http://www.tlrsystems.com

Urine Alert Technical Solutions Australia: http://www.tecsol.com.au/

BASIC TEXTBOOKS ON APPLIED BEHAVIOR ANALYSIS

Beginning Level

Martin, G., and J. Pear. 1992. *Behavior Modification: What It Is and How to Do It.* 4th ed. Englewood Cliffs, N.J.: Prentice Hall.

Advanced Level

Cooper, J. O., T. E. Heron, and W. L. Heward. 1987. *Applied Behavior Analysis.* Upper Saddle River, N.J.: Prentice-Hall.

References

American Psychiatric Association. 2000. *Diagnostic and Statistical Manual of Mental Disorders (DSM-IV-TR)*. 4th ed. Text revision. Washington, D.C.: American Psychiatric Association.

Carr, E. G., and V. M. Durand. 1985. Reducing behavior problems through functional communication training. *Journal of Applied Behavior Analysis* 18:111–26.

Fenske, F. C., S. Zalenski, P. J. Krantz, and L. E. McClannahan. 1985. Age at intervention and treatment outcome for autistic children in a comprehensive intervention program. *Analysis and Intervention in Developmental Disabilities* 5:49–58.

Kendall, P. C. 1992. *Coping Cat Workbook*. Ardmore, Penn.: Workbook Pub Inc.

Lockshin, S., J. Gillis, and R. G. Romanczyk. 2004. *Defying Autism: Keeping Your Sanity and Taking Control*. New York: DRL Books.

Lovaas, O. I. 1987. Behavioral treatment and normal education and intellectual functioning in young autistic children. *Journal of Consulting and Clinical Psychology* 55:3–9.

Maurice, C., G. Green, and S. C. Luce, eds. 1996. *Behavioral Intervention for Young Children with Autism: A Manual for Parents and Professionals*. Austin, Tex.: Pro-Ed.

McEachin, J. J., T. Smith, and O. I. Lovaas. 1993. Long-term outcome for children with autism who received early intensive behavioral treatment. *American Journal of Mental Retardation* 97:359–72.

Romanczyk, R. G., S. B. Lockshin, and L. Matey. 2000. *Individualized Goal Selection Curriculum*. Apalachin, N.Y.: CBT Associates.

Scheuerman, B., and J. Webber. 2002. *Autism: Teaching Does Make a Difference*. Belmont, Calif.: Wadsworth Publishing.

Stephanie B. Lockshin, Ph.D., BCBA, has over twenty-five year's experience with autism spectrum disorders. She is a licensed clinical psychologist, director of clinical services at the Institute for Child Development, and a board-certified behavior analyst. She is also actively involved in private practice and in training students and professionals in the provision of family services. She has coauthored book chapters and research publications on autism spectrum disorders and coauthored the *IGS Curriculum*, a guide for goal selection in educational and clinical practice.

Jennifer M. Gillis, MA, BCBA, is a board-certified behavior analyst at the Institute for Child Development. She coordinates EI services and outreach programs by providing ABA consultation to families, school districts, classroom teachers, early intervention service providers and programs. She has published in numerous books and journals, and has addressed regional, national, and international professional conferences.

Raymond G. Romanczyk, Ph.D., BCBA, is professor of clinical psychology at the State University of New York at Binghamton, a fellow of the American Psychological Association, a board-certified behavior analyst, and founder and director of the Institute for Child Development. For over thirty years, he has provided services to children and families and has been involved in advocacy, program development, and the judicial and legislative process as an expert witness. He serves as a member of the editorial board and reviewer for numerous professional journals, has published in many journals and books, and has presented several hundred addresses at regional, national, and international professional conferences.

Some Other
New Harbinger Titles

The Courage to Trust, Item 3805 $14.95

The Gift of ADHD, Item 3899 $14.95

The Power of Two Workbook, Item 3341 $19.95

Adult Children of Divorce, Item 3368 $14.95

Fifty Great Tips, Tricks, and Techniques to Connect with Your Teen, Item 3597 $10.95

Helping Your Child with OCD, Item 3325 $19.95

Helping Your Depressed Child, Item 3228 $14.95

The Couples's Guide to Love and Money, Item 3112 $18.95

50 Wonderful Ways to be a Single-Parent Family, Item 3082 $12.95

Caring for Your Grieving Child, Item 3066 $14.95

Helping Your Child Overcome an Eating Disorder, Item 3104 $16.95

Helping Your Angry Child, Item 3120 $17.95

The Stepparent's Survival Guide, Item 3058 $17.95

Drugs and Your Kid, Item 3015 $15.95

The Daughter-In-Law's Survival Guide, Item 2817 $12.95

Whose Life Is It Anyway?, Item 2892 $14.95

It Happened to Me, Item 2795 $17.95

Act it Out, Item 2906 $19.95

Parenting Your Older Adopted Child, Item 2841 $16.95

Boy Talk, Item 271X $14.95

Talking to Alzheimer's, Item 2701 $12.95

Helping a Child with Nonverbal Learning Disorder or Asperger's Syndrome, Item 2779 $14.95

The 50 Best Ways to Simplify Your Life, Item 2558 $11.95

When Anger Hurts Your Relationship, Item 2604 $13.95

The Couple's Survival Workbook, Item 254X $18.95

Loving Your Teenage Daughter, Item 2620 $14.95

The Hidden Feeling of Motherhood, Item 2458 $14.95

Parenting Well When You're Depressed, Item 2515 $17.95

Thinking Pregnant, Item 2302 $13.95

Call **toll free, 1-800-748-6273,** or log on to our online bookstore at **www.newharbinger.com** to order. Have your Visa or Mastercard number ready. Or send a check for the titles you want to New Harbinger Publications, Inc., 5674 Shattuck Ave., Oakland, CA 94609. Include $4.50 for the first book and 75¢ for each additional book, to cover shipping and handling. (California residents please include appropriate sales tax.) Allow two to five weeks for delivery.

Prices subject to change without notice.